MRS. GASKELL AND HER FRIENDS

E. C. Gaskell

From a drawing by George Richmond, R.A., in the National Portrait Gallery

MRS. GASKELL
AND HER FRIENDS

ELIZABETH HALDANE, C. H.

HODDER AND STOUGHTON
LIMITED   LONDON

22328

823GAS
823.8
GAS/HAL

X101523857.

Made and Printed in 1930 for Hodder and Stoughton Limited, London, E.C.4
by Wyman & Sons Ltd., London Reading and Fakenham

CONTENTS

CHAPTER   PAGE

PREFATORY NOTE - - - - - - - vii

I ELIZABETH GASKELL—HER SURROUNDINGS AND EARLY DAYS - - - - - - - - - 1

II MRS. GASKELL'S VENTURE INTO AUTHORSHIP : NOVELS WITH A PURPOSE - - - - - - - 33

III PEACE AFTER STORM : " CRANFORD " - - - 69

IV FLORENCE NIGHTINGALE AND " NORTH AND SOUTH " - 89

V ELIZABETH GASKELL AND CHARLOTTE BRONTË : THEIR EARLY FRIENDSHIP - - - - - - 119

VI ELIZABETH GASKELL AND CHARLOTTE BRONTË : VISIT TO HAWORTH AND MISS BRONTË'S MARRIAGE - 141

VII ELIZABETH GASKELL AND CHARLOTTE BRONTË : THE WRITING OF THE BIOGRAPHY - - - - 162

VIII THE SHORT STORIES : ROBBERS AND GHOSTS - - 191

IX MATURITY : " SYLVIA'S LOVERS " AND " COUSIN PHILLIS " - - - - - - - - 210

X MRS. GASKELL AS A LETTER-WRITER - - - 228

XI THE FINAL EFFORT—"WIVES AND DAUGHTERS" - 272

CONCLUSION - - - - - - - 304

LIST OF ILLUSTRATIONS

E. C. GASKELL - - - - - - - *Frontispiece*

FLORENCE NIGHTINGALE - - - - - *Facing Page* 88

CHARLOTTE BRONTË - - - - - - - ,, 140

CATHERINE WINKWORTH - - - - - - ,, 190

MADAME MOHL - - - - - - - ,, 272

FOR many years there was no Biography of Mrs. Gaskell, though a good many books have been written about her and her surroundings. There was, for instance, Mrs. Ellis H. Chadwick's " Mrs. Gaskell : Haunts, Homes, and Stories," which contains a good deal of interesting information collected in a somewhat heterogeneous way. Mrs. Gaskell's unmarried daughters disliked the idea of any Life being written as being against their mother's wishes, though other members of the family thought differently. But it was soon evident that the embargo could not be maintained, for it was not possible to appraise the work of Mrs. Gaskell without knowing something of the conditions under which it appeared. She herself, with all the reticence claimed for her, had the courage to come into the open and also to maintain her position against critics when she deemed it desirable, and in her life she had nothing to hide.

Two books of importance regarding Elizabeth Gaskell's life have recently appeared. The first is a short Life by Mr. A. Stanton Whitfield, who finished the study in 1925, but owing to his having been in Japan and far from libraries he did not succeed in publishing it till 1928. The second comes from America and is a well documented and very useful book by Dr. Gerald De Witt Sanders, with a Bibliography by Dr. Clark S. Northup, which claims to be a study rather than a Life. It does, however, give a clear record of the facts of Mrs. Gaskell's life, and corrects certain errors in previous records. There is also a " Brief Biography " by the Rev. George A. Payne, of Knutsford.

It has happened that through the kindness of Lord Brotherton I have been allowed to look through a mass of Gaskell Correspondence now in his Library at Leeds. I have also had the great advantage of seeing unpublished letters that belonged to the Winkworth sisters, one of whom became Mrs. Shaen, and all of whom were close friends of the Gaskells : some of these are of especial interest as dealing with Charlotte Brontë and Florence Nightingale. They were lent to me by Miss Margaret Shaen, to whose kind help I am deeply indebted. Mr. Bryan Holland, a grandson of Mrs. Gaskell, also gave me his assistance. Then the late Mr. Clement Shorter had systematically collected material with the view of writing a Biography, which he unfortunately was unable to accomplish, and Mrs. Shorter has been most kind in allowing me to use this in accordance with his wish expressed before his death.

This book endeavours to study Mrs. Gaskell in relation to the friends who were intertwined with her life. Men and women are judged largely by the friendships that are made by them, and Elizabeth Gaskell had several very interesting friendships. The first, of course, was with Charlotte Brontë whose Biography she wrote, the second with Florence Nightingale, the third with Madame Mohl of Paris, and finally there was that with the Winkworth sisters, the best known of whom is the translator of the *Lyra Germanica,* the hymns that are sung throughout the English-speaking world.

E. S. H.

WHEN we look back on the writers, and especially the novelists, of our country there are some who without aspiring to the highest place in her annals yet have a peculiar distinction in our minds owing to the fact that they depict the life and times of their day not only with accuracy but also with distinction. They have, in fact, the same value in literature that " Conversation Pieces " have in art. They tell us so much that we want to know and that historians forget to record, about the atmosphere of the time, the nuances that are so small and yet so important if we wish to understand what people thought, spoke of, and liked in an age not our own.

Of course there were the great figures who did this in a pre-eminent way. We think of Smollett and Fielding, of " Tristram Shandy " and of " Tom Jones " almost automatically when we speak of the period to which they belonged. And then we have our Scott, by whose novels the meaning and aspirations of the country of his birth are more clearly revealed to us than could have been done by tomes of history books. And after that we come on to Dickens, Thackeray, Disraeli, Kingsley and George Eliot, all in their different way true historians of their time. Should we ever have realised what country-town England, and rural people generally, looked like, thought and said, without the descriptions of the latter ? And could we have known town life or its fun, its comedies and tragedies without our Dickens, or the significance of the Industrial Revolution without Disraeli's mordant pictures of the life in manufacturing towns? There were writers, of course, who were not pre-eminently historians of their day and yet who brought before us vividly the way in which people lived. There was Jane Austen, for instance, to whom the war that was devastating Europe was but a background of no importance except as it might affect the employment of some of her characters, and who troubled herself not at all with the economic condition of the people who were outside her delightful little circle of men and women, and not very much over descriptions of the scenery unless natural conditions affected the action of her story and had hence to be detailed. This is perhaps what gives us the sense of rest and peace that comes to us in reading her tales.

We have to acknowledge that Elizabeth Gaskell was of the minor sort in that she had not the creative genius of the latter. Her value to us is that she was pre-eminently of her time, and both a representative and an accurate describer of it. She was a typical Victorian; we have only to look at her portrait to assure ourselves of that; but Victorianism was a wonderfully mingled product, little as the present generation realise it. It was in her case a product not alone of the conventionalism which is supposed to be its chief characteristic—she had indeed plenty of that—but even more of the influences of the revolution which was taking place in life as well as industry, and which took on itself many and different phases. Then again, though a Realist in many ways, she was largely influenced by the Romantic move-ment of the early part of last century. Despite the

Romanticism of Scott and others of his school, there was, of course, nothing in this country approaching to the sentimentalism of Germany. Dickens, indeed, came nearest it in later days, but to the stolid Englishman it had usually seemed something to be ashamed of. Still Dickens made sentiment a reality and Elizabeth Gaskell adored her Dickens. She had a girlish love of the exciting and improbable which continued all through her life. Ghosts and murderers had a special attraction for her, just as they had for Dickens, who loved to get her to write for the Christmas numbers of his magazine. It is necessary to get at the very varied influences that surrounded this ordinary-looking, prosperous Englishwoman to understand her view-point. It seemed quite inconsistent with her love of dreadful deeds and wicked men that she should be the wife of a Nonconformist minister of the best type, that her life should be apparently devoted to the education of her children and to carrying on the usual activities of a minister's life, teaching Sunday school, holding mothers' meetings and the like.

One comes to feel, of course, that below this placid exterior there was no real moral dullness but that there existed whole possibilities of rebellion. One was not born a Unitarian in those days without having a tradition of protest in one's bones. The sect was small but extraordinarily intellectual and efficient, and if born within it, it was impossible not to gaze at the world from a rather superior angle, though always with a touch of self-consciousness. As to religion itself, on Mrs. Gaskell's part, it is difficult to say. Conventionally it was all there, but with her there is much more emphasis placed on consistency in conduct and belief than in the simple faith that used to be regarded as true spiritual religion—at least of the evangelical sort. Of course, the Unitarians were not of the evangelical faith as were the Baptists or Methodists—far from it. They took a calm and judicial view of things spiritual and material which relieved them from the religious excitements common to their day and allowed them to carry on their daily lives as good citizens without conflict with the ordinary man and woman of the world.

Mrs. Gaskell had, all the same, the rebel hidden away behind her calm exterior—the rebel that so constantly betrayed itself despite the repression of the time. For in those days repression was very real in regard to women ; and women had but little chance if they had literary aspirations, or indeed any aspirations outside the ordinary. They were subject to be treated as Southey treated Charlotte Brontë, as somewhat naughty children who had to be bluntly but kindly put in their places. Both these women, who as friends and contemporaries form an interesting comparison, suffered under the same inhibitions, but more or less conquered them. Elizabeth Gaskell did so by being carried away by the sufferings of her fellow beings in the " Hungry Forties." For she lived amongst these common people and knew what they had to endure. And she lived also amongst intelligent people who recognised their duties. It is true that those she knew best were of the " *Laisser Aller* " school and believed that trade must at all costs be left to work its own way out of its difficulties. But she was the mother of a young family, the wife of a minister who saw clearly what was happening around him, and she was impelled to write about it all. Her husband, indeed, would have been content had her literary aspirations gone no further than verses on the Annals of the poor after the manner of the object of their particular admiration, the poet Crabbe. But this was not the wife's idea ; she looked at the poor in no idyllic fashion, but as suffering humanity at her door, and she felt she must write from the depths of her heart what she saw and knew beneath the exterior of correct propriety that she presented to the world.

This was the origin of " Mary Barton " which represented Elizabeth Gaskell's first awakening to the realities of life and showed her the powers she possessed. From the time she began to write that book other powers developed in the strange way that they do when once awakened almost by force. Having come into touch with the world as it is, she went on to see its beauties and its humours in a new way. One wonders whether she could have written " Cranford " had she not begun with " Mary Barton " and " Ruth." In " Cranford " she saw the absurdities of ordinary life and the pathos that underlay them all. But these things are not seen by those whose eyes are not opened.

Of course there were other writings of a different kind. There were first of all those numerous short tales, ghost stories, murder stories ; some of them very good and others pot-boilers, journalistic efforts not worthy of their writer. Many of these are difficult to classify, but they evidently gave their author pleasure to write. She had a curiously inventive mind that adored setting out the marvellous, the terrible, and indeed the impossible. Perhaps she wanted to escape from the ordinary and banal, the dimness and monotony of Manchester middle-class life. And then again there was the short story that was a perfectly thought-out idyll, like the immortal "Cousin Phillis" or perhaps the "Moorland Cottage." After she had once wakened up, Elizabeth Gaskell broke away from complete immersion in her surroundings—no easy task in those days. She saw her friends, she travelled, became what is now called a modern woman, who had, little as the outsider might think it, all the impulses of such a woman. One of the most interesting things in Elizabeth Gaskell's life is to compare hers with her friend, Charlotte Brontë; the latter shy, reserved, proud to a painful degree but sensible of being, beyond her reserve and lack of capacity to meet the demands of outside society her "own woman"; and wondering whether this bright, happy soul to whom the world seemed to bring all good things and few evil, could prevent herself from being constrained to see, not Truth, but what she wished to see. How few are the people who can do this; perhaps it is necessary to be reared on some bleak soil and to have none of the distractions given to most well-to-do women by the world if we are to reach this end. In any case, whether by these means or others, Charlotte Brontë and her sisters rose above the conditions of their circumstances and joined the select circle of the immortals to whom genius gives a special place of honour.

It is not implied that Mrs. Gaskell was lacking in genius of a kind, real of its sort. She had her own work, a different one from the Brontës'—the work of interpreting her own age and time as it was to the ordinary man who looked at it with inside knowledge. The Brontës never had that knowledge. They had no conception of what even their nearest neighbours were talking or thinking of in common life. They told of exceptional people and exceptional circumstances. One wonders what " Cranford " would have meant to them. They could not have endured the life of the gossiping little town any more than they could have endured the drawing-room conversations that Jane Austen loves to record. Charlotte's strictures on Jane Austen's writings are amusingly comprehensible. She writes of her as ruffling her reader by nothing vehement, disturbing him by nothing profound and of her delineation of character as " a carefully-fenced, highly cultivated garden, with neat borders and delicate flowers. . . . I should hardly like to live with her ladies and gentlemen in their elegant but confined homes." Nor could she have lived with them in fact without misery to both !

If we take Mrs. Gaskell as symbolic of Victorianism at its best—its hey-day was during the period of her writing ; a few years after her death it became sullied by the modernist spirit—we may ask what was its basis ? First of all undoubtedly there was, inherently and fundamentally, the tremendous regard for Family. At no period, surely, was that bond of family regard and family duty so vividly put before the world. In all Elizabeth Gaskell's writings this side of life was emphasised—we never have heroines isolated from their progenitors as we often have elsewhere—and it was equally emphasised in her life. In some ways it proved a real drag on women's lives and it often implied work of an almost unbearable kind, just as happened in Charlotte Brontë's case in respect of her father. In Mrs. Gaskell's life this bond was happier ; her husband and she dwelt in amity, though she might possibly have wished him to take a more imaginative view of things ; and to her children she was the ideal mother of the standard kind, making herself responsible for every part of their lives, and not allowing them to stray far away from their home and its influence ; this was the Victorian Domesticity at its best.

Then there was the newly begotten work to set right certain abuses of which there were but too many, and respecting which men and women had but just become conscious. There was the beginning of the end here, for it was soon found that the glossing-over process of shutting one's eyes—women's eyes, at least—to this terrible side of life, and teaching a general doctrine of optimism, would not work ; and this is how Elizabeth Gaskell first broke open her bonds and found herself an author and a reformer. This, on the part of womankind, is one of the most valuable and interesting contributions made by the age to the life of the Nation. It was one that bore with it weighty consequences in time to come.

There was finally, in spite of new ventures, the obvious bowing to the conventions of the day that we associate most definitely with the time. This had two sides—one the fact that life was thereby made easier. People knew what they were expected to do and they did it. They left the ordinary things of life to be settled for them as they left conventions to be settled by conventionality, to put it in the language of a great philosopher, and thus they held themselves free to do the more important things. Unluckily this process had also a stultifying effect on society by making it stiff and fossilised instead of fresh and growing. It was, perhaps, more definitely harmful in provincial society than in metropolitan, and though Mrs. Gaskell was fully conscious of it and smiled at it, she could not but be in a great measure in its clutches.

Her life was in no way remarkable. It had no striking event ; it led its passive way along what might seem a well-beaten track. It was a life like a hundred others ; no tempestuous youth or mental crises such as those through which George Eliot was passing at the same age. Mrs. Gaskell's childhood was only sad in that she was deprived of a mother's care through death ; her young womanhood was not unhappy and her first love was apparently her only love, though others were obviously attracted to her. Her married life was even and contented. Children were given to her, and she was a model mother. Her husband was attractive and worthy; of the necessities of life she was well supplied, and as no one can be said to have lived happily till death reaches them, the end of her life was peaceful and painless.

Such a life seems to give little material for a biographer. It is only when we look below the surface that we see what every life means, and when we do that we know well that the most ordinary life is full of its tragedies and comedies. There is no such thing as dullness where life exists. We turn over piles of faded letters, letters commonplace and domestic for the most part, but every now and then we see into the deep places of the heart—places that in those days were so carefully guarded by the society in which Mrs. Gaskell, the dissenting minister's wife, lived. She keeps her secrets well, and had she never written her books we should never have known they existed. But though she hardly ever speaks of her writings in her family letters, or if she does mention them, like her fellow authoresses of the day only does so to beg for reticence on the part of her correspondents, the writings are still there and tell their own tale. Women writers of last century were more autobiographical than men because their lives and experiences were so severely limited; they had a restricted area to deal with and knew nothing to speak of outside it. How could they? But this had its good side as well as its bad because they wrote of what they knew and knew intimately. " Villette," " Wives and Daughters," " The Mill on the Floss " tell us all we want to know about their authors.

We must now just sketch the life of the girl Elizabeth Stevenson, who became the wife of the Rev. William Gaskell, of Manchester.

Her life, as has been implied, was not an exciting one as the world judges, and her dislike to bringing her personal experiences before the public was intensified by the trouble brought upon her through her biography of Charlotte Brontë. But time obliterates these objections and men and women who make themselves famous must realise that fame makes them subject to certain claims on the part of their fellow men ; and one of these claims is that of satisfying the demand which requires that their life story should bear a certain relationship to their writings. How are we to understand the one without taking heed of the other ?

Elizabeth Cleghorn Stevenson—the bearer of a thoroughly north-country name—was born in a house in Lindsey Row, Chelsea, now known through the investigations of her biographer, the late Mrs. Ellis H. Chadwick, as 93, Cheyne Walk, opposite Battersea Bridge and close to the home of Carlyle.

The date of her birth was September 29th, 1810, so that she was exactly nine years older than that other great Victorian woman novelist, George Eliot, and the same number of years older than Queen Victoria herself. She was born about the time Jane Austen was contemplating the anonymous publication of " Sense and Sensibility." It is curious that her forebears bore a certain resemblance to those of George Eliot, for her mother was Elizabeth Holland, daughter of a certain Samuel Holland, farmer and land agent of Sandlebridge, Cheshire, and George Eliot's father was of the same profession. Her second name came from a close friend of her father's, who was an agriculturist in Berwickshire. It was the solid, honest middle-classes of the best nonconformist order that produced women like Elizabeth Gaskell, Harriet Martineau and George Eliot. It is easy to condemn these classes by a name, and Philistine comes glibly to the tongue of those who see their failings more clearly than their merits. But in their sometimes commonplace lives there was a depth only unperceived by the superficial observer.

Elizabeth's mother died a year (or thirteen months, to be accurate) after her birth. Poor soul, she had borne seven children before this one, and since her marriage at Knutsford in Cheshire in 1797 to the date of her death in London in October, 1811, she had lost all but one of those seven children, and now a twelve-year-old boy and the infant daughter alone remained. She herself was forty years of age when she died, and the Eugenists would have said that the baby girl had not the best chance in life. It is curious that quite a number of the great in the world of letters lost their mothers at birth or soon after. On his wife's death the father hardly knew what to do with his infant child. He had by this time moved to Beaufort Row, now Beaufort Street, also in the town of Chelsea. Very fortunately, in his view, his sister-in-law, Mrs. Lumb, offered to take his child and bring it up for him. It was rather a melancholy home to which to bring the infant girl had she been old enough to realise it. Mrs. Lumb had married a man who proved to be insane, and she had a young daughter who was very delicate and a cripple, having leapt out of the window from her nurse's arms to reach her mother outside, and thereby injured herself for life. This daughter, still a child, writes to her mother a most pathetic letter begging her to allow the infant Elizabeth to live with them as their own, saying she would make all necessary sacrifices of time and pleasure if she would only grant the request.

Mrs. Lumb left her husband and established herself in a comfortable house at Knutsford, which as a result became famous in literature as Cranford. The poor, kind little cousin died, and then Elizabeth became a daughter to her aunt, a truly happy relationship it seems to have been. Mrs. Gaskell and her eldest child were with Mrs. Lumb at her death.

Middle-class provincial life, such as Mrs. Gaskell lived in and was to describe so successfully, has great attraction for us in these days of hurry and unrest. Even the journey from London to Knutsford by coach must really have been an adventure for the benevolent friend who took charge of the child. Once established at her destination, the girl had the same sort of joys that were enjoyed by Mary Anne Evans. Both drove about in dog-carts—the first with her father, the land agent, the second with her uncle, Dr. Peter Holland, while he was making his rounds. Both girls were observant ; the scenes and speech of their surroundings made a deep impression on their minds. It is difficult to believe that the same impression would be made by similar journeys by motor-car. But when we go back to Jane Austen we seem to feel that it was unnecessary to voyage at all. All that was required was to sit quietly at home, watching, without being thought to be watching, every phase of conduct and expression ! So that we need not think travel necessary for education even when it takes the mild form of driving in a dog-cart. There was plenty of matter for observation. The little town was quaint enough indeed with its old superstitions and its old customs, such as that of " sanding the pavement " for those about to be married. An old lady had left a legacy to be spent on paving the narrow side-walks on condition that they should never be widened because she had all her life objected to seeing man and woman " linking."

Mrs. Lumb was a Unitarian, like her brother-in-law, Elizabeth Stevenson's father. The history of the latter, William Stevenson, is specially interesting and worthy of being recorded, for a hundred years ago Unitarianism stood for freedom in thought and act in a way that was done by no other section of Dissent. Mr. Stevenson belonged to a Border family, and had many north country characteristics. He was the son of a naval officer, and was born at Berwick-on-Tweed in 1772. Whether or no the family was of Norse origin, as has been asserted, it had seamanship in the blood, and Mrs. Gaskell's elder brother entered the mercantile service and disappeared mysteriously, as did poor Peter in " Cranford." But there were literary traditions in the family as well, for her grandmother, Isabella

Thomson, was related to the author of " The Seasons." Her father, William Stevenson, soon made it clear that he wished to follow a studious career, and the evident way to do so was to enter the Ministry. From the grammar school at Berwick he went on to prepare for his future work, and when still very young was appointed to a Unitarian chapel near Manchester while also teaching in the Academy. It is possible that his association with literary society in Manchester unsettled his views. Anyhow, he had conscientious scruples which caused him to cease to be a minister, and after serving an apprenticeship in East Lothian became a farmer near Edinburgh. It was when he rented a small farm that he took the occasion to marry Elizabeth Holland, of whom we have spoken. She was of Sandlebridge, near Knutsford, in Cheshire, the daughter of a man well known in agriculture, who lived in what is known to us as Hope Farm in " Cousin Phillis," that immortal idyll of rural life. But Saughton Mills, the farm in which the young couple settled close to Edinburgh, was not much of a success, despite the efforts of the wife, who was considerably more knowledgeable in rural matters than her husband. The times were bad, as they usually are to farmers. If only the effects of the war had come, all might have been well, as was the case not so long afterwards when landlords and farmers flourished abundantly. Just then there were unrealised fears that made for financial instability, and in the year 1802 the couple moved to Edinburgh and set up a boarding house for students in Drummond Street, close to the university. It was the Edinburgh of Scott's youth when he was still a young advocate living in Castle Street. But it was also the Edinburgh of Cockburn

and Francis Horner, of Jeffrey, and Brougham and
Sydney Smith. Jeffrey lived near the young couple
in Buccleuch Place, and there the *Edinburgh* had its
birth. The strange thing is that Mr. Stevenson had
sufficient education to maintain his position in an
intellectual centre—such as Edinburgh then was—
as a literary man. The boarding-house was cared
for by the unfortunate wife whose babies were
coming apace, and the father acted as coach to
students, and contributed to all the best-known
reviews of the day. It was no mean thing to be a
contributor to the *Edinburgh,* and also to the
Westminster Review and *Brewster's Encyclopædia.*
Finally, in 1803, and through Constable, he became
editor of the *Scots Magazine,* the one monthly in
Edinburgh which in 1816 was replaced by William
Blackwood's new venture, and a known and respected
figure in the city. Stevenson got the "Ettrick
Shepherd" to contribute, and he had other literary,
scientific and farmer friends about him. The wife or
mother of one James Cleghorn of Saughton Mills
was kind to the young couple and their daughter
was given her name. It was, however, a precarious
livelihood that Stevenson made, in spite of hard
and conscientious work, and when the Whig Earl
of Lauderdale of the day, who had in 1806 been
offered the Governor-Generalship of India, proposed
to him to be his private secretary, he gladly accepted
the offer. Doubtless this foreign work appealed to
the ambitious and still young man, though we do
not know how it presented itself to his wife, struggling
to maintain a boarding-house and have her babies.
There was, however, no reason for any one to be
disturbed on the subject, for the East India Company objected to the appointment, and it was not

ratified, even though Fox had pressed it. But since by this time Stevenson had gone to London to help in Lord Lauderdale's preparations for India, the latter felt obliged to try to find for him another job. In these days noblemen could find jobs rather easily. The end was that Stevenson was appointed as keeper of the Treasury Records. This Civil Service appointment proved to be the final professional occupation of the preacher-farmer editor and tutor, and for its sake he refused, it is said, a more exciting offer of a professorship in Russia. Perhaps he thought of his wife in this regard ; we cannot tell.

It thus appears that the infant Elizabeth had anyhow intellectual antecedents and traditions of hard work and serious thought. She was always proud of her father—a " minister-farmer " and man of letters. We do not know a great deal of her mother, but we do know a considerable amount of her mother's family. She came of the well known Cheshire family of Hollands. The grandfather, Samuel Holland, of Sandlebridge, was a man of strong character, and his son, Elizabeth's uncle, was Peter Holland, a physician well known in Knutsford, and his son again, Elizabeth's cousin, was Sir Henry Holland, the eminent physician and Fellow of the Royal Society, from whom is descended Lord Knutsford. The present Viscount Knutsford, the " king of beggars," has a notable ancestry in medical matters, and he carries on the tradition of his family nobly ; for, though not himself a physician, he has spent his life in helping the medical profession in material ways and giving an example to the world of what can be accomplished in regard to dealing with the sick on scientific lines through voluntary effort. Lord Knutsford still preserves relics of the old

Sandlebridge days, including the shuffle-board *
used by the family there. The original Samuel
Holland had that same splendid optimism that
carries men through the greatest difficulties scathe-
less.

Thus Elizabeth Stevenson came of good stock.
Sandlebridge Farm, her mother's early home, had
come into the family possession by marriage with a
certain Mary Colthurst, also of good ancestry. A
cousin, brother of Sir Henry, was named Peter
Holland, like his uncle, and was one of those admirable country surgeons who were famous all over the
district round Knutsford and whom his relation is
supposed to have immortalised as Dr. Gibson of
" Wives and Daughters." There were other con-
nections, if not relations, in the Wedgwoods of
pottery fame, and consequently in the Darwins.
Nearly all were Unitarians, and in that district, at
any rate, this was tantamount to saying that they
were intelligent and educated people. There were
noted Unitarian ministers amongst them like the
family of Turner ; in those days Nonconformists
tended to keep together, so that nearly all the
families intermarried like Royalty.

However, Elizabeth Stevenson did not open her
eyes in any more cheerful surroundings than those
of Chelsea in the house then rented by her father,
a man of moderate means, at £20 per annum.
Another nought would have to be added to the rent
of such a mansion now, and probably considerably
more.

The move to Knutsford was a happy one to more

* A shuffle board of the old days was an unusually long table
standing upon legs of oak with many drawers and cupboards underneath. Counters were jerked from one end to the other.

than the little motherless girl. It has given the
world an immortal picture of the life in a small
country town in the early nineteenth century as
accurate as Trollope's Barchester. Mrs. Gaskell
never knew the clerical life of a cathedral town, but
she did know, and that very thoroughly, the life
of the intelligent Nonconformist or Evangelical
Churchman of the same period in history. And she
had the wit to observe every manner in the behaviour
of the people, and the humour to enjoy the amusing
side of it without forgetting the more serious. So
we all know Knutsford because we all know Cranford,
and when we talk of our little town as a " veritable
Cranford " we understand to an iota what we mean.
Mrs. Lumb, her aunt, and Peter Holland, her uncle,
were responsible for Elizabeth's welfare, and the
occasional visit to Chelsea to see the father who
had now remarried and whose wife bore him yet
another son and daughter, were but rather unhappy
interludes. There were, however, delightful occasions when her own brother John—the mischievous
jolly John—came to pay a brief visit. Then there
were wigs on the green !

The Unitarians of those days were, of course,
ardent philanthropists, and little Elizabeth was set
to teach a class in Sunday school before she was
fourteen. This was the usual thing amongst the
Nonconformists of the day. A Sunday school
was a new venture, disapproved of by the high
and dry, and keenly supported by those who
were interested in education, religious and secular.
A child intelligent as to scholarship and versed
in the Scriptures was eagerly pressed into the
service, and this particular child adored little
children.

A happy home it must have been, though an
uneventful and quiet one. Mrs. Lumb—the name
itself is attractive—had a little farm, bred pigs,
poultry and geese—what could be more delightful ?
The girl had the Holland cousins to play with, but
her learning appears to have been given by, or for
the main part derived from her relatives. In
housekeeping she had much and thorough instruction from Aunt Lumb. Perhaps this sort of happy-
go-lucky education is as satisfactory to an intelligent
girl as that of a modern High School, since, though
there are sure to be big gaps in it, the main part, the
developing of intelligence, is likely to be present.
So at least it was with Elizabeth Stevenson. One
thing she did learn as an only child, and that was
not to be afraid of expressing her opinion. In an
age when girls were looked on as creatures expected
to defer their views to whoever was older than
themselves and to those who were considered to be
their betters, Elizabeth—the only child—wrote and
spoke what she thought. This rare gift was worth
much to the future novelist, though it brought her
often enough into disfavour. The few letters that
remain from an early date are delightfully un-
self-conscious.

There was in Knutsford an excellent dancing
master, once the instructor of William Pitt, whose
name was Rogier, and who also taught Elizabeth
the French language. With him she made wonderful progress. She describes him in the paper
termed *My French Master*, though, of course, under
a different name, and in this record tells how he
hated dirty boots, and how the children were told
to give him the driest part of the path, and how it
was impossible to make him keep to that part, and

how, despite his politeness in choosing the mud for his portion of the road, his polished boots returned without a speck, while his companions' were covered with dirt.   The dancing master was also a botanist, and in this taste little Elizabeth sympathised, being particularly interested in a wild saxifrage which was to be found in the vicinity of her home.   Her aunt's home was one of those big red-brick houses built on the edge of the common and full of comfortable corners and window-seats.   There was a small garden in front which divided it from the heath, and a large flower garden behind, with a vegetable garden behind that.   In the centre of the lawn in front was a large old fir tree under which little Elizabeth used to sit and do her sewing.   Indeed, her lessons were sometimes conducted out-of-doors, when she was permitted to take out table and chairs.   There were two kitchens, one with no less than four ovens, and here, as in many farm-houses, all the baking and cooking was conducted, and it was here that the future Mrs. Gaskell learned the art of cooking, baking, and brewing.   Altogether her child-life was just the life she was to write about. Church House, where the kind Dr. Peter Holland lived, was close by ; one could see the old house where Lord Clive as a boy used to spring from one pier to another at the risk of his life.   Sandlebridge, Dr. Holland's mother's and father's dwelling, was about three miles off.   Church House owned the family pew—a big square one—in the old church of Knutsford, and, though Dissenters, the Hollands kept a tenacious hold upon it, although it was used only occasionally by visitors not of their faith.   Her grandfather, the land-agent and farmer, died when Elizabeth was but six years old.

At the age of fourteen, Elizabeth was sent to a boarding school at Stratford-on-Avon, kept by three sisters named Byerley : sisters usually combined to carry on a school in those days ; before this time there was a party of five spinster ladies who owned the school. The family had, as was likewise a common occurrence then with schoolmistresses' families, got into financial difficulties, and hence the launching into school teaching. As usual, there was one of the Byerley sisters, Miss Catherine, who was the attractive sister beloved by her pupils. Another sister was unfortunately deaf as a post. The old schoolhouse of Avonbank was said to have been for a brief period the home of Shakespeare in 1602, and in any case it had been ecclesiastical property and the residence of certain Benedictine monks of Worcester, and had, as the House of St. Mary, been used as a school from the beginning of the fifteenth century. In Shakespeare's day it was owned by his cousin, Thomas Greene. Why it was allowed to be destroyed in 1866 one cannot fathom. The present Avonbank was built near it. One can hardly imagine any outside circumstance more likely to arouse the imaginative powers of a young girl than to have her lessons in the house in which Shakespeare lived, and where he may have written part of " Hamlet." The school was a good one as schools went in those days ; the teaching in girls' schools of the time has been too much decried. The girl had plenty of amusement and learned there French, Italian, music and deportment with success. It was not cheap, for a little later it cost about £148 a year to board a girl there—a large sum for those days, though this included holiday time and necessary articles of dress. But the main point—the crux—

in all girls' schools lies in the head mistress ; and in this case Miss Byerley, the daughter of the manager for the Wedgwoods, and great-niece of the famous Josiah Wedgwood, had good traditions and apparently some ideas, advanced for her age, about the position of her sex. Two of her pupils were granddaughters of Dr. Joseph Priestley, sent from America, where Priestley had taken refuge after the burning of his house in Manchester. There is a letter written to William Howitt, telling of Elizabeth's visits as a schoolgirl, with other schoolgirls, to Clopton Hall, about a mile from Stratford-on-Avon, the home of one of their companions. There she heard the ghost story which made so great an impression upon her and which came to be published later on.

In 1827, Elizabeth left school and returned to her beloved aunt. Her stay with her was, however, brief, for this was the time when the poor brother disappeared so mysteriously in India ; the father's health also broke down so that he sent for the girl, now seventeen years old, to join him at Chelsea. There two very sad years were spent just when they might have been so happy with good Aunt Lumb. It was a difficult relationship, that with a step-mother and a father only seen on occasional visits to Chelsea, a half-brother William and a half-sister Catherine. However, to 3, Beaufort Row she went, and there she endeavoured to carry on her studies in Latin, French and Italian under her father's directions.

The poor girl was, in fact, miserably unhappy in her new surroundings. This is what she says of this time : " Long ago I lived in Chelsea occasionally with my father and stepmother, and *very, very* unhappy I used to be ; and if it had not been for the beautiful grand river, which was an inexplicable comfort to me, and a family of the name of Kennett, I think my child's heart would have broken." It was a great deal for one of her reticence in family matters to confess.

Her father's health was gradually giving way and after a long and painful illness he had a paralytic stroke and died on March 22nd, 1829. He was buried in St. Luke's burial ground in King's Road. The tragedy was that the girl was just coming to love the almost unknown father and, indeed, she tended him to the best of her powers. His affairs were left in a bad state and there were his widow and younger children to provide for. A rich relative, Mr. Swinton Holland, took Elizabeth to his house in Park Lane for a visit—a change of scene for her—and then she went to her kind Aunt Lumb at Knutsford once more. Eight years later Mrs. Lumb died, leaving her the reversion of half of her estate, so that she had an income of her own of £80 a year. The invalid daughter inherited a fortune on her father's death and wished to settle it on her cousin Elizabeth after her mother's death, but died herself before the deed was made out.

For some reason, not very clear, Aunt Lumb thought the girl should, at this time, go elsewhere to live. Elizabeth's cousin in London, Sir Henry Holland, who lived in Brook Street, as befitted a prosperous physician, had been the pupil of the Rev. William Turner, of Newcastle, in his early days and had resided with him. Thus it was possibly he who suggested the girl paying Mrs. Turner a visit so that her ideas might be enlarged, and her education completed, and considering the nature of her life so far, the suggestion seemed a wise one. She spent two successive winters with the Turners. Mr. Turner was one of a family which had for generations been Unitarian ministers and he carried on his work in a famous Newcastle church for more than half a century. He was also one of those remarkable men who were not only teachers and ministers but extremely useful citizens. His name is honoured in Newcastle still. At this time he was in full vigour despite advanced years, and as his first wife had been a Holland, a cousin of Elizabeth's mother, he was the more disposed to help her. His second wife was, indeed, a connection also, for, as has been noticed, all these intelligent Unitarian families had apparently, like the Friends, intermarried. The Turner connection gave the future Mrs. Gaskell much of the material used in " Ruth," which she used to call her " Newcastle story."

It was a happy circumstance that brought the young girl to a home of so much intelligence and keenness, for these were the days when the new Literary and Philosophical Societies were being set on foot and public lectures instituted, and in all these new social ventures Mr. Turner was deeply interested, as well as in the institution of Sunday schools. He was likewise a valued friend and helper to the young engineer, George Stephenson.

About 1830, Elizabeth left Newcastle and, with Mr. Turner's daughter, Ann, went to Edinburgh to live in lodgings there. The change might very likely have been due to the outbreak of cholera, which was specially virulent in Newcastle. The life in Edinburgh, without many introductions, must have seemed dull and drab after the society of Newcastle where Mr. Turner was a well-known figure, acquainted with the important people of the town. The girl must have thought of the early life of her parents, who had enjoyed the literary society of the place, with some longing after the same. The *Scots Magazine*, edited by her father, was dead and *Blackwood's Magazine* reigned in its stead. Scott was struggling bravely on between Abbotsford and Edinburgh. Probably the two young women had themselves a certain number of friends, however, and Elizabeth had grown into a beautiful girl, so striking a girl was she that a lovely miniature was painted of her by an artist named Thompson, and a bust was made by a sculptor of the day, David Dunbar, Allan Cuningham's friend and Chantry's pupil.* Who arranged for these to be done we do not know. In any case the charm of Edinburgh impressed itself upon her, for later on she writes to Ellen Nussey, the friend of Charlotte Brontë : " Edinburgh, compared to London, is like a vivid page of history compared to a dull lecture on political economy." This winter was but the forerunner of many visits in later life.

But now there was to be a change in Elizabeth Stevenson's life. The daughter of Mr. Turner, of Newcastle, had married Mr. John Gooch Robberds, the minister of the Cross Street Unitarian Church at Manchester. At their house Elizabeth met the junior minister, her future husband, William Gaskell. The Robberds had been rather intimate friends of the family and Elizabeth paid them visits when at Knutsford. They lived at Greenheys, then the rural district described in " Mary Barton." The matter soon developed and William Gaskell came to

* A replica of this bust from the studio of Mr. Hamo Thornycroft is in the Library of Owens College.

C

Knutsford where she then was, to see the young lady of his admiration, and in an amusing letter to her future sister-in-law she tells of the visit to " darling Aunt Lumb " who had been ill. " You can't think what rude speeches she makes to me. To give you a slight specimen : ' Why, Elizabeth, how could this man ever take a fancy to such a little giddy, thoughtless thing as you ? ' and many other equally pretty speeches."

The marriage took place in August, 1832, in St. John's Parish Church, Knutsford, for in those days weddings were not solemnised in dissenting chapels.   The bride's uncle, Mr. Peter Holland, gave Elizabeth away, and it is recorded, what we can well believe, that the two principal actors in the ceremony were an extraordinarily handsome couple.

William Gaskell, whose father had studied at the Warrington Academy, and knew the Aikins, one of whom became Mrs. Barbauld, was also educated at Warrington, along with Josiah Wedgwood's sons. Afterwards he graduated at Glasgow University, and then he entered the theological training college for Unitarian ministers at York. This college was transferred from York to Manchester and became the " Manchester New College." Later on it removed to London and subsequently to its present abode at Oxford, where it still preserves its name as Manchester College. At Manchester Mr. Gaskell held the Professorship of English History and Literature in the college along with his Cross Street pastorate. He held the latter charge for over fifty years, during twenty-six of which years he was joint minister with Mr. Robberds. As a teacher he was a grave, serious man, but not without wit as a story shows. One of his pupils at the New College where he was Professor of English History and Literature blundered egregiously. The lecturer sprang to his feet with such vehemence that his chair, already rickety, went to pieces with the hasty movement. Mr. Gaskell glanced over his shoulder and exclaimed : " Mr. ——, the very chair can't stand it ! "

Now the bride was set up in her little home in Dover Street, Manchester, and the life must have been simple and economical to begin with. Later on Mrs. Lynn Linton talks of the plainness of young Mrs. Gaskell's attire : " Her beautiful white arms were bare to the shoulder, and as destitute of bracelets as her hands were of gloves." The young woman was still a girl in nature in the year 1832. Certainly she had lighted on an unexceptionable bridegroom, slender and distinguished-looking, standing six feet high, one who " walked with stately graciousness," " there was something clean and sweet and refined and pure in his very presence." The character thus given appears to have been no exaggeration. Indeed, all who knew William Gaskell give evidence to the same effect, and as Elizabeth was a beautiful young woman the two must have made a striking couple.

The honeymoon in North Wales was a time of enormous enjoyment judging from their letters. The young husband writes in his enthusiasm : " My bonny wee wife—*My* bonny wee wife—grows I do think more bonny than ever." The couple returned to take up house on the bride's twenty-second birth-day. The house was convenient for the chapel, in a semi-rural district near the old Manchester High School for Girls and not far from the University, then Owens College. Young Mrs. Gaskell threw herself into her husband's work and soon got to know the factory hands.

The chapel dated back to 1694 and was said to be the first Dissenting place of worship in Manchester. It suffered on one occasion from the violence of the Jacobite mob in 1715, for it had no dealings with the Stewarts. Its creed in former times seems to have been uncertain and to have been termed Unitarian or Presbyterian indifferently. It is still an important chapel, now, of course, in the middle of the great city but still typically surrounded by a graveyard. The chapel claimed amongst its members many of the most intelligent as well as philanthropic of the citizens of the place and there was a chapel library possessing many rare theological books.

In 1833, the year after her marriage, the first child came, but, alas, stillborn—a very touching poem was written on the event ; the following year a girl arrived and named Marianne ; she was followed by three other daughters. In early days the Gaskells had thoughts of turning to literature in a mild way, and in 1837, five years after their marriage, they published jointly a poem called " Sketches Among the Poor " (No. 1) in *Blackwood's Magazine*. No. 2 did not follow, so presumably the young authors received little encouragement from the editor of " Maga." Mrs. Gaskell spoke of this abortive scheme as " spoken near a dog-rose " and therefore unsuccessful. If she did not write for publication Elizabeth Gaskell wrote letters copiously, all in the beautiful Italian hand of the day and frequently crossed. Amongst her correspondents was Mary Howitt; but many of her letters were said to have been destroyed by the dishonesty of a page-boy who sold them as waste-paper.

The life of the young people was domestic without being carried away by domesticity. They were living in a busy and growing manufacturing town overflowing with life and interest and took full part in its work. Manchester in the thirties was really a sad spot ; indeed, there was little but misery in town and country at this time so far as the working people were concerned. The Industrial Revolution had done its best or worst with the people of the land and had to bear the consequences. The measure of political power given in 1832 only seemed to make their sufferings more articulate. The agitation for political power and for the abolition of the corn tax was at its height when the Gaskells married. There was misery in the rural districts which was brutally punished, and there was equal misery in the industrial districts where starvation faced the suffering masses. Rioting was common and the homes of the well-to-do were often barricaded at nights in fear of what might happen. There is no wonder that these things sank into the hearts of the young people and especially into that of a mother.

Besides their work outside, they read, the two ; and Mr. Gaskell prepared his lectures on " The Poets and Poetry of Humble Life " in the manner of his favourite authors, Crabbe and Hood ; his wife naturally (in those days) helped in the search for suitable facts. Probably Mr. Gaskell looked at the events of the day from the somewhat Olympian heights of the preacher and lecturer to working men. But there was nothing Olympian in the manner Mrs. Gaskell regarded the events of the day. She was by nature bright and merry, but the sufferings of the mill workers were very real to her : she was busy with her young children and wifely duties and had not much time to concentrate on other work during the early part of her married life. These things, however, were sinking into her heart and preparing the way for the outburst that was to follow, when arguments of patience, of *laissez-faire*, of the political economy of the day, were met by the rough words : " Have yo' seen your child clemmed to death ? " There was the plain truth that made the Poetry of Humble Life ring false.

So far, however, this had not come to pass. Mr. Gaskell was a sensible man, fully conscious of his civic duties. His wife was still the same bright girl, thought to be somewhat flighty. It was one of the successful marriages which never cease to surprise the onlooker. William Gaskell, serious, dignified, informing, with a love of writing pamphlets and hymns and giving lectures of an improving sort—a man of real education of an old-fashioned type and a most useful citizen to whom his work was his paramount interest—had allied himself to a bright, pretty girl who had all the traditions of her age as to wifely and motherly duty, who was ready to play her part conscientiously as a minister's wife, but who yet had an adventurous spirit within her, that if awakened might carry her into a world undreamt of by her grave husband. She was like many women of her period, taught to accept the lot put before her and be guided by those to whom she had committed her life. But the awakening came, first of all in her feelings for those around her, which was so intense that she was compelled to do something to record publicly what these feelings were.

The Gaskells were living in a live town with people of interest like Francis Newman, the Cardinal's younger brother who became a professor in Manchester New College, and many others, and Mr. Gaskell came into touch with them through his connection with Owens College and also through his public work. But though the town was still, comparatively speaking, small, having only about 300,000 inhabitants, it was suffering terribly from unemployment. More than a hundred mills and other works were standing idle, thousands of dwellings and many shops and offices were unoccupied. And it was estimated that there were eight thousand people whose weekly income only averaged one-and-twopence-halfpenny. No wonder there were riots, for the people were literally starving. It seemed a depressing surrounding into which to bring a young wife. She and her husband did their best, giving away what they could. He served on a Public Health Committee which made what preparations could be made to prevent a further epidemic of cholera by taking preventive steps in good time and thereby forestalling the work of the " Medical Officer of Health " who followed later on. This good voluntary work must have been of great use in a time when the sanitary condition of towns was little thought of and when manufacturing towns rushed up unwholesome buildings to accommodate the overflowing factory operatives. It seems odd to us to think that it was considered incongruous that a dissenting minister should have the " honour " of moving the first resolution at a public meeting called to consider the health conditions of the town ! Mr. Gaskell was chairman of the Portico Library, still a famous institution, and then a place where, as its name implies, discussions took a high level. They were also hot discussions, but the chairman appeared to have been able to keep the peace. All those outside occupations along with his lectures, the Principalship of the Unitarian Home

Missionary College, and other Church work kept him busy and much away from home. People were waking up to the fact that something must be done to stem the flood of misery that was around them, and on the political side the Free Trade controversy was in full swing. There were those who blamed intemperance for much of the poverty amongst the people, regarding it as cause rather than effect. So Temperance reforms were set on foot, and Mr. Gaskell served on another committee for the better regulation of beer-houses and places of amusement. In those days women were not, of course, called upon to undertake public work. He was not, as this shows, extreme in his views on such matters, any more than his wife, though teetotalism was coming to be fashionable; nor was he himself a teetotaller. On the whole Manchester was regarded as the home of progress in science and politics. It had, whether owing to its political and social circumstances or not, produced a number of eminent men such as Dalton, Joule and Roscoe, while its famous Grammar school educated De Quincey and Harrison Ainsworth. Cobden's house it was that became the first home of the College founded by John Owens* : this was the College in which Mr. Gaskell lectured.

* Now Victoria University.

IT was a formidable thing in those days for a woman to plunge into authorship, and indeed in young Mrs. Gaskell's case the " plunge " was a very gradual one as befitted her sex and age. When she was at school at Stratford, Elizabeth Stevenson had visited an old house called Clopton Hall, reputed to be haunted. Ghosts and haunted houses and all stories connected with them had an immense attraction for her, and she wrote an account of this visit to her friend, William Howitt, in the form of a letter. Now William Howitt and his wife, Mary, were veritable bookmakers—they are said to have had a hundred and fifty to their credit between them—and being bent on encouraging improving literature, the two at once urged this promising new writer to " use her pen for the public benefit " as it was expressed in the stilted language of the day. Mary Howitt says in her autobiography that a letter signed E. C. Gaskell was sent to her husband on the announcement of his intended " Visits to Remarkable Places," so that she probably began the correspondence. Of course, any advice from persons of much literary experience and considerably her seniors must have made a deep impression on Elizabeth Gaskell, but it can hardly be said that they were the instigators of her later work. The Howitts were great travellers, especially in Germany, and the acquaintanceship with them began during a wonderful tour up the Rhine in which they were her companions. This took place in the year 1841, when Elizabeth was thirty-one years of age. Incited by her first contact with literary people this tour was the source of various short stories which came to be published later on.

This extract is from a letter to William and Mary Howitt thanking them for the pleasure they have given her by their charming descriptions of natural scenery :

I was brought up in a country town, and my lot is now to live in or rather on the borders of a great manufacturing town, but when spring days first come and the bursting leaves and sweet earthy smells tell me that " Somer is y comen in," I feel a stirring instinct and long to be off into the deep grassy solitudes of the country, just like a bird wakens up from its content at the change of the seasons and wends its way to some well-known but till then forgotten land. But as I happen to be a woman instead of a bird, and as I have ties at home, and duties to perform, and as, moreover, I have no wings like a dove to fly away, but if I travel I must go by coach, and " remember the coachman," why I must stay at home and content myself with recalling the happy scenes which your books bring up before me.

It shows how the young woman was prepared to respond to anything that touched her innate sense of natural beauty.

The idea of authorship was now established, but so far it was but amateurish : there was no driving force behind. Circumstances made the vision into a reality.

By the time this question arose, Mrs. Gaskell had been married for nine years and three daughters had arrived.   In 1842 a move was made from 14, Dover Street, to 121, Upper Rumford Street, a larger and more commodious house.   The drawing-room was refurnished and a new piano bought which meant stability and continuity.   Then in 1843, the first and only boy was born.   Ten months later, this little Willie, named after his father, was taken with his sister to Festiniog in North Wales, the place the parents had visited on their honeymoon, and the residence of a certain Charles Holland, a relative. There the girl contracted scarlet fever, and after moving to Portmadoc, a short distance off, the baby developed the disease and died.   This sorrow left a permanent effect on the mother's life : she never really got over it.

There followed a black time in Mrs. Gaskell's history.   Not only was she smitten by her own sorrow and filled with grief and depression of spirit ; there was besides this grief which, as she says, the banal words of comfort then the custom to administer seemed only to increase, an intense feeling of sympathy with the sufferings of the people around her. Her husband had the wisdom to see that self-expression was the best and only way to meet the blank sense of absolute despair, and he encouraged her to write.   He saw that for her the old-fashioned method of working for the poor and giving or administering alms was not enough.   His wife felt constrained in some way or other to move people's hearts, and possibly she had the power to do so by her pen.   Perhaps, he must have told himself, she might by her writings do what other writers were doing at the time, and help to redress grievous wrongs. Were not Dickens, Charles Reade and Disraeli doing (or about to do in Reade's case) the same ?

Anyhow this time of blackness had its result, and " Mary Barton " came into existence, though it was not published till 1848, for the actual publication was no easy matter for an unknown author. The impetus to write, if it were lacking, was finally given by the words of a mill-worker spoken of before, to whom Mrs. Gaskell was trying to inculcate patience : " Ay, ma'am, but have yo' ever seen a child clemmed to death ? " This plain speaking clinched the matter for her—she spoke no more of patience, something must be done.

The time she described was avowedly rather earlier than the date at which she wrote (1845–47) but not very much so. It referred to the very early forties, the time which Disraeli also treats in his novels. " Sybil " was published in 1845 before " Mary Barton," but there is no evidence that there was any special connection between the two works. There had been bad harvests in the later thirties, and the rejection of the great Chartist petition in 1838–39—the People's Charter—with its ten points, made feeling very bitter, for more than a million people had, or were supposed to have, signed it. The account of John Barton's visit to London as a delegate on this occasion, and the bitter sense of disappointment on the refusal of the House of Commons to consider the Charter, represents faithfully what really occurred. After that date things grew desperate, and there was seething discontent till 1842, when riots broke out in the county of Lancashire. Then later on came the further Petition for the six points of the People's Charter, and when the House of Commons still refused to hear these petitions, not only riots but a General Strike began, and workers were forced to leave the mills. The rioting was of course dealt with by the police, but men's minds were now awakening to the desperate condition of things ; Lord Ashley (afterwards Lord Shaftesbury) brought to light many of the hardships that were being undergone ; his reforms in regard to the prevention of young children's work were not always appreciated by their parents, as is shown in " Mary Barton," but they moved people's hearts, and money was collected for relief, so that something at least was accomplished before the Repeal of the Corn Laws. The *Manchester Guardian*, not the advanced paper it afterwards became, wrote about the " morbid sensibility to the conditions of the operatives " displayed by Mrs. Gaskell in accordance with the fashion set in of late among " the gentry and landed aristocracy."* This looked as if it were the class Disraeli hoped so much from rather than the middle classes that were taking up the cudgels for the poor. But this is not certain, for the agitation for Reform was mainly middle class, though it was not at all in favour of interfering with the established relationship between capital and labour, and Chartism repudiated any alliance with middle class radicalism. Naturally from these Olympic heights Mrs. Gaskell, as a woman, was told that the matters she dealt with were " either above the comprehension of the authoress or beyond her sphere of knowledge."

Elizabeth Gaskell had suffered and she knew what it was to suffer. This time of sorrow and deep

* February 28th, 1849. Quoted by Prof. Ward in his Introduction to " Mary Barton."

feeling brushed aside the conventionalities that had
hitherto governed her life.   So far she had been a
good mother of children, a " faithful " minister's
wife, a charming hostess in a quiet way amongst
pleasant and intelligent friends.   Now at last " she
found herself " ;   she came to know what had been
unknown to her, she found latent powers of observation that she herself knew nothing of.   In fact
she broke through the chrysalis of conventionality,
and probably none in the present day know what
it was to do this for a well brought up young woman
in the middle of last century.

Anyhow she wrote with a bitter pen of those who
were in a state where " lamentations and tears are
thrown aside as useless, but in which the lips are
compressed for curses, and the hands clenched and
ready to smite."   Strange words for the wife of the
minister of the respectable old chapel to use :   to us
the strangeness is not only in the awakening to that
which we feel the blind might almost have seen, but
to the fact that it opened up not just the life of the
factory hands of Manchester before her, but also
that of the men and women of " Cranford."

The story of " Mary Barton " is not as well known
now as it was years ago when it aroused so much
feeling in England, and made a sensation not much
less than that made by " Sybil," though it did not
bear the same political consequences.   All Mrs.
Gaskell's tales that count are drawn very closely
from real life, a somewhat embarrassing fact for her
friends and acquaintances, perhaps, but one that
was very evident.   After all, it has been so in many
of the best novels of this time and of every time.
In pure Romance figures must be invented, and that
was done in some of Elizabeth Gaskell's strange and

romantic short tales ; probably it is so in regard to wholly humorous writing, but in that she played comparatively little part. In the character studies of Mrs. Gaskell or Charlotte Brontë or Trollope, or a dozen other such writers, the characters are quite evidently drawn from individual men and women whom the writers have known. In regard to places the same was true. Green Heys Fields, where the story opens, was as well known to Manchester people under a very similar name as were some of the characters. Not that each of the characters was portrayed from an individual known to the author. That, of course, could not have been. But the principal characters certainly were so, and the minor ones were taken from the people known generally to her in daily life. As to the facts of the story, the author herself says : " In ' Mary Barton ' nobody and nothing was real but the character of John Barton ; the circumstances are different, but the character and some of the speeches are exactly those of a poor man I know. . . . I told the story according to a fancy of my own ; to really *see* the scenes I tried to describe (and they *were* as real as my own life at the time) and then to tell them as nearly as I could, as if I were speaking to a friend over the fire on a winter's night and describing real occurrences."

There is the trade unionist John Barton driven to extremities by the hard facts of life, and finally becoming a murderer ; there is the heroine Mary Barton, his daughter, who is flattered by the attentions of young Mr. Carson, his employer's son, and who goes through much tribulation before she is mated to her faithful Jem, wrongfully accused of having committed the murder owing to jealousy of his rival; and there are a number of minor characters generally well and carefully drawn from men and women within the writer's knowledge. It is only near the close that the didactic element appears too clearly, and this was partly forced upon her by her literary advisers. Job Leigh, a character in the book, argues with Mr. Carson, the representative of the employers' interests—argues against the *laissez-faire* doctrines of the orthodox economists who would let each man be self-reliant and fend for himself : " Facts have proved, and are daily proving, how much better it is for every man to be independent of help and self-reliant." Job's reply was : " You can never work facts as you would fixed quantities, and say, given two facts and the product is so and so. God has given men feelings and passions which cannot be worked into the problem, because they are for ever changing and uncertain. God has also made some weak ; not in any one way, but in all. One is weak in body, another in mind, another in steadiness of purpose, a fourth cannot tell right from wrong, and so on ; or if he can tell the right, he wants strength to hold by it. Now to my thinking, them that is strong in any of God's gifts is meant to help the weak, be hanged to the facts ! "

Mr. Carson, who is depicted at the trial as bitterly and really brutally disposed to the supposed murderer of his son, is made to become at least a more considerate employer, and though the habits and manners of former days remained, so that he was considered hard and cold at heart, he altered, and many of the improvements carried out in the system of employment in Manchester are said to owe their origin to his stern, thoughtful mind. It was an unfortunate thing that an employer had really been murdered, though under very different circumstances, and that his name became quite unjustly associated with the story.* Mrs. Gaskell was not appreciative of the fact in writing her tale that this was quite likely to be the case, though perhaps she ought to have been so. Probably indeed she was more influenced by certain Scottish trials earlier in the century of men driven desperate in the same way. She wrote a little later the following letter to Sir John Potter which makes the whole matter clear :

I wish to give "Mary Barton" and another little book to the Free Library. But before I do so I should like to make a private inquiry of you (with whom the Institution has become so honourably identified) as to how far my giving the former of these books would be distasteful to you. Of course, I cannot be unaware of the opinions which you and your brother have so frequently and openly expressed with regard to "Mary Barton" ; and, as I feel great respect for all your exertions in behalf of the Library, it appeared to me as if it would be an impertinence on my part to send the obnoxious book to any collection in which you took an

* Thomas Ashton of Pole Bank was murdered in consequence of a dispute with the trade union. His brother James had gone to a dance and he went to the mill that evening in his place. The last person who spoke to him was his sister Mary, a girl of twelve years old. Within an hour of leaving her the body was carried into the house. The older girl of fifteen was playing on the piano to her parents when they heard the shot and trusted nothing serious had happened. Shortly afterwards the servant called Mr. Ashton out, and Mrs. Ashton followed to find the body of their son in the hall.

Mr. Arthur Potter writes that Mary married his father, Thomas B. Potter, of Bride Hall, Pendleton, a member of Cross Street Chapel. In 1849 his mother started reading "Mary Barton," and when she came to the account of the murder she fainted. Mr. Potter's father and his uncle, Sir John Potter, blamed Mrs. Gaskell for reviving this tragedy, but the explanatory letter written by her removed all ill feeling.

interest without previously asking you to tell me honestly if you would really rather that it was not included in the Catalogue ? May I add one word ? Of course, I had heard of young Mr. Ashton's murder at the time when it took place ; but I knew none of the details, nothing about the family, never read the trial (if trial there were, which I do not to this day know) : and if the circumstances were present to my mind at the time of my writing " Mary Barton " it was so unconsciously, although its occurrence, and that of one or two similar cases at Glasgow at the time of a strike, were, I have no doubt, suggestive of the plot, as having shown me to what lengths the animosity of irritated workmen would go. I have been exceedingly grieved to find how much pain I have unintentionally given to a family of whom I know nothing but that they have suffered a great sorrow ; I can hardly wonder that they, not knowing me, and believing what they did, should have been angry ; but I would infinitely rather never have written the book than have been guilty of the want of all common feeling, and respect for misfortune, which I should have shown if I had made Mr. Ashton's death into a mere subject for a story. May I request you to consider this note as private ? I shall not name either it, or the purport of your answer to any one, except my husband, who is at present ignorant of my writing to you.

Yours truly,
E. C. Gaskell.

One of the most interesting parts of the book is the description of Barton's journey to London to present the Charter, and the feelings of the Chartists on its rejection by Parliament, and another the **description** of Job Leigh's journey from **London** bringing back an infant grandchild whose parents had died there of fever.   Job's experiences remind one of the experiences of Silas Marner, also left with an infant to tend without knowledge.   Job and the other grandfather who was with him had to rest in an inn, and as the chambermaid was able to pacify the crying child, a bright thought occurred to the two men :

" ' Young woman, have you gotten a spare night cap ? '

" ' Missis always keeps night caps for gentlemen as does not like to unpack,' says she rather quick.

" ' Ay, but, young woman, it's one of your night caps I want.   Th' babby seems to have taken a mind to you ; and may be in th' dark it might take me for yo if I'd gotten your night cap on.'

" The chambermaid smirked and went for the cap, but I laughed outright at th' oud bearded chap thinking he'd make hissel like a woman just by putting on a woman's cap.   Howe'er he'd not be laughed out on't, so I held the babby till he were in bed.   Such a night as we had on it !   Babby began to scream o' th' ould fashion and we took turn and turn about to sit up and rock it.   My heart were very sore for the little one, as it groped about wi' its mouth ; but for a' that I could scarce keep fra' smiling at th' thought o' us two oud chaps, th' one wi' a woman's night cap on, sitting on our hinder ends for half the night hushabying a babby as wouldn't be hushabied ! ' "

This is a humorous part of the tale, but most of it is sad.   There are too many bedside scenes, scenes of death, for popular taste, and here and there the authoress breaks into reflections on the sufferings of the people and tells of how these sufferers " wept first and then cursed."   How, she asks, could such hardships such as starvation and sleeping on cold hearthstones for weeks and weeks in damp cellars fail to produce acts of ferocious precipitation ? It is a terrible indictment of the individualism of the time and it drew force from the fact that it was written in no exaggerated style but was taken from the sights that the writer had seen with her own eyes and from words that she had heard from men and women grown desperate. This is a foretaste of what was to follow so soon, in the agitation regarding land-values and the socialistic point of view generally.

" ' Why, the very land as fetched but sixty pound twenty years agone is now worth six hundred, and that, too, is owing to our labour ; but look at yo, and see me and poor Davenport yonder ; whatten better are we ?

" ' I don't want money, child ! D—n their charity and their money ! I want work, and it is my right. I want work.' "

This is language Elizabeth Gaskell probably heard with her own ears and it sank into her heart.

At the time " Mary Barton " was, of course, said by its critics not to be a true representation of the facts and to be a libel on the employers. It was declared to be an incitement to class hatred : why, it was asked, did a minister's wife not point out that the spirit of improvidence brought about the sad results in Barton's case ? The *Edinburgh Review* considered such books " likely to be mischievous in the South from the lack of stress on artisan improvidence " (the North was evidently esteemed better trained !). The employers, it was declared, were not the selfish beings they were depicted as being, nor were the conditions such as she described. In her next book, however, " North and South," an employer is depicted as making an effort to get on good terms with his people, and in no case are the employed drawn as models of virtue. They are, what is far more important, ordinary men and women with the faults and virtues of ordinary men and women whether rich or poor. Disraeli took another line and made the condition of the poor a party cry. Perhaps he did more for the end in view than did Mrs. Gaskell by taking the political view and waking up a political party, but both helped in bringing home to the people of this land the desperate results of the Industrial Revolution. It was not in the writer's power as a woman and mother to look for any grandiose solution of the problem such as Disraeli affected. " England once more possessing a free monarchy and a privileged and prosperous people " meant as little to her as did Coningsby's vision of the town of Manchester when he " entered chambers vaster than are told of in Arabian fables and peopled with inhabitants more wondrous than Afrite or Peri. In there he beheld in long-continued ranks, those mysterious forms full of existence without life, that perform with facility, and in an instant, what man can fulfil only with difficulty and in days." To her machinery was but machinery, and men were men, and it was for men and women as they were at the time she wrote that she cared supremely : the nature of the " Nation " that was to rescue them was not her concern. Years of toil were not going to succeed in obliterating the evil done by losing sight of humanity in the search for prosperity. In the meantime it brought on Elizabeth Gaskell personal enmity and journalistic censure, serious things for her to face as a woman living in the best circles of a great provincial town. It is curious to learn from a letter written in February, 1849, to Mr. W. S. Williams that Miss Brontë had been reading the book, which she calls a "clever though painful tale," and that she was a little dismayed to find herself "in some measure anticipated both in subject and incident." She asks Mr. Williams's opinion in this regard. One can see but little similarity between "Mary Barton" and "Shirley," which is probably what was meant.

The letters that followed the publication in the autumn of 1848 were of course of all sorts, but chiefly critical. Mrs. Gaskell wanted the authorship to be concealed and writes to her friend Miss Ewart, who apparently divined the real state of the case:

I did write it, but how did you find it out? I do want it to be concealed if possible, and I don't think anybody here has the least idea who is the author. . . . I am almost frightened at my own action in writing it. . . . I can only say I wanted to represent the subject in the light in which some of the workmen certainly consider to be true *; not that I dare to say is the abstract absolute truth.*

That some of the men do view the subject in the way I have tried to represent, I have personal evidence ; and I think somewhere in the first volume you may find a sentence stating that my intention was simply to represent the view many of the workpeople took. I do think that we must all acknowledge that there are duties connected with the manufacturing system not fully understood as yet, and evils existing in relation to it which may be remedied in some degree, although we as yet do not see how ; but surely there is no harm in directing the attention to the existence of such evils. No one can feel more deeply than I how wicked *it is to do anything to excite class against class ; and it has*

been most unconscious if I have done so . . . no praise
could compensate me for the self-reproach I shall feel
if I have written unjustly.

One would imagine that the daughter of a Liberal
member of Parliament (Mr. Ewart), the instigator of
the first Public Libraries Act, would have been
sympathetic with any attempt to grapple with the
evils of the Industrial Revolution, the effects of which
were to defeat the efforts of generations of reformers.
Susanna Winkworth, her great friend, tells how
Mrs. Gaskell lent the book to a certain family of
Chartists, zealous followers of Feargus O'Connor,
industrious respectable people, but very poor, and
the husband well read but " full of the bitterest
feelings against the middle and upper classes."
They had been so delighted with it that " they sat up
at night to read it and cried over it." So little did
it apparently take of sympathy to touch these poor
people. Carlyle's letter is one of the most striking
of all the many letters Mrs. Gaskell received and it
must have cheered her in her troubles. It is dated
from Chelsea, 1848.

Dear Madam,
 (For I catch the treble of that fine melodious voice
very well)—We have read your book here, my wife first
and then I ; both of us with real pleasure. A beautiful,
cheerfully pious, social, clear and observant character
is everywhere recognisable in the writer, which sense is
the welcomest sight any writer can show in his books ;
your field is moreover new, important, full of rich
material (which, as is usual, required a soul of true
opulence to recognise them as such). The result is a
Book deserving to take its place far above the ordinary

garbage of Novels—a book which every intelligent person
may read with entertainment; and which it will do
every one good to read. I gratefully accept it as a real
contribution (about the first real one) towards developing
a huge subject, which has lain dumb too long, and really
ought to speak for itself, and tell us its meaning a little,
if there be any voice in it at all. Speech or literature
(which is, or should be, select speech) could hardly find
a more rational function, I think, at present. You
will probably give us other books on the same matter;
and " Mary Barton," according to my auguries of its
reception here, is likely to procure you sufficient in-
vitation. May you do it well and ever better ! Your
writing is already very beautiful, soft, clear and natural.
On the side of veracity, or devout earnestness of mind,
I find you already strong. May you live long to write
good books.

T. Carlyle.

This was indeed praise from the highest living
authority and one not easily satisfied. The two
seemed to be better suited in impersonal correspondence than in personal contact, as appears later.

Any anonymity had soon to be given up, for false
reports arose such as that the author was a Mrs.
Wheeler, a clergyman's wife who wrote " Cotton
Land." Whewell admired the book and saw a
likeness in an incident in it to one in " Hermann und
Dorothea." Samuel Bamford, author of " Passages
in the Life of a Radical," says of it : " A sorrow-
fully beautiful production it is, few being able to
contemplate it with tearless eyes—of John Bartons
I have known hundreds." Maria Edgeworth's praise
was unstinted, but not knowing the author she was
inclined to attribute it to Harriet Martineau, " who

had intimate knowledge of manufacturers' miseries."
Most sympathetic readers seem to have wept over
it—tears were more easily called up in these days :
" a story over which Statesmen weep " was not
exaggerated. Walter Savage Landor burst into
verse :

> " Some there are whose names will live
> Not in the memories but in the hearts of men ;
> Because those hearts they comforted and raised,
> And, when they saw God's image cast down,
> Lifted them up again, and blew the dust
> From the worn feature and disfigured limb.
> Such thou art, Mighty Master "—

and much more of the same kind.   Dickens, always
impressed by the sensational, wishes to come to
Manchester to discuss getting the authoress to write
for him.   His admiration for writing of the kind
which meant raising the down-trodden was indeed
sincere.   M. Guizot said to Senior when he visited
him that his delight was in reading English novels :
" Miss Austen, Miss Brontë, Mrs. Gaskell and George
Eliot form a school which in their excellence re-
sembles the clouds of dramatic poets of the great
Athenian age."   M. Emile Montégut, in the *Revue
des deux Mondes* of 1853, expresses his admiration of
Mrs. Gaskell's work and specially of " Mary Barton."
We may think all this praise exaggerated, and
perhaps it was.   But the reason was not far to seek,
because this book touched strings that were ready
to vibrate to the chord which reached them.   Men
and women had been told time and again that trade
must be carried on as trade, that the workers must
be treated as hands taking their part in a great
machine which had to operate regardless of the
ordinary demands of humanity, that any interference from outside in the direction of diminishing

hours and raising wages could put the whole gear
out of order. And at last humanity revolted.
Something truer and deeper than any laws of
political economy arose and declared itself appalled,
and said these inhuman conditions must cease.
And Elizabeth Gaskell was one of the mouthpieces
for this cry of indignation, just as was another
admirer of hers, Elizabeth Barrett Browning, who
put her cry into verse. The tears of her many
readers, rich and poor, were no crocodile tears.
They were the tears of indignation as well as pity.

The book is not a great book : it is crude and
sometimes melodramatic. The characters are often
made to talk with the tongue of the authoress and
to give utterance to the thoughts in her mind in
the language she might have used but that they
would not have used. Mrs. Gaskell had not wholly
learned the art of book-writing. But it came at
what in common parlance is called the psychological
moment ; the time when men were awakening to
the injustices of the people concerned and feeling
a responsibility for them. And on the whole as
this book had more real knowledge of facts than
had Disraeli's, though perhaps not more than Charles
Reade's, it drew attention of a kind which went
beyond the mere attention it would have otherwise
received. The day was when writers of this kind
still justified their writing of fiction on the ground
that it was " doing good." And, indeed, this book
did more for the cause it advocated—the according
of sympathy and help to the oppressed—than many
serious essays and benevolent institutions.

The natural consequence of all that had occurred,
the criticism and praise, the sensation which arose
in the intelligent part of the community, was that

a new life opened up for the quiet minister's wife ; she leapt beyond the stage of writing homely verses such as those with which her husband occupied himself in leisure moments, and with which he probably adorned the headings of her chapters, terming them " Manchester Songs." Now she came into contact with the outside world itself and began to know the men and women who lived in that world of intellect hitherto beyond her ken.

The process was not always happy. Mrs. Gaskell had been relieved to find that her Sunday class, the working people, appreciated her efforts instead of resenting them, as she feared they might ; but the formidable William Rathbone Greg, as critic, was on her heels. Like many of her fellow citizens who did not venture into print, he felt it his duty to expose what he considered the misrepresentation of the masters whose champion he considered himself to be, since he was of a well-known employer family. In a paper reprinted in the volume " Mistaken Aims and Attainable Ideals of the Working Classes " he insisted on the charitable efforts of the employers, in spite of the fact that they, too, were sufferers, though their suffering was of a kind that their dependents could not follow. Also he emphasised, what was true, that the rural population was suffering equally and that not only the industrialists were concerned. As to the suffering of the masters, Job himself is made to say : " It's in things for show they cut short, while for such as me it's in things for life we've to stint," which is a good answer to W. R. Greg. Her critic, however, appreciated certain phases of her work and its insight into the sympathy given by the poor to the poor. Still, it was clear that this straightforward book, written from the heart and from what the writer knew as fact and felt impelled to write down, was going to bring a cart of bricks upon her head.

The very publication of the anonymous book had been a worry. Many publishers rejected it, but at last Mr. Forster, who " read " for Chapman & Hall, accepted it, not without many criticisms—some probably well deserved—and after dwelling for a year in the publishers' receptacles, so that the author said she " had forgotten all about it," it saw the light in 1848, as by " Cotton Mather Mills " (a man's name being chosen to give more confidence), William Howitt helping as regards business terms.* Of course this name was soon judged to be fictitious. The publishers insisted, much to the author's chagrin, in having some pages inserted near the end which might well have been omitted, since they included unnecessary reflections and explanations.

When " Mary Barton " did appear things were in a ferment. The courts were sentencing Chartist agitators to transportation for life. Besides this, novels were pouring on the market from Lytton, Disraeli, Dickens, Thackeray and many others. Publishers might have thought there was an *embarras des richesses*, and that a story dealing with so contentious a subject would have but little chance of success. Of all those who wrote on the subject Mrs. Gaskell had one qualification possessed by no other. She was a mother ; there was no woman novel writer of the time who was the same : Harriet Martineau, Maria Edgeworth, the Brontë sisters, George Eliot, all missed this quality, just as Jane Austen, Miss Burney and Miss Ferrier in former days were childless women. And because it is difficult for a woman

* £100 was given for the copyright.

to write who has the responsibilities of a family to consider, we honour her, and recognise that she had a certain advantage over them, at least in the particular vein she had chosen. For we have the sense that she herself has known the subtle relationship between mother, husband and child, and gained a certain fullness of life thereby. She knew, besides, the pain of seeing her child taken from her.*
Unfortunately there were disadvantages to be weighed against these gains, and of them we shall speak : to be a wife and mother in those days was no easy task, nor, owing to its conditions, was it ever conducive to self-expression. Elizabeth Gaskell sat at her little table surrounded by husband and children, and finds " bustle " (as she called it) everywhere ; most of the others could get quiet if nothing more.

In the interval before publication the indefatigable Howitts, who felt they had made a real discovery, got the writer to give them certain tales of Manchester life under the same name for their *Journal*.†
The tales are too didactic for present-day reading and might be called " pot-boilers," but they all have more than a touch of reality and not much false sentiment.

Things were, in the main, looking brighter for the still young couple and their three children. Despite its critics, the book had in the end a striking success,

---

* There is a little Diary written by Mrs. Gaskell during the babyhood of her first daughter, Marianne (twenty-five copies of which were published by Mr. Shorter with the consent of Mr. Bryan Holland, Marianne's son), that expresses her feelings on this subject. She speaks of " How all a woman's life, at least as it seems to me now, ought to have a reference to the period when she will be fulfilling one of her greatest and highest duties, that of a mother." There was nothing of the ultra-feminist about Elizabeth Gaskell.

† " Libbie Marsh's Three Eras," " The Sexton's Hero " and " Christmas Storms and Sunshine."

and the year after publication (1849) the third edition appeared. Then came introductions to famous men. Indeed quite suddenly at the age of forty Elizabeth Gaskell's fame became acknowledged. It is curious that she and her almost contemporary woman writer, George Eliot, commenced their important imaginative work about the same age, and this though women are supposed to develop earlier than men. One conceives that in the last century the conventions held them more tightly in their grasp, and made it more difficult for them to discover early their true life work. In the one case there was the line of work pointed out by friends of the other sex and of strong mentality ; in the other there was the obvious and recognised first duty of a young and beautiful woman to marry, bear children and be a helpmeet to her husband. In both cases the " woman movement " was beginning ; in George Eliot's consciously, as the more intellectual and detached ; in Elizabeth Gaskell's unconsciously ; for though she was living in an atmosphere of intelligence she never dreamt of breaking through the bonds that custom had imposed on married womanhood.

At this stage in her career, indeed, we find Mrs. Gaskell doing the work of her household, managing things there, training her servants as servants were trained in those days, teaching the girls in her Sunday class literature and geography, and arranging sewing classes for poor women, as well as superintending the education of her daughters. She was, indeed, the ideal mother and wife of the period. And yet she was something more, for she had found courage to go into a new country and to write of real things deep down in human nature.

In the year 1849 she had an adventure, for she went to Shottery alone and saw a ghost! She writes : " I didn't come home straight as you thought I did. Your mesmeric clairvoyance ought to have carried you to a very pretty, really old-fashioned cottage at Shottery, the village where Shakespeare's wife lived in her maiden days, a cottage where one's head was literally in danger of being bumped by low doors, and where the windows were casements, where the rooms were all entered by a step up, or a step down, where the scents through the open hall door were all of sweet briar and lilies of the valley : where we slept with our windows open to hear the nightingale's jug-jug, and where the very shadows in the drawing-room had a green tinge from the leafy trees which hung over the windows. Could there be a greater contrast to dear, charming, dingy, dirty Panton Square ? We had rainy days for rest ; when we sat with open windows, revelling in the sound of the raindrops pattering among the trees ; and we had brilliantly fine days when we went long drives ; in one of which (to a place where I believed the Sleeping Beauty lived, it was so overgrown and hidden up by woods) *I saw* a ghost ! Yes, I did."

Then she tells how, after having her fortune told by a gipsy, she turned home-sick and rushed home (to Rumford Street) and found her husband at the station in Manchester. " We joggled home ; our home is a mile and a half from the *very* middle of Manchester ; the last house countrywards of an interminably long street, the other end of which touches the town, while we look into fields, not very pretty or rural fields it must be owned, but in which the children can see cows milked and hay made in summer-time." " I do think our house is very bright." It all seems like ideally happy conditions for a contented wife to live in.

The other book of the same nature as " Mary Barton " (of which, though it comes later, it is better to speak here) is " Ruth," which was not published till 1853, five years after the other. It was of the same nature in that it was also a bold effort to deal with a difficult social problem, and, like " Mary Barton," it showed real courage in the act. For the days of looking leniently on the " unmarried mother " and the agitation for equality of the sexes had not yet come and was not to come for many years. Therefore it took courage for a minister's wife living in the midst of conventional surroundings, to write a tale in which the heroine was what was termed a " fallen woman." In some men's minds the greatest error was in the action of the principal male character, the Dissenting minister, whose character is otherwise not only above reproach but a very beautiful one, and yet who seemed not only to condone but also to conceal sin. In this there was some justice. But the main objection was that the story dealt with a breach of the Seventh Commandment without sufficiently condemning it.

The history of " Ruth " is not an unusual one. She was a beautiful orphan girl apprenticed to a dressmaker, and before the days of regulation of hours kept hard at work far into the night. She was one of those selected to go to the great Hunt Ball to attend to any of the dancers whose dress in those days of frills and furbelows might come to grief. There she met a gentleman who had accompanied one of the ladies whilst her frock was being repaired. The acquaintance improved over an

accident to a child and gradually it ripened and they
walked together ; she was seen by her employer
under what she considered compromising circumstances and dismissed on the spot, and after that
the girl accepted her friend's offer to take her with
him to Wales. Mrs. Gaskell loved describing her
favourite spots, and North Wales was the place
where she had spent her happiest days. But there
is no account of any happiness in the life so far as
Ruth was concerned. She played a negative part, and
the end was what might have been expected. Her
friend took ill and all sorts of complications arose ;
finally, however, she was deserted with nothing but
a gift of money to console her, and this money she
would not accept. She was taken pity on by a
certain Thurston Benson, a rather wonderful and
unusual type of Nonconformist minister, somewhat
deformed, who persuaded his sister to join with him
in taking the girl into their own home after her
baby was born. Ruth's joy in her prospect of
motherhood was drawn from the writer's inmost
soul. The character of Thurston is well conceived
and evidently from life. He was one of those who
saw beyond the narrow limits of Christianity as it
was then understood, and who could understand
that virtue and conventionality were not the same
thing. He really belongs to a later era than that
in which he lived. The part of his conduct that is
susceptible of criticism was that Ruth was tacitly
accepted and passed off as a widow; this indeed
resulted in the discovery of the truth by a pharisaical
neighbour, Mr. Bradshaw, in whose family she had
been teaching and in his ceasing to have any dealings
with the pastor whose ministrations he had formerly
attended and whom he financially supported.

E

Altogether the circumstances were tragic, for Mr. Benson saw that he had acted wrongly in concealing the truth and the little Leonard, Ruth's boy, was " gloomily silent and apparently hard and cold," and she could hardly manage him. She herself dreaded going out into the streets after her story had become known. Old Sally the servant of sixty only hoped she would not lose her character by her association with Ruth—" and me a parish clerk's daughter." The minister could no longer accept the fourth part of his meagre salary of eighty pounds a year as pastor which came from Mr. Bradshaw, his quondam supporter, and for two years Ruth lived in misery, as her opportunity for teaching had gone and she could earn but a pittance by her needle. The boy was delicate and nervous so that the mother felt that " her sharpest punishment came through him," and finally Ruth made up her mind to become a nurse. When she declared her intention to a friend, the latter said : " ' You, a sick nurse ! ' " involuntarily glancing over the beautiful lithe figure and the lovely refinement of Ruth's face. " My dear Ruth, I don't think you are fitted for it ! ' " Ruth protested that she would love the work and try to be watchful and patient. " It was not in that way I meant that you were not fitted for it, I meant that you were fitted for something better. Why, Ruth, you are better educated than I am ! " Ruth thought her education might be useful, even her knowledge of Latin to read the prescriptions which her friend unkindly said the doctors would not wish her to do. " All your taste and refinement will be in your way and will unfit you for your work ; a person unfit for anything else may move quietly, and speak gently, and give medicine

when the doctor orders it, and keep awake at night ;
and those are the best qualities I ever heard of in a
sick nurse."

This showed the way in which sick nursing was
regarded in those pre-Florence Nightingale days.
Ruth however became a nurse for the paupers and
" had enough self-command to control herself from
expressing any sign of repugnance." She found a
use for all her powers, and her harmony and refinement of manner, voice and gesture were useful to
her in her devoted work. If remuneration were
offered to her she took it simply for her child's
subsistence. No doubt the new idea of service to the
sick was coming into existence and Miss Nightingale
herself approved of the manner in which Ruth was
made to learn her task, though indeed the lesson
was merely learned on the " decaying frames " of
the poor : there was no other method available.

Gradually friends came to the rescue. Mr. Bradshaw's son-in-law wished to send Ruth's boy to
school. Mr. Benson thought there might be
" allusions to his peculiar position that might touch
the raw spot in his mind," so sensitive were people
in those days to what was esteemed disgrace. But
things worked out in the end for Mr. Benson's
advantage. Mr. Bradshaw's son was found to have
forged the minister's signature and taken his money,
and his father was consumed with grief and shame
and returned to his pew in the chapel. A terrible
fever broke out, one of the physicians died and the
nurses " shrank from being drafted into the pesti-
lential fever ward," and when high wages failed to
tempt any to what, on their part, they considered
as certain death, Ruth became the matron of
the fever ward. Her work was well and successfully

done and the one who had been so decried
became a heroine in the town. Her last patient
was, however, her former lover, now Member of
Parliament for the town, and after nursing him,
poor Ruth herself died. " She will be in the light
of God's countenance when you and I are afar off."
The words used of her were words actually used by
the writer's old friend, William Turner, of Newcastle.

The story is as usual with Mrs. Gaskell's earlier
tales, full of exciting, almost melodramatic incidents,
with tragedy predominating. But there is not by
any means an entire absence of comedy. Sally, the
Bensons' servant, is as amusing a character as can
be desired, and her account of her sweethearts and
how she repulsed them is extremely entertaining.
" It was Saturday night, and I'd my baize apron
on, and the tails of my bed-gown pinned together
behind, down on my knees pipe-claying the kitchen
when a knock comes at the back-door. ' Come in ! '
says I ; but it knocked again, as if it were too
stately to open the door for itself ; so I got up,
rather cross and opened the door and there stood
Jerry Dixon." Jerry insisted on coming in and sat
down by the oven. " Well, it seemed no use standing waiting for my gentleman to go ; not that he
had much to see either ; but he kept twirling his
hat round and round, and smoothing the nap on't
with the back of his hand. So at last I squatted
down to my work, and thinks I, I shall be on my
knees all ready if he puts up a prayer, for I knew
he was a Methodie by bringing-up, and had only
lately turned to master's way of thinking ; and
them Methodies are terrible hands at unexpected
prayers when one least looks for 'em. I can't say
I like their way of taking one by surprise as it were ;

but then I'm a parish-clerk's daughter, and could never demean myself to dissenting fashions. . . . I'd been caught once or twice unawares, so this time I thought I'd be up to it, and I moved a dry duster wherever I went, to kneel upon in case he began when I were in a wet place. By and by I thought, if the man would pray it would be a blessing, for it would prevent his sending his eyes after me wherever I went ; for when they takes to praying they shuts their eyes, and quiver th' lids in a queer kind o' way—them Dissenters does. . . . At length he clears his throat uncommon loud ; so I spreads my duster, and shuts my eyes all ready ; but when nought comed of it, I opened my eyes a little but to see what he were about. My word! if there he wasn't down on his knees right facing me, staring as hard as he could." Of course Jerry wished not to pray but to make a proposal of marriage, which he duly did, but received no encouragement !

Still, on the whole the story, like its predecessors, is a sad one, and one does not wonder that it was thought so. No one in modern days—few people, at least—would condemn Ruth's conduct in a general way, but many would say with truth that Thurston did not act honourably as a minister of high moral principles ought to have done, by deliberately calling Ruth a widow in order that she might gain a status in the society in which she moved. And Ruth herself, who is made to have such high ideals of conduct, would hardly have consented to the deception imposed by others. In any case the authoress suffered—and suffered acutely —from the criticism of her friends.

The tale is such a common one in novels that one cannot but ask who has best succeeded in

telling it ?   Is it George Eliot, or Dickens, or some
of our more modern writers like Hardy ?   Or does
it take a supreme genius like Goethe to get a grasp
of the situation in its universality ?   To most
novelists it is the individual side that counts ;   the
pathos of the woman hounded down by her fellows.
The personal aspect is too much dwelt on by Mrs.
Gaskell and not allowed to develop of itself in its
full tragic significance as would have been the case
in the highest form of writing.   That, at least, is
how it strikes one in the present day.

The following letter shows how deeply the
criticism of the book grieved her.   It was in reply
to a letter of thanks for the gift of a copy of
" Ruth " :   " You are mistaken about either letters
or congratulations.   As yet I have had hardly any
of the former ;   indeed I anticipate so much pain
from them that in several instances I have *forbidden*
people to write, for their expressions of disapproval
(although I have known that the feeling would
exist in them) would be very painful and stinging
at the time.   ' An unfit subject for fiction ' is the
thing they say about it.   I knew all this before ;
but I determined notwithstanding to speak my
mind out about it ;   only now I shrink with more
pain than I can tell you from what people are
saying, though I could do every jot of it over again
to-morrow.   ' Deep regret ' is what my friends
here feel and express.   In short, the only comparison I can find for myself is to St. Sebastian tied
to a tree to be shot at with arrows ;   but I knew it
before so it comes upon me as no surprise—as what
must be endured with as quiet *seeming*, and as little
inward pain as I can. . . . I have spoken out my
mind in the best way I can, and I have no doubt

that what was meant so earnestly must do some good, though perhaps not all the good, or not the *very* good I meant. I am in a quiver of pain about it. I can't tell you how much I need strength." And then the unfortunate authoress goes on : " I had a terrible fit of crying all Saty. night at the unkind things people were saying. . . . I wanted to have gone to see you before ' Ruth ' was published. I have taken leave of my ' respectable friends ' up and down the country ; *you* I don't call respectable, but you are surrounded by respectabilities and I can't encounter their ' shocks.' " And again : " Don't fancy me overwhelmed with letters and congratulations. I have not had one yet ; and all the fruits thereof have been bitter."

To her friend, Miss Fox, she writes : " About ' Ruth ' one of your London Libraries (Bell, I believe) has had to withdraw it from circulation on account of ' its being unfit for family reading,' and *Spectator*, *Literary Gazette*, *Sharpe's Magazine*, *Colborn* have all abused it as roundly as may be. *Literary Gazette* in every form of abuse—' insufferably dull,' ' style offensive from affectation ' [of all sins the one Mrs. Gaskell was least guilty of], ' deep regret that we and all admirers of " Mary Barton " must feel at the author's loss of reputation.' ' Thoroughly commonplace,' etc. etc. I don't know of a newspaper which praised it but the *Examiner* which was bound to for Chapman's sake—and that's *that*, and be hanged to it."

To understand this extraordinary onslaught on what appears to us in these days a perfectly harmless book dealing with a very common situation in a high-minded and pure-minded way, we must remember the times, and that Josephine Butler had just married the man who was to help her in her campaign against the sham morality of the day. It throws a wonderful light on Victorian sensibility to think that a book of this kind, written with the highest motives, and almost painfully moral, should have such a reception. To us it is almost incredible that it should be so. We cannot but respect the woman who moving in the best Nonconformist circles of the day—a mother of a family of carefully brought up daughters and the wife of a highly regarded minister—should have had the courage to write simply and sincerely what she felt to be the truth. Her friend Catherine Winkworth tells her sister how she had tried to take out superfluous epithets and sentences which seemed to give the book a slightly sentimental twang. There is something of this, but little in comparison to what one would find in Dickens.

Naturally there were people in the world of a very different outlook and they were not slow to express their feelings and somewhat to reassure the depressed author. John Forster, the faithful, was so touched by it that he could hardly sleep, and he saw in it nothing false or exaggerated. As a hardened and dignified critic he confessed that he had a " good cry " over the final chapters. How many readers do the same over any tragic tale in these unsentimental days ? Mrs. Gaskell told her friend Emily Shaen that Monckton Milnes had written in praise of " Ruth " as " highly poetic without losing its simplicity—a rare feat in prose." And Emily Taylor, who was advanced in her views, said the Benson lie was a clear result of our present savage state of opinion and cruel way of thinking.

Charlotte Brontë was consulted in the inception

of the tale and her criticism reads equally strangely
now that most dramas end tragically and are thought
to be pandering to false sentiment if they do otherwise. She asks the question of the creator of
Ruth : " Why should she die ? Why are we to
shut up the book weeping ? " " My heart fails at
the pang it will have to undergo." For one whose
heart never failed over what her own creations had
to suffer in mind or body this indeed sounds
curious, even if modified to the extent of stating
that if the writer's inspiration so commanded it, no
one had the right to stay the sacrificial knife.
When the time of publication came near Miss
Brontë expressed to Mr. Smith, her publisher,
reluctance to come in the way of " Ruth " with
" Villette." She writes from her publisher's house
in London affectionately but guardedly : " Not
that I think she (bless her very sweet face. I have
already devoured Vol. I) would suffer from contact
with ' Villette.' " . . . " Of the delineation of
character I shall be better able to judge when I get
to the end ; but may say in passing that Sally, the
old servant, seems to be ' an apple of gold,' deserving
to be ' set in a picture of silver.' "

Charlotte Brontë never could write a book for its
moral, or take up a philanthropic scheme, but she
honoured Mrs. Beecher Stowe for doing it, and so
she honoured Mrs. Gaskell, for there is no doubt
that there is plenty of propaganda in " Ruth," just
as there was in " Mary Barton." It is quite clear
that when Mrs. Gaskell submitted the outline of
her story to Charlotte Brontë she did not respond
by sending a manuscript of her own, though
" Villette " was of course available. She writes to
her friend in reference to the two books about to

be published about the same time : " I dare say, arrange as we may, we shall not be able wholly to prevent comparison ; it is the nature of some critics to be invidious ; but we need not care ; we can set them at defiance ; they *shall* not make us foes, they *shall* not mingle with our mutual feelings one taint of jealousy ; there is my hand on that ; I know you will give clasp for clasp. ' Villette ' has, indeed, no right to print itself before ' Ruth.' There is a goodness, a philanthropic purpose, a social use in the latter, to which the former cannot for an instant pretend ; nor can it claim precedence on the ground of surpassing power."

Miss Brontë was no narrow critic of the just in literature though she knew well her own feelings in its regard. She saw too the snag which would be laid hold of by the critics who would see in the good minister Mr. Benson one who was a dissembler all the while in passing off Ruth as a married woman. The writer also knew this to have been wrong, but *pace* her critics Mrs. Gaskell makes the sympathy of the reader go out to the erring mortal and so she was thought to have made adultery attractive. It was not all condemnation, however, for the excellent and intelligent Mrs. Fletcher, who knew Mrs. Gaskell's parents when they lived in Edinburgh, liked and admired the book. Archdeacon and Mrs. Hare were enthusiastic supporters, and the former's remark regarding those who committed it to the flames was, " Well, the Bible has been burned." Cobden liked it, of course Dickens ; and Kingsley who thirsted for more books of the same nature. Guizot admired it greatly, and a daughter of his translated it into French, but one of the most valued testimonies to its merits came in 1859 from Florence Nightingale,

who said : " It is a beautiful novel, and I think
I like it better than when I first read it six years
ago." George Eliot admired " Ruth," especially
the finish and fullness of its style, but she was
inclined to think that it " would not be an enduring
or classical fiction " since the author had too great
a love of dramatic effects and was not contented
with the half-tints of real life." But her descriptions of the attic in the minister's house, and the rich
humour of Sally, delighted her. Her criticisms have
proved correct. " Ruth " is too much of the
moment to be a lasting tale ; but this may in a
degree apply to the better conceived " Adam Bede,"
in which the topic is in the main the same.

Mrs. Jameson, the author of " Sacred and Profane
Art," thought the writer's voice had been lifted up
against " demoralising laxity of principle," quite
another view from most. Cobden " blessed the
authoress, as he closed her book, for her courage
and humanity." Frederick Denison Maurice thought
the tale " as true to human experience as it is to
divinest morality," and Dean Stanley's mother,
whose opinion Mrs. Gaskell valued, adored it. There
was still in the background, however, the formidable
critic of former days, W. R. Greg, who tackled it in
" The False Morality of Lady Novelists," strange to
say, as far as Mrs. Gaskell was concerned, from quite
a different angle and rather an interesting one in
those days. He thought the tale a very beautiful
one, but considered that the writer had made the
common mistake of erring in her estimate of the
relative culpability of certain sins, failings and back-
slidings. " Should a woman, however young and
ignorant, once have ' fallen ' (a cruel word) she
is painted without discrimination as the most

sunken of sinners " ; and he blames the writer in
this case of having, though in a mild form, acquiesced
in this erroneous moral estimate. He thought she
should have taken a firmer and bolder stand. The
pharisaic Bradshaw, who turns so brutally on poor
Ruth, was the real villain in the piece ; Ruth the
saint as regards whom there should not have been
any conventional and mysterious language about
her grievous sin.

Nowadays this criticism would be assented to,
but though Thurston Benson and his sister are
characters which should always live, their deception
can hardly be morally justified, though it may well
be condoned.

Mrs. Gaskell writes to Catherine Winkworth
(whom she calls Katie, asking her to call her Lily) :
" The *North British Review* had a *delicious* review
of ' Ruth ' in it. Who the deuce could have written
it ? It is so truly religious, it makes me swear with
delight. I think it is one of the Christian Socialists,
but I can't make out which. I must make Will
[Mr. Gaskell] find out." So it is that the author
gets over her drubbings and is able to express herself
on her pleasure like a young woman of the twentieth
century might have done, regardless of Mrs. Grundy
round the corner.

AFTER the publication of "Mary Barton" in 1850, Mrs. Gaskell wrote several short stories, some of which did not greatly add to their author's reputation. There was doubtless more than a tendency on the writer's part to be drawn into journalism, following on her first experience with the stories written for the Howitts before "Mary" found a publisher. Most probably when the long delay occurred, the writer was discouraged, and thought her serious effort not likely to succeed, and hence was persuaded to write what other women of the day were writing, stories of a moral and Sunday school sort. They were lucrative in a small way and there was a constant demand for them. Then, again, after "Mary Barton" did appear, Mrs. Gaskell might indeed have been forced back into her shell by criticism, so trying to a woman of her nature ; but on the other hand London became aware of what she had written and she was beginning to realise that she counted in that great world. Above all, Dickens, who now had his magazine *Household Words* on hand, with his quick eye for what would take, was concerned to get her to write for him. He gave a great dinner to celebrate the publication of his own great work "David Copperfield," and Mrs. Gaskell was invited to meet such distinguished company as the Carlyles, Thackeray, Rogers, Hablot Browne, and Douglas Jerrold. Then

Samuel Rogers had her to breakfast—one of his famous breakfasts—to meet Forster and the Macreadys. On her journey back Mr. Stanton Whitfield tells us she travelled with J. A. Froude and had much talk with him. While in London she went also to visit the Carlyles and spent an hour with the sage whilst he talked mostly of his own books : " Lolling and fidgeting in his chair all the time." The rather prim, good-looking minister's wife possibly did not impress the rugged Scot who was engaged in denouncing the respectabilities of life, and the two were clearly not born to understand one another, despite his appreciation of " Mary Barton." Emily Winkworth wrote indignantly to her sister in 1849 that Mrs. Carlyle had sent Mrs. Gaskell a long and very nice note begging her to call, and saying how much her husband wanted to see her ; and when she duly went to the house she was kept an hour with Mrs. Carlyle, looking out into the garden " where her great rude husband " was walking backwards and forwards in a dirty Scotch plaid smoking ; he had to be sent for four times before he would come in.* Later on he became more appreciative and went so far, in 1851, as to offer a visit to the Gaskells on his way from Scotland. Jane had been staying in Manchester with her friend Geraldine Jewsbury, whom Carlyle did not love (" that ill-natured old maid," as he called her), and his wife evidently deemed it expedient to advise him to offer this visit to the home of the Gaskells, their house being " very large and in the midst of a shrubbery and garden near Miss Jewsbury's," so that she (Mrs. Carlyle) was able to come in to breakfast. Mrs. Gaskell had before that taken Mrs.

* " Life of Catherine Winkworth," p. 176.

Carlyle for a drive when she was staying with her friend. " She is," Mrs. Carlyle says, "a very kind cheery woman in her own home ; but there is an atmosphere of moral dullness about all Socinian women." Just the sort of acrid remark that clever, bitter-tongued woman would have made. Later on (1852) Mrs. Lynn Linton, not always the kindest critic, met Mrs. Gaskell at Dr. Chapman's (of the *Westminster Review*), when he gave a dinner to Carlyle and Emerson which was joined by Froude and Mrs. Gaskell. She says, in "My Literary Life," " Her manner to me was perfect. I was a young beginner and she at the zenith of her fame ; but she neither snubbed nor patronised. It was the fine manner of a woman to a girl."

Mrs. Gaskell also met other famous men : Monck-ton Milnes, Guizot, Archdeacon Hare and Frederick Denison Maurice, who were all fervent admirers of her work. Mrs. Salis Schwabe, a Manchester friend, likewise invited her to meet Chevalier Bunsen. When she spent a vacation at Skelwith, near Amble-side, she met a greater man still in Wordsworth, through the mediacy of Crabb Robinson, who loved to make such contacts, but we have no account of that event and it must have been just a few months before Wordsworth's death.

In 1849 the Gaskells moved from the little house in Rumford Street to the much more elegant " detached " house at 42, Plymouth Grove which, though conveniently situated for the town, had trees and fields around it. It was not a " common house," but was built in an unusual way with one room leading into another. It is not difficult for us to realise the difference it made to a woman of Mrs. Gaskell's nature to have a comfortable and roomy home in which she could get some quiet and conveniently entertain her guests. Things were looking rather better for the operatives since the repealing of the Corn Laws when trade began to revive. Money was not really a pressing need for the Gaskell household, since Mr. Gaskell, in addition to his salary, had a certain income from his father, who had been engaged in a sail-making business, and Mrs. Gaskell had also her private income from Aunt Lumb ; but there were now four daughters to educate, the last having been born in 1846.* To earn on one's own account, however small the earnings may be, gives a woman a wonderful sense of independence, and short stories brought in immediate and satisfactory returns. The wife's private income went automatically in those days to the husband, and she had to look to him for everything she wore or purchased for her children. However kind a husband might be—and Mr. Gaskell was very kind—this was cramping indeed. Unfortunately Mr. Gaskell, like other husbands of the day, thought the same rule applied to " earned income," as by law it did. We read in a letter to Miss Fox a little later (in 1850) : " Do you know they sent me £10 for ' Lizzie Leigh ' ? I stared and wondered if I was swindling them (i.e. editor of *Household Words*), but I suppose I am not ; and William has composedly buttoned it up in his pocket. He has promised I may have some for my Refuge ! "

How would this action strike a young authoress of the present day ?

Mr. Gaskell was deep in his work ; he had private pupils, including the three clever Winkworth girls

* Mr. Clement Shorter states that the Gaskells had inherited £500 per annum from Mr. Holbrook Gaskell some years before the move to Plymouth Grove.

is as usual at this time of year dining out almost every day."

The Christian Socialist movement naturally interested Mrs. Gaskell since she had so many personal links with it. It was also the sort of medium point of view to which she was veering, once the bitter feelings described in "Mary Barton" had somewhat passed. She writes to her friend, Miss Fox: "I mean to copy you out some lines of my *hero*, Mr. Kingsley ; and I want to ask you and Mr. Fox if you know of a co-operative tailor's shop established by Prof. Maurice, Archdeacon Hare, Mr. Ludlow and Kingsley (many clergymen) on Louis Blanc's principle ? " Then there were the other friends like Froude and Newman, the Cardinal's brother. This letter is to Miss Gaskell, her sister-in-law :

Marianne is practising gorgeous litanies to the Virgin with Mrs. Froude which she has brought from Rome [the first Mrs. Froude had strong Catholic leanings] ; *and I am going through a course of John Henry Newman's Sermons.* Our *own Mr. Newman is just going to publish something on public worship, and Mr. Froude's " Life of Tacitus " gets on grandly (in imagination his wife says). Your ears ought to have tingled last Saturday week when Miss Martineau and I spoke about you.*

In another letter to Miss Fox about an occasion on which Mr. Froude was present :

W. Connington was telling me that Emerson refers to Mr. Froude when he speaks of the " languid gentleman at Oxford who says nothing is new, nothing is true, and it does not signify." Mr. C. stammers and twitches awfully and he had got into this story before Mr. Froude was aware. When he heard what he was saying he tried to check him by nods and winks and anything but wreathed smiles. Mr. C., however, was not to be stopped, especially as he had puckered up his eyes for a good stammer. He twitched and made grimaces, and at length he jerked it out with the air of a man who has done a great action, and opened his eyes to Mr. Froude's angry face.

Francis W. Newman, the younger brother of the Cardinal, who was professor at Manchester New College from 1840–46, became an esteemed fellow citizen and friend. His views were so divergent from those of John Henry that communications ceased between them, but the other party esteemed him highly. Mrs. Gaskell writes to her sister-in-law : " I *do* know my dear Mr. Newman, we all reverence him with true reverence as you would if you knew him. He is so holy ! His life, his spiritual and religious life, is very interesting—the face and voice at first sight told ' He had been with Christ.' I never during a six-year pretty intimate acquaintance heard or saw anything which took off that first conviction. Oh, dear ! I long for the days back again when he came dropping in in the dusk and lost no time in pouring out what his heart was full of," and again " His voice and pronunciation are perfect ; I do like that rich melodious accent which Oxford men have, though it is called bumptious. But Mr. Newman's self is not bumptious. He dresses so shabbily you would not see his full beauty." Francis Newman after leaving Manchester became a professor in University College, London, which was open to men of his modernist views.

One of the many visitors to Manchester was Macready the actor. "I wish I had seen more of him," Mrs. Gaskell writes to the same correspondent. "I had a little bit of talk with him, extremely interesting as soon as the little bit of stiff stateliness had gone off. I only grudge the evening being so short." "I did like him very much." . . . And then reminding one of changes in social custom, " I wonder if you are puzzled about the shaking hands ceremony as I am, never knowing when (in what stage of intimacy) it begins, so Macready and I backwards and forwards our hands and ended by not shaking at all. . . . I wish you would remember me very kindly to Mrs. Macready. I don't want her to forget me."

Another letter of 1849 to Miss Fox, the same friend, who was the daughter of a well-known Unitarian member of Parliament, is amusing as showing the surprise caused by the fact that a Bishop's wife should call on the wife of a Unitarian minister, however distinguished he might be : " We are going to call on the Bishop and Mrs. Lee, who took the dreaded step of calling upon us (Units) the other day. Don't congratulate us too soon, my dear ! " This is the subsequent account of the visit ; evidently the Church " was less to be dreaded than some of the Evangelicals."

" And now I'll tell you a bit about our call on the Bishop. As luck would have it it was a visitation or something-ation, and upwards of 20 clergymen were there. Such fun ! We were tumbled into the drawing-room to them ; archdeacon and all ! Mrs. Lee is a little, timid woman. *I* should make a better Bishop's wife if the Unitarians ever come uppermost in my day ; and she thinks me ' satirical ' and is afraid of me, Mrs. Schwabe says. So you may imagine the malàproposness of the whole affair ; Mr. Stowell was there and all the cursing Evangelicals. . . . We got on pretty well till the Bishop came in. I thought I would watch him and see how he took the affair ; if he skirted Unitarianism as a subject, as he generally talks about it to William. But no ! he pounced on the subject at once ; it was funny to watch the clergymen of the evangelical set who looked as if a bombshell was going off among them."

The two outstanding stories of this period are " Lizzie Leigh " and the " Moorland Cottage," both published in 1850. The first appeared in *Household Words* and is on the same theme as " Ruth " —what was then called a " fall from virtue " and the intense sense of disgrace to the family that this lapse entailed. It is a thoroughly Lancastrian tale, worked out in a sensational and somewhat film-like fashion. The second, a Christmas story published by Chapman & Hall, was much better thought out, and is really a beautiful story of an idyllic kind : " As sweet, as pure, as fresh as an unopened morning daisy," says Charlotte Brontë, who, strange to say, sent her sister's " Wuthering Heights " in return ; and later she writes : " I told you that book opened like a daisy. I now tell you that it finished like a herb—a balsamic herb with healing in its leaves. That small volume has beauty for commencement, gathers power in progress, and closes in pathos." This is indeed high testimony from a fellow novelist but the " leal-hearted Maggie " she speaks of does take more than our fancy and there is in the tale what is nearer to German Romanticism than ordinary English tragedy. From the date it is

appears to us to be a complete conception and gives us such a true picture of life of its time and place and of all time, and is written with such literary skill, that we accept it as part of our language. For the denizens of " Cranford " are, with really slight alteration in modes and manners, with us still. We all know Miss Matty, though she no longer wears a " gigot " sleeve or " helmet-shaped bonnet." The characters are drawn to life and are therefore enduring through the ages as all life-drawn pictures are, since with all its differences humanity remains the same. All our grandmothers have told us that things are changed since their day ; that there are no more " Cranfords " since the steam engine, the aeroplane, and the char-à-bancs have destroyed them ; that there are no servants like the faithful Sally in Mr. Benson's house, that simplicity has gone and with it calm thought and reflection. And we all know how untrue this is, and that there are the same good things and good people if we look for them, and that our very great grandmothers used to say exactly the same thing as those who came generations later. Hence we still call our gossiping little towns " Cranfords," and know that it is only our blind eyes that prevent our seeing the pathos and kindliness of the lives in them, and that make us turn aside with a scornful ridicule at the less attractive features which we allow ourselves to dwell on at the expense of those more attractive. When Cowper tells us that God made the country, we are apt in our ignorance to say the Devil must have made the country town, knowing something of its character, or thinking we do so.

Mrs. Gaskell was the happy soul who was able to teach us all the real things, and that without any undue sentimentality such as has spoiled the descriptions of other writers who have in these later days attempted the same task ; she has brought out the inherent *humanity* of simple people living dull, quiet lives, unnoticed by the busy world outside. And she tells her tale with a delightful humour such as gives the most crabbed of us pleasure.

Knutsford, the home of her youth, was of course the origin of the book. The observant little girl who lived there with " Aunt Lumb " had let nothing pass her unnoticed. Just as Jane Austen was observing every turn in the talk of her more distinguished company, and wrote before she had ever learned to spell, so had this far from precocious child stored up in her little head everything that passed, the poor burned cow with the flannel waistcoat and drawers, the little shop, the innocent but untruthful snobbery (always noticed by children), the funny little pretences that made life " genteel," and all the rest. How dull would life be without pretence as all children know, for their happiness is made up of pretence, and therefore they don't condemn it in their elders as one would imagine they might do.

We may thank Dickens for insisting in his insinuating way that " Cranford " was to be carried on after the first few numbers. It had really completed itself at the end of Chapter II when poor Captain Brown was made to meet a tragic fate by being killed " by one of them nasty cruel railroads." We regret his death (and to tell the truth so did his author) and that of Miss Debōrah Jenkyns (to be pronounced Debōrah since her father, the Rector, said it was so in the Hebrew) described just afterwards ; but they signified that the short tale was brought to a conclusion, and death was usually the means taken to finish a story with satisfaction to everyone. It is a real delight to us that after the lapse of let us say ten years, from the time we may be said to date Miss Jenkyn's death, the observant writer was invited to renew her stay at " Cranford." It is indeed true that it is difficult to understand how Miss Jenkyns was before her death to be described as old and feeble, for her sister (who was clearly not many years her junior) was years later only fifty-one. However, people, especially women, grew older wonderfully early in these days and in any case the matter is of no import. There are other funny little discrepancies of the same kind.

The really important point is the truthfulness of the descriptions, and the delicious humour that is so delicate that it never lapses into exaggeration on the one hand or vulgarity on the other. Naturally John Forster and Dickens were delighted. Dickens indeed gave slight offence by his modesty in changing the book read by the Captain before he lost his life: Hood's poems instead of " Pickwick," his own immortal work, was said to be the work in which he was immersed. The authoress was very decided in respect that she did not wish her work so tampered with, indeed she always had clear views about alterations in her writings since she had suffered from changes made in " Mary Barton." Charlotte Brontë admired this new book "with that sort of pleasure which seems always too brief in its duration." She read it aloud to her father. " I wished the paper had been twice as long." It was "graphic, pithy, penetrating, shrewd, yet kind and indulgent." Ruskin flew into a passion over Captain Brown's death (with some reason), but his mother coaxed him into starting again. " I do not know that I have ever read a more finished piece of study of human nature (a very great and good thing when it is not spoiled). I can't think why you left it off. You might have killed Miss Matty as you're fond of killing nice people and then gone on with Jessie's children." This letter immensely pleased the recipient who tells Ruskin how she had actually seen the cow that wore the grey flannel jacket and known the cat that swallowed the lace, that belonged to the lady that sent for the doctor that gave the emetic, etc. etc. And she goes on to tell an even more amusing (and true) tale of how people she knew, having got a new carpet with white spaces on it, had taught their young servant to vault or jump gracefully over these for fear of soiling them with her dirty feet! She seemed to have a wealth of such stories. All the realistic little touches make one sensible that Mrs. Gaskell was in fact one of the favoured folk who see and hear where others are blind and deaf. When one comes to think of it (and one does as one reads), we have all met the widow in rustling black silk when " bombazine would have shown a deeper sense of her loss "! And do we not all know someone who has nervous tremors in going to bed, though she may not hit on the ingenious expedient of rolling the ball underneath it, or of hiring a boy to sleep with her late husband, the Major's, sword, edge towards the head of the bed at the top of his pillow—the boy, it is true, slept so soundly that he had to be well shaken or cold-jugged in the morning, but that obviated the danger of his using the sword on Jenny in the early dawn when she got up to wash!

Then there is dear old Miss Matty's oracular remark when she heard that two of her acquaintances

in Cranford were about to be joined in matrimony:
"Two people that we know going to be married!
It's coming very near!" And how true is the
saying of the faithful, if rough, Martha, the
servant: "Many a one has been comforted in
their sorrow by seeing a good dish coming upon the
table."

There is again the exciting visit of the Aga Peter
and his extenuation of his confessed sacrilege of
having shot a cherubim by explaining that he had
been "long among savages—all of whom were
heathens—some of them, he was afraid, downright
Dissenters!"

And in the end the tragedy of poor Miss Matty
who has lost the lover who, though rejected perforce
in youth, is still the love of her heart to the end.
She shows no outward sign but the request to the
milliner to make her caps something like the Hon.
Mrs. Jameson's.

"But she wears widow's caps, ma'am!"

"Oh, I only meant something in that style; not
widow's of course, but rather like Mrs. Jameson's."

What could be sadder?

Mrs. Gaskell had an inherent sense of humour, so
often lacking in women writers; she writes of two
young men she had met abroad: "I am afraid they
had a want to me in their composition—a want of
sense of humour that Dr. Arnold had too—but it is
a want." "Cranford" was, however, the only
book she wrote that was in this key and so delicate
in pathos. The narrator, the Mary who came in as
an outsider to help the old ladies, is made not to
look at the life simply as a visitor, but to partake
of the peaceful happiness of the life herself. She

could not have told us the tale as she does had she kept herself merely as a spectator from outside. She did as the others did and never looked at a man but as something a little apart and different, to be treated as not quite coming into the picture. Of course there must have been a real Mary behind, who understood the humour of it all, and she was the author herself. The actors were the beloved spinsters and widows who were living lives of " genteel economy " in the miniature world, the world of Amazons, that cared nothing for what was happening outside excepting as it affected itself. The kindnesses that were done, the unselfishness shewn in that miniature society were epitomes of what might be happening in the big rough world outside, and we examine the actions with the same loving care that one bestows on a beautiful little Alpine flower. One has the feeling with " Cranford " that criticism would be sacrilege.

Herbert Paul in an article on " The Apotheosis of the Novel," in the *Nineteenth Century* of 1897, says, " If in creative power and imaginative range Mrs. Gaskell hardly ranks with Dickens or Thackeray, with George Eliot or Charlotte Brontë, she is one of the most charming and exquisite writers of English fiction that ever lived. The grace of her style and quaintness of her humour remind one of Charles Lamb." Cardinal Newman admired Mrs. Gaskell, his biographer tells us. In the region of poetry and fiction, it is said, the Cardinal never admired what he did not like " and he liked nothing the general tendency of which he did not regard as making for righteousness."

Lord Houghton says of " Cranford " that it is " The finest piece of humanistic description that has been added to English literature since Charles Lamb," once more taking Lamb in comparison. Another competent critic*, writing of Mrs. Gaskell at her Centenary, says, " She had the true comic spirit, urbane, lucent, and cool. . . . In pure comedy she never missed. Her comedy not only keeps its youth ; it is younger than we, with everlasting youth and gaiety." He goes on to say that we have little of essential comedy in our literature excluding Shakespeare, Goldsmith, Lamb, Jane Austen and Meredith (a pretty fair exemption), so that we often find it difficult to differentiate it from satire, travesty or farce. In " Cranford," he claims, " Comedy walks through the pages radiant, alert and contained." Certainly Mrs. Gaskell's comic vein was imperturbable : it came to her without an effort and accordingly gives one no sense of effort or strain ; hence comes our entire enjoyment of it. The evils she wrote of in " Mary Barton " and " Ruth " may pass away in the course of civilisation and then their work is done, and their value is only that of historical documents. But the delicate comedy of " Cranford " remains as a permanent possession, a possession which animates our imagination and helps us to understand the world we live in —to make it a more cheerful place for ourselves and others ; to add to the joy of life.

This was the only one of her books Mrs. Gaskell cared to read again. " Sometimes when I am ailing or ill I take ' Cranford ' and I was going to say enjoy it (but that would not be pretty), laugh over it afresh," she wrote to Ruskin.

Mrs. Gaskell wrote because she loved to write. There was no compulsion ; it came naturally to her

* Professor Herford.

to put her thoughts into words.   Her place is high,
but not among the highest, for she does not reach
to the highest passion.   Her characters are not
drawn with the precision of an Austen : they are
loosely constructed compared with hers.   But she
does portray English life and English feeling about
life in a way which will always give her an honourable
place so long as these are held in estimation amongst
us.

Miss Florence Nightingale.
at Embley.
December 28th 1857.

FLORENCE NIGHTINGALE
From a drawing in the National Gallery by Sir George Scharf

ELIZABETH GASKELL was fortunate in coming into relation with two of the most remarkable women of her time. George Eliot and Harriet Martineau she never knew as friends, but she did form friendships with Florence Nightingale and Charlotte Brontë, for she had the power of appreciating women very different from herself, and was ready to give unstinted admiration where she believed admiration to be due.

She writes to Emily Winkworth (now become Mrs. Shaen) so interesting a letter from Lea Hurst, Miss Nightingale's home, that, although it is long, it is worth reproducing, especially as it has not, so far as I know, been published before. Mr. and Mrs. Nightingale, who had come to know Mrs. Gaskell through their daughter, invited her to stay at their beautiful home so that she might have a quiet time for writing "North and South," and so considerate were they that she was asked to remain in these restful surroundings as long as she wished after the family had left it. They, or their daughter, realised how much quiet and rest were needed by the busy woman. Of course, it was not the days of the Crimean War as yet, but these were very near. One sees from these letters the enormous influence that Florence Nightingale exerted on those with whom she came into contact, even before she reached the distinguished position she held through her work for the benefit of the fighting Forces.

Lea Hurst,
Oct. 27th, 1854.

Well! I vow I won't write letters ; but it is no use, and I must answer you. You have *done me so much good, dearest Nem ; more than anyone else in my life—(that I am aware of) except my own darling Aunt Lumb and Miss Mitchell. I always feel raised higher when I am near you, and* held up *in a calmer and truer atmosphere than my usual anxious, poor, impatient one. One person may act on some and not on others—it's no cause for despair because, darling, you can't work on everybody ; very few* can—*only such people as F. N. I'll enclose you two pieces of Mr. S. Gaskell* to show how* he's *carried off his feet. When I* told *him of Miss F. N. before he saw her, he called her my enthusiastic young lady and irritated me by speaking very contemptuously of her ; as well-meaning, etc. Now here's his first piece and his second piece, and* you need not return *'em. Oh ! I wish I were with you, my dear E., to nurse you a bit, and pour into you. But I'll do the best I can to-morrow answering your questions. By the way, I've written in such a hurry to Katie† that she has misunderstood me. The Egyptian letters are to be* printed;‡ *only not some bits, which I thought specially beautiful and touching, and telling of individual character. . . . Mrs. Nightingale says she was a " dreamy " child. Did I tell you of her* 18 *dolls all ill in rows in bed, when she was quite a little thing ? These two girls*

---

* Mr. Sam Gaskell, a relative.
† Catherine Winkworth.
‡ The letters from Miss Nightingale from Egpyt which she visited. She was deeply interested in Egyptian Mythology.

*had a governess for two and a half years—from 7 to
9½ with F. N.   Then she married, and they'd another
whom they did not like, so then Mr. N. took his girls
in hand, and taught them himself.   He is a very
superior man ;   full of great interests ;   took high
honours at college—and worked away at classics and
metaphysics, and mathematics with them ;   especially
F. N., who, he said, had quite a man's mind.   She
does not sound to have been wayward—only carried
away by a sense of the " Father's Work " that she
ought to be about.   She was early struck by all sorts
of Catholic legends—(not that she's a bit Catholic,
except as feeling that that is a living faith).   One day
she said (I can't remember many of her sayings, but
I'll try and recollect all I can, and then remember
they're private bits).   " There are two churches in
Europe that are dead, the Anglican and the Greek—
and two that are alive, the Roman Catholic and the
Lutheran.   The two former can be galvanised into
action, but the actual living soul has departed out of
them."   I used to ask Parthe N.* a great deal about
F. N.   Parthe is plain, clever and apparently nothing
out of the common way as to character ;   but she is
for all that.   She is devoted—her sense of existence is
lost in Florence's.   I never saw such adoring love.
To set F. at liberty to do her great work, Parthe has
annihilated herself, her own tastes, her own wishes in
order to take up all the little duties of home, to parents,
to poor, to society, to servants—all the small things
that fritter away time and life, all these Parthe does,
for fear if anything was neglected people might blame
F. as well as from feeling these duties imperative as
if they were grand things.   Well !   but to return I
was asking Parthe about F. and I never saw such*

* Parthenope Nightingale, afterwards Lady Verney.

*intense affection as that with which she spoke of her.
She said that she never saw anyone like Florence for
the natural intense love of God—as a personal being.
She says F. does not care for* individuals—*(which is
curiously true)—but for the whole race as being God's
creatures. One little speech of Florence's Parthe
told me—"I look to 30 as the age when Our Saviour
took up his work. I am trying to prepare myself
to follow his steps when I am as old as He is." Now
she is 33 Florence takes up one thing at a time and
bends her whole soul to that. Music was it once.
When they were 17 and 18 Mr. and Mrs. N. took
them to Italy before they were presented. And F.
worked at music; the scientific part; and for the
time cared for nothing but music. She has never cared
in the least for art. Then again the study of the truth
as disguised in the myths and hieroglyphics of the
Egyptian religion as the root of other religions, took
hold of her; (you will see the exquisite beauty of her
ideas on this head when you get her letters)—and for
a year and a half in Egypt and in Athens she was
absorbed in this. Now all this is swept away. They
were correcting the proofs of her Egyptian letters
when she was here—and had to refer to her about the
myth about Thotte. She could remember nothing about
it. She did not even care to try and remember. She
never reads any book now. She has not time for it, to
begin with; and secondly she says life is so vivid
that books seem poor. The latter volumes of Bunsen
are the only books that she even looked into here. She
used to sit with her head bent a little forwards, one
hand lying in repose over the other on her knees looking in that steady way which means that people are
not seeing the real actual before them. The only thing
she talked much about that I knew was suggested by*

Bunsen, who stated something like this—that among the Japhetic races individuals *had not so much influence as among the Shemetic.* Mr. Nightingale *said that that was a finer state of society when individuals were not so much ahead of those about them, etc., and she took up the other side very warmly, and said that her admiration of the heroic was of itself so fine a quality, and was lost—along with epic poetry, etc., where heroes were none, etc. etc. etc.* It was *very interesting, but I make a mess of it in repeating. I'll tell you one or two more of her speeches—only mind! I felt that I heard them as being received into the family, not as addressed to myself, so they are rather private. Speaking of the cholera in the Middlesex Hospital, she said, " The prostitutes come in perpetually—poor creatures staggering off their beat! It took worse hold of them than of any. One poor girl, loathsomely filthy, came in, and was dead in four hours. I held her in my arms and I heard her saying something. I bent down to hear. ' Pray God, that you may never be in the despair I am in at this time.' I said, ' Oh, my girl, are you not now more merciful than the God you think you are going to ? Yet the real God is far more merciful than any human creature ever was, or can ever imagine.' " Then, again, I never heard such capital mimicry as she gave of a poor woman, who was brought in one night, when F. N. and a porter were the only people up—every other nurse worn out for the time. Three medical students came up, smoking cigars, and went away. F. N. undressed the woman, who was half tipsy but kept saying, " You would not think it, ma'am, but a week ago I was in silk and satins ; in silk and satins, dancing at Woolwich. Yes! ma'am, for all I am so dirty I am draped in silks and satins sometimes. Real*

*French silks and satins." This woman was a nurse
earning her five guineas a week with nursing ladies.
She got better. F.N. has very seldom told her family of
her plans till they were pretty well matured; then they
remembered back for years little speeches (like that
about our Saviour at 30), which show that the thoughts
have been in her mind for years. I saw a little instance
of this while she was here. She had had the toothache,
and an abscess in her mouth, and Mrs. N. was very
anxious about her, as she was evidently not strong.
On Monday she said, " I am going to-morrow." This
took them quite by surprise as she evidently was still
very poorly; and Mrs. N. remonstrated. But it
turned out she had written and made so many arrangements depending on her presence, before she had even
spoken about it to her family, that they had nothing to
do but to yield; and it struck me that, considering how
decidedly this step of hers was against their judgment
as well as against their wishes, it was very beautiful
to see how silently and diligently they all tried " to
speed the parting guest." Indeed, Parthe one day
said, " She seems led by something higher than I can
see, and all I can do is to move every obstacle in my
power out of her path "; and so it is with them all.
That text always jarred against me, that " Who is my
mother and my brethren?"—and there is just that
jar in F.N. to me. She has no friend—and she
wants none. She stands perfectly alone, half-way
between God and His creatures. She used to go a
great deal among the villagers here, who dote upon her.
One poor woman lost a boy seven years ago of white
swelling in his knee, and F.N. went twice a day to
dress it. The boy shrank from death; F.N. took an
engraving from some Italian master, a figure of Christ
as the Good Shepherd carrying a little lamb in His*

*arms, and told the boy that so tenderly would Christ
carry him, etc. The mother speaks of F. N.—did to
me only yesterday—as of a heavenly angel. Yet the
father of this dead child—the husband of this poor
woman—died last 5th of September, and I was witness
to the extreme difficulty with which Parthe induced
Florence to go and see this childless widow once
whilst she was here; and though the woman entreated
her to come again she never did. She will not go
among the villagers now because her heart and soul
are absorbed by her hospital plans, and as she says she
can only attend to one thing at once. She is so excessively soft and gentle in voice, manner, and movement that one never feels the unbendableness of her
character when one is near her. Her powers are
astonishing. In one way you will see that in the
Egyptian letters. In another way in what she has
done in the Ladies' Hospital in Harley Street. She
has been night-nurse and day-nurse—housekeeper (and
reduced the household expenses one-third from the
previous housekeeper who had been accustomed to
economy all her life), mixer-up of medicine, secretary,
attended all the operations—and rubbed cold feet
perpetually at night—which last I name because they
found that one lady jumped out of bed when F. N.
was coming round and stood with her feet upon the
hearthstone in order to have them rubbed. To go back
to F. N.'s previous life, I believe there is no end to
the offers she has had—for nine years Mr. M. Milnes
was at her feet; but Parthe says she never knew her
care for one man more than another in any way at
any time. Mr. and Mrs. Bracebridge (named in
S. G.'s letter) went with her into Egypt. I long for
these Egyptian letters. They must come out before
your confinement. She and I had a grand quarrel*

one day. She is, I think, too much for institutions, sisterhoods and associations, and she said if she had influence enough not a mother should bring up a child herself; there should be crêches for the rich as well as the poor. If she had twenty children she would send them all to a crêche, seeing, of course, that it was a well-managed crêche. That exactly tells of what seems to me the *want—but then this want of love for individuals becomes a gift and a very rare one, if one takes it in conjunction with her intense love for the* race *; her utter unselfishness in serving and ministering. I think I have told you all—even to impressions—but she is really so extraordinary a creature that impressions may be erroneous, and anything like a judgment of her must be presumptuous, and what a letter I have written! Only if you are on the sofa it won't tire you as it might do if you were busy.*

I have told Meta* she may begin to prepare herself for entering upon a nurse's life of devotion when she is thirty or so, by going about among sick now, and that all the help I can give in letting her see hospitals, etc., if she wishes she may have. I doubt if she has purpose enough to do all this; but I have taken great care not to damp her—and if she has purpose, I will help her, as I propose, to lead such a life; tho' it is not everyone who can be Miss N. I wish, my darling, you were here for a day only. It is so lovely; so very lovely, and still, and out of the world; to say nothing of air more pure than I ever yet felt.

This letter is especially interesting as showing by very acute criticism the rather inhuman side of this wonderful woman. The personal relations were evidently, in Mrs. Gaskell's view, swallowed up in

* Her daughter.

the larger and impersonal side ; the individual
with its affections and idiosyncrasies is merged in
the race. It rather justifies the criticism made,
for instance, by Lytton Strachey in his study of
Florence Nightingale. Perhaps it is impossible that
it should have been otherwise. The modern tendency
is doubtless in this direction as socialistic views
develop, but it could not appeal to the very personal
and human Elizabeth Gaskell.

There follows a reference to the development
of " Margaret Hale " (to be called eventually
" North and South "), with which the author was
evidently making good progress in her quiet
surroundings.

*I've got to (with Margaret—I'm off at her now
following your letter) when they've quarrelled, silently,
after the lie and she knows she loves him, and he is
trying not to love her ; and Frederick is gone back to
Spain and Mrs. Hale is dead and Mr. Bell has come
to stay with the Hales, and Mr. Thornton ought to
be developing himself—and Mr. Hale ought to die—
and if I could get over this next piece I could swim
through the London life beautifully into the sunset
glory of the last scene. But hitherto Thornton is good ;
and I'm afraid of a touch marring him ; and I want
to keep his character consistent with itself, and large
and strong and tender, and* yet a master. *That's my
next puzzle. I am enough on not to hurry ; and yet
I don't know if waiting and thinking will bring any
new ideas about him. I wish you'd give me some.
I go to Captain Holland's, Ashbourne Hall, Derbyshire, to-morrow and home on Tuesday next.*

Your own grateful and affectionate,

Lily.

Portions of the following letter to Catherine Winkworth, Emily Shaen's sister, are given in Miss Nightingale's Life, by E. T. Cook, but much of interest is omitted there. It also is written during the delightful time of rest and quiet which was so sorely needed.

Lea Hurst, near Matlock,
October 20th, 1854.

My dearest Kate,

I am going to begin a letter to you, which you must forward to Emily, please. . . . Miss Florence Nightingale went on the 31st *of August to take superintendence of the cholera patients in the Middlesex Hospital (where they were obliged to send out their usual patients in order to take in the patients brought in every half-hour from the Soho district, Broad Street, etc.). She says cholera is not infectious from person to person. Only two of the nurses had it, one of them died, the other recovered ; that none of the porters, etc., had it. She herself was up day and night from Friday afternoon (Sept.* 1) *to Sunday afternoon, receiving the poor creatures (chiefly fallen women of that neighbourhood, they had it the worst) who were being constantly brought in—undressing them . . . putting on turpentine stupes, etc., herself, to as many as she could manage, never even had a touch of the complaint. She says, moreover, that one week the chances of recovery seemed as* 1 *to* 10, *but that since then the chances of recovery are as* 20 *to* 1.

Oh! Katie! I wish you could see her—outsidedly only! She is tall ; very slight and willowy in figure ; thick shortish rich brown hair ; very delicate pretty complexion, rather like my Flossy's, only more delicate colouring ; grey eyes which are generally pensive and drooping, but when they choose can be the merriest eyes I ever saw ; and perfect teeth, making her smile the sweetest I ever saw. Put a long piece of soft net, say 1¼ yards long and half a yard wide, and tie it round this beautifully-shaped head, so as to form a soft white framework for the full oval of her face (for she had the tooth-ache and so wore this little piece of drapery), and dress her up in black silk high up to the long white round throat, and a black shawl on —and you may get near an idea of her perfect grace and lovely appearance.

She is so like a saint. Mrs. Nightingale tells me that when a girl of 15 or so she was often missing in the evening, and Mrs. N. would take a lantern and go up into the village to find her sitting by the bedside of some one who was ill, and saying she could not sit down to a grand 7 o'clock dinner while this was going on, etc. Then Mr. and Mrs. Nightingale took their two daughters to Italy, and they lived there till it was time for them to be presented at Court. In London she was excessively admired and had (this I have heard from other people) no end of offers—but she studied hard with her father, and is a perfect Greek and Latin scholar ; so perfect that when she went to travel a few years later with Mr. and Mrs. Bracebridge, and they were in Transylvania, she was always chosen to address the old Abbots, etc., at the convents in Latin, to state their wants. She travelled for a year and a half with them, going to Athens and all sorts of classical Greek places ; then up the Nile to the Second Cataract with these Bracebridges. Her mother says that when she started, they equipped her en princesse, and when she came back, she had little besides the clothes she had on ; she had given away her linen, etc., right and left to those who wanted it.

Then she said that life was too serious a thing to be wasted in pleasure-seeking ; and she went to Kaiserswerth, and was there for three months, taking her turn as a Deaconess, scouring rooms and all the other menial work, etc. Then she went to Paris, where she studied nursing in the hospitals, in the dress of a nun or abbess ; and besides was for a month serving at a bureau in an arrondissement, *in order to learn from the Sisters of their mode of visiting the poor.*

And now she is at the head of the " Establishment for Invalid Gentlewomen " ; nursing continually, and present at every operation. *She has a great deal of fun, and is carried along by that, I think. She mimics most capitally ; mimics for instance the way of talking of some of the poor Governesses in the Establishment, with their delight at having a man servant, and at having* Lady Canning *and* Lady Monteagle *to do this and that for them. And then at that cholera time she went off, leaving word where she could be sent for, for she considered her " Gentlewomen " to have a prior claim on her services to the Middlesex Hospital, etc. I came in here for the end of her fortnight of holiday in the year. Is it not like St. Elizabeth of Hungary ? The efforts of her family to interest her in other occupations by allowing her to travel, etc.—but the clinging to one object ! Now I must go to dress for dinner. We dine at* 7.

She continues later on, taking the same subject, and showing the immense influence this extra-ordinary woman had on another woman.

She must be a creature of another race, so high and mighty and angelic, doing things by impulse or some divine inspiration—not by effort and struggle of will.

But she seems almost too holy to be talked about as a mere wonder. Mrs. Nightingale says, with tears in her eyes (alluding to Andersen's " Fairy Tales "), that they are ducks and have hatched a wild swan. She seems as completely led by God as Joan of Arc.

I never heard of any one like her. It makes me feel the livingness of God more than ever to think how straight He is sending His spirit down into her, as into the prophets and saints of old. I dare say all this sounds rather like " bosh "—but indeed if you had heard all about her that I have, you would feel as I do. You must take a good deal upon trust.

* * * * *

Saturday Evening. *And now they are all gone, and the house is cleared; and I am left alone, established high up in two rooms, opening one out of the other—the old nurseries; the inner one—very barely furnished—is my bedroom now, but usually Miss Nightingale's. It is curious how simple it is compared even to that of our girls. The old carpet does not cover the floor. The furniture is painted wood; no easy chair, no sofa, a little curtainless bed, a small glass, not so large as mine at home. One of the windows looks out upon a battlement, from which, high as Lea Hurst is, one can see the clouds careering round one; one seems on the Devil's pinnacle of the Temple. It is curious to see how simply these two young women have been brought up. This place has nothing of the magnificence of Embley, their house in Hampshire, still it is a stately enough kind of abode, yet here is the eldest daughter's room. In the outer room—the former day nursery—Miss Florence's room when she is at home, everything is equally simple; now of course the bed is re-converted into a sofa, two*

*small tables, a few bookshelves, a drab carpet only
partially covering the clean boards, and stone-coloured
walls—as cold in colouring as need to be, but with one
low window on one side, trellissed over with Virginian
Creepers as gorgeous as can be ; and opposite one, by
which I am writing, looking over such country !   First
a garden with stone terraces and flights of steps, and
old stone columns with globes on the top of them in
every direction ; the borders of these terraces being
perfectly gorgeous with masses of hollyhocks, dahlias,
nasturtiums, geraniums, etc.   Then a sloping meadow
losing itself in a steep wooded descent (such tints over
the wood !) to the river Derwent, the rocks on the other
side of which form the first distance and are of a red
colour streaked with misty purple.   Beyond this,
interlacing hills forming three ranges of distance ; the
first, deep brown with decaying heather, the next in
some purple shadow, and the last catching some pale
watery sun-light ; I don't know where it comes from !
In every direction the walks are most beautiful ; old
English Sir Roger de Coverley kind of villages are
hidden in the moorland hills about here.*

This gives an account of the life at Lea Hurst :

*It is getting dark, I am to have my tea up in my
turret at six.   And after that, I shall lock my outer
door, and write.   I am stocked with coals and candles
up here ; for I am a quarter of a mile of staircases
and odd intricate passages away from everyone in the
house.   Could solitude be more complete ?   The house
is in a wild park, along which I hardly yet know my
way, so as to get to the different gates.   I went to lunch
at the Arkwrights at Willersley on Thursday, and they
asked me to go often there ; and wanted me to go with*

*their large party in the house and make excursions in
the country, but I declined manfully. They are the
only people who can rout me out. Lady Coltman has
a house seven miles off, but I have refused to go there,
and she goes to Brighton on Tuesday, so ought not
" Margaret Hale" to stand a good chance? I do
think she is going on nicely ; I have not written much,
but so* well! *There's modesty for you. I have not
half told you about Miss F. N. It must keep till I see
you. But she is thinking (don't name this ; it is a
secret as yet) of becoming the Matron of one of the
great London Hospitals as soon as she has got this small
establishment in Harley Street into training.*

*All this time I have never thanked you, dearest Kate,
for your letter, and the pains you have taken to get me
that information about mercantile failures. . . . And
now I'm going to tell you bits of fun, etc. They have
had Mr. Hallam, Lord Monteagle, Sir Francis Doyle,
and several others staying here, and all the talk was
about Dr. Whewell's book, " The Plurality of Worlds,"
Lord Ellesmere said : " Well! Nature has but been
able to produce* one *Whewell. I think it is a great
evidence of the benevolence of the Almighty." Sir
Francis Doyle (he who last year, when a very clever
satirical Mrs. Milnes Gaskell said she wished people
would not look at her as if she were the author of
" Ruth," etc., replied : " Can't you tell them, my
dear, that you're Ruthless?") made this epigram on
Whewell :*

> " Should a man through all space to far galaxies travel,
> And of nebulous films the remotest unravel,
> He will find, should he venture to fathom Infinity,
> That the great work of God, is the Master of Trinity."

Do write. What do you think of a fire burning

down Mr. Thornton's mills and houses as a help to failure ? Then Margaret would rebuild them larger and better, and need not go to live there when she's married. Tell me what you think. Margaret has just told the lie, and is gathering herself up after her dead faint ; very weak and stunned and humble.

One companion I have got—an owl. Miss Florence Nightingale picked it up, thrown out of its nest in the Parthenon ;—nursed the little round puff-ball and here he is (just like the owls beside Minerva, and on the old Greek drachmas)—a regular mischievous intelligent pet.

Your very affectionate,
Lily.

A letter written to Mrs. Gaskell much later on from Florence's elder sister Parthenope, tells of the effect of Florence's work upon the country and gives her impression of Mrs. Gaskell's new book.

Embley.
If I could tell you how overdone with writing I am, you wd. not wonder at my not having thanked you for your letter and that very pretty " war music " before. Every week I think the flood of English benevolence must come to an end, and every week a fresh wave comes down upon us. In December it was preserved meats, wine and money. Now we have reverted to shirts, knitted things and books, and I have only had 3 fifty pound notes in the whole 28 days which I take very ill. Really it is very beautiful, the gifts come from every kind and sort of person from the sugar refiner's clerk and his 6 shirts, to the splendid ball of the " ladies of Ind " ; the contribution of a mill, a Countess's offer to set a village to work on

whatever is most wanted, an invalid's sympathetic pairs of muffetees, the small clergyman's wife's packet of little books and stockings, the old linen from a farmer's wife, etc., etc. Truly " North and South " have mingled their good thoughts in this. I believe much charity to our neighbours and love of God is brought forth by the war. The storm of bigotry too has done good, it has made the liberal speak out, while they are rather apt to keep their sense to themselves, as wisdom is not listened to when she cries in the streets now whatever she may have been.

By the bye, I must say what a deal of wisdom there seems to me in " N. & S." It has instructed me exceedingly. You hold the balance very evenly and it must be a hard task. I am quite sorry to part with it, and wish it had not ended so soon, or so abruptly, but I am afraid you are right, for I am afraid Margaret will not be happy, tho' she will make him so; he is too old to mould, and the poetry of her nature will suffer under the iron mark which has compressed his so long. And then Mrs. Thornton will never forgive her for having reinstated her son, that hard, coarse, ungenerous woman will never consent to take an obligation, as he does so beautifully (for I think that is one of the best things you have done—he is too proud to be annoyed at being obliged to his wife and loves her too deeply to know that it is a burthen). They (Mrs. T. & M.) cannot live together and be happy and yet she cannot be turned out of the house, but when do one's friends' marriages satisfy one ? They are the most melancholy things generally one goes through. However, I have a pleasant one in prospect just now so I ought not to say so.

As for Scutari where we are living all day, and at night " for then begins a journey in my head, to work

H

my mind when body's work's expired." The news is not good. The enormous amount of sick that are come and coming down upon them is so fearful, the proportion of deaths increasing, then the sick are in such an exhausted state, " almost insensible to everything, not like the wounded, who were always men and brave ones. These poor fellows, when they arrive, have to be fed with a spoon often, and can neither speak nor move " say the B's. Her work is perfectly incessant. The last letter described the day before, one afternoon's work; ' a ship load had arrived, who were dosed with arrowroot and wine at 8, at 9 I went to look them up again, at 10 I found her and Mrs. Roberts (her head nurse) still there, a man had a ball extracted from under the eye, several badly wounded were dressed, 2 died, the whole were looked to again and fed, but it took till 12 p.m. to do this.' An officer just come back says she is here, there and everywhere, and the men would all lose their heads for her. We hear stories and testimonies to her without end from perfect strangers very touching to us. This morning came the account of the thanks one may say of the Houses of Parliament, both sides, the Duke of Leeds, Ld. Derby, Duke of Newcastle, Mr. Herbert, a pretty message to her from the Queen, the usual flood of letters from every class in the land, from peers to cottagers offering help or asking for news, a beautiful little tribute, a gold Scarabæus inscribed " without alloy as is the approbation you inspire," and with this storm of applause a letter from Scutari, so full of anxiety, giving such an account of the strain on body and mind, which no nature can endure for long; the contrast was almost more than one could bear.

Another morning I had letters from America, France, Italy and Germany together about her, the

American saying the interest there was as great as in England.

Sunday—a Scutari letter but I have no time to tell anything, it enclosed orders for 25 letters to be writ. thanks for things etc., also £135, and usual home allowance of letters.

The only letter I have seen from Mrs. Gaskell to Miss Nightingale is dated December 31st, 1858, and is given in her Life. It refers to the second treatise on Female Nursing in Military Hospitals which was really a treatise on nursing at large. Mrs. Gaskell writes : " I read the Subsidiary Notes first. It was so interesting I could not leave it. I finished it at one long morning sitting—hardly stirring between breakfast and dinner. I cannot tell you how much I like it, and for such a number of reasons. First, because you know of a varnish which is as good or better than black-lead for grates (only I wonder what it is). Next because of the little sentences of real deep wisdom which from their depth and true foundation may be real help in every direction and to every person ; and for the quiet, devout references to God which make the book a holy one."

The two women were so different in nature that it is difficult to see how they could become real friends. The story the older woman was writing would, of course, appeal to one who, like Miss Nightingale, appreciated the modern movement in theology and its consequences. Mrs. Gaskell had no call to outside public work and made her home the real centre of her life. But the women who were her friends realised the value of her work as she did theirs and this is testimony to the wide-mindedness of all. It takes many to make a world.

Florence Nightingale, having the stronger character, broke from tradition more thoroughly than ever could have done her gentle contemporary. And yet such a hold did it have on the women of that time that in some respects she returned to the standards of Victorianism in later life ; anyhow she resented John Stuart Mill's blandishments in regard to " coming out into the open." It is difficult to picture Miss Nightingale living quite the conventional life of a well-born Englishwoman of her period, and yet had she succumbed to the many efforts made to get her to give up her independent womanhood (which indeed one can hardly figure to oneself), married a clergyman and had four daughters, what would have resulted ? The truth is that both —the one consciously, the other unconsciously— were breaking down the walls that Mrs. Grundy had built round women's lives in the nineteenth century. Miss Nightingale had no use for the sentimentality that was controlling the emotions and leading them into the beaten tracks of ordinary social life. Mrs. Gaskell had much of the romantic in her, but she was carried along by force with the life of her time and the manners of her time, and though she wrote of freedom from the shackles of the customs and conventions of her day it was perhaps only in her short romantic tales that she entirely escaped from their thraldom.

In her next novel, already referred to, which she wrote partly at Embley and which was called " North and South " (Mr. Forster wished it called so rather than " Margaret Hale "), she deals with another moral question very different from that treated of in " Ruth," but one which was troubling many good men and a few good women of the day. The question was one of the conflict of moral ideas, and it was one that would have appealed strongly to Miss Nightingale, who was grappling with just such ideas. A clergyman, the husband of a good, ordinary, matter-of-fact clergyman's wife, and the father of a charming daughter, Margaret Hale, realises that he does not believe in the doctrines he is preaching, and must give up his living in an attractive country parish in the New Forest where he and his family are adored by the people. Mrs. Gaskell's father had done something of the kind in ceasing to be a minister and trying his fortunes in another line of life without too much success, so that she had an idea of what it would mean to leave a pleasant parsonage and go with an unsympathetic wife to " labour " in a smoky northern industrial town and to face obloquy on account of his beliefs. The story is well told, though lacking in the unction of a later writer, Mrs. Humphry Ward, who dealt with a similar subject, and we can picture the feelings of the women of the family and their " superior " maid at finding themselves ensconced in dingy rooms costing thirty pounds a year, all they could afford, with overloaded cornices and a gaudy paper of pink and blue roses with yellow leaves, though indeed they were saved from the worst by a millowner whom Margaret to begin with held in disdain. The heroine herself is vividly described as she appeared to the same rough millowner, whom eventually she was to marry, however unlikely it seemed at first. " Her dress was very plain ; a close straw bonnet of the best material and shape, trimmed with white ribbon ; a dark silk gown, without any trimming or flounce ; a large Indian shawl, which hung about her in heavy folds, and

which she wore as an empress wears her drapery."
It sounds extraordinarily unlike the attire of a
modern girl while house-hunting; but Mrs. Gaskell
loved clothes, and, being famed for her good taste
in them, liked to describe them. This was evidently
the ideal wear of the time and no doubt it was
becoming.

Mr. Hale had to act as tutor to such as he could
get to instruct in order to make a livelihood. His
whole action was no doubt guided by the highest
dictates of conscience, but it strikes us at the
same time as extremely selfish in its manner. The
way in which not only the decision but the plans
are made without once consulting the querulous but
faithful wife, is typical of the attitude to the family
so often adopted in those days by its head. The
girl was marvellously loyal, but the maid who had
always been in the " best families " had no com-
punction in setting forth her views. " And master
thinking of turning Dissenter at his time of life,
when, if it is not to be said he's done well in the
Church, he's not done badly after all. I had a
cousin, miss, who turned Methodist preacher after
he was fifty years of age, and a tailor all his life ;
but then he had never been able to make a pair of
trousers to fit, for as long as he had been in the
trade, so it was no wonder."

The life at Milton (Manchester of course) is well
described, the heavy smoky air and the rough outspoken factory workers whom gradually the girl
came to understand and love after their independent
ways ceased to astonish. Then comes the strike and
the importation of Irish labour which drove the men
into rioting, and Margaret's part in endeavouring
to quell the riot and help Mr. Thornton, the mill-

owner. The strike fails as did the general strike it is founded on, and then there is much talk of the Union, its benefits and faults. It is evident that the writer has had all the arguments of the " economists " pressed upon her since the days of " Mary Barton." Her deep sympathy with the " hands " and their suffering (we are not spared death-bed scenes in this tale, though they are not so frequent as before) are as real as ever, and her observation and description of their lives is as accurate. But the study is mainly from the point of view of the employer. Thornton is the typical employer of the straight, unbending kind who expects to be served well, and if he is not from his point of view, is adamant. Then there is the working man Higgins and his relations with his employer. Higgins is as independent as his master, and when they fall out and he loses his job, he is in a parlous state, especially as he takes over the care of the children of a fellow worker who drowned himself. The rights of the union and the action of the masters who will not take " union " men are dealt with very fairly. Mrs. Gaskell sees that the " South " has nothing to offer for these hard-headed workers, with its labour all the day long for nine shillings a week, the sameness of the toil deadening their imaginations as they were not deadened in a manufacturing town. At night these men were, as she says, brutishly tired and could think of nothing. She does indeed give a very true account of what the life of labourers was at that time in the Southern counties of which she knew from her country life before her marriage. They were no better and perhaps worse than those in the North.

Margaret's wooing, her father's death, and the

account of the Oxford don, the friend of her father, who came into her life and made her his heiress is the best part of the book. Mrs. Gaskell excels in her description of the type that Thornton represents ; she is at home in all her descriptions of his life and of the life of Milton ; where she fails is when Margaret leaves her old surroundings and goes to live with the rich aunt and cousin in London. The life there is drawn conventionally and the rival lover does not interest us.

For some reason—perhaps the course of time, but more because her point of view had mellowed—this book did not arouse the storm of protest that did " Mary Barton." The critical W. R. Greg thought it had not the genius of " Mary Barton " which, " in spite of my criticism I admired," but he thought the spirit and execution excellent, the delineation being delicate and just.

It appeared in 1855, just after Dickens had written " Hard Times " ; whether that suggested to Mrs. Gaskell to revert to Manchester life or not one cannot tell, but Dickens encouraged her in her work. She dealt with a time somewhat later than the " hungry forties " described in " Mary Barton," though the relations between employer and employed were still far from what they might be. Mr. Thornton, a man of great will and power of thought, is never depicted in quite such a bad light as the employer in " Mary Barton." He is a hard man but not an unfeeling man, and when he comes to know Higgins, a typical independent Lancastrian operative, and through him to understand his fellow workers, largely influenced of course by Margaret, on whom he pours his love and admiration, he shows the best side of his character. Mrs.

Gaskell has tried hard to keep the balance this time between master and man. Perhaps it was easier now that times were a little better for all.

Mrs. Jameson (mentioned before) was always a faithful critic. She writes as follows :—

If you are to be found in passing thro' London though but for half an hour and will let me know where —I should like so much to see you! Now in regard to your charming Tale—I am so grateful to it and to you that criticism seems ungracious—but since you ask my opinion so distinctly you shall have it. I do think the conclusion hurried—and what you call huddled up; there should be more gradation in effect, and the rapidity of the incidents at the close destroys the proportions *of your story as a work of art—I mean the end is not in proportion with the beginning. This is a fault of* construction—*but what* is *done is so beautiful and complete that it is only in considering the work as a whole that we feel that too great compression—we want to know something more about the other characters. I do not know whether to advise you to alter it—what has been once thrown warm off the mind and has run into the mould seldom bears alteration—but do not, with your powers, engage to write periodically; it has had a mischievous effect, I think, on Dickens and Thackeray—and it enrages me to lose that beautiful picture of the gradual opening of the mutual mind and heart of the two beings you have created with such an intense vitality and which you would have given with such delicacy and power—so here you have my opinion most crudely and unceremoniously but most truly—and pray send me a copy— for I shall indeed value it.*

Mrs. Gaskell took the criticism of Mrs. Jameson

in good part and thanked her for it. She was fully conscious of the necessity of looking at the literary life seriously. She writes again, on October 29th, 1851* : " I think that Miss Brontë had hold of the true idea when she said to me last summer : ' If I had to earn my living I would go out as a governess again, much as I dislike the life ; I think one should only write out of the fullness of one's heart spontaneously.' " She had often felt in despair about the working out of her plots, hurried as she was by serial publication. " I had," she writes, " to write pretty hard without waiting for the happy leisure hours, so that the story got ' muddled and hurried up.' Every page was grudged me just at last, and I was compelled to desperate compression." However, the story (" North and South ") was to be republished, and the author began to feel the end was not as bad as she had feared ; in fact the changes pressed upon her did not after all have to be made, and Mr. Thornton and Margaret were allowed to develop in the manner intended.

Curiously enough Charlotte Brontë " was concerned mostly about the early chapter when Mr. Hale announces his decision to leave the Church." She thought the subject difficult ; " if you had any narrowness of views or bitterness of feeling towards the Church or her clergy, I should groan over it still " ; but she is satisfied that no attack is meant, but only defence of those who feel it a duty to leave her fold. " Well, it is a good ground, but still rugged for the step of fiction. Stony—thorny will it prove at times, I fear." One remembers how Charlotte Brontë (possibly under the influence of Mr. Nicholls) and her friend Miss Nussey would not

* Clement Shorter's privately printed letters of Charlotte Brontë.

attend at Mr. Gaskell's chapel at Cross Street and Charlotte's husband detested all dissenters. Mrs. Gaskell herself was not by nature speculative, and she took her churchmanship to all appearances lightly, though loyal enough to her husband's views; but she detested bigotry and lack of charity, and she had seen a good deal of both. Perhaps as she depicted Mr. Hale she had Mr. Gaskell a little in mind, sitting in his overheated study working at the *Unitarian Herald*, preparing the lectures, and only on view at meal time. But he was, as indeed was Mr. Hale, thoroughly conscientious and honourable, and in those days it was the man's work that counted. It was a world's wonder when Florence Nightingale, after the Crimean War, made herself to be reckoned as a factor in government so far as sanitary reform was concerned, and even she was never thought of as a member of the Royal Commission on the Health of the Army, though it was her *own* Royal Commission, appointed solely by her efforts. Mrs. Gaskell was much taken up by her home affairs, and only to her outside friends like Miss Fox and the Winkworths does she in her earlier days write about books or politics, though she thought about both a great deal. There was not time for talk in winter, and her husband when he went on holiday preferred to go alone, usually to the Edmund Potters in Scotland. He liked his work and worked hard, avoiding fuss or social functions such as the British Association meeting brought with it. Quiet was what he wanted, and he was only got to travel to Rome by tremendous effort. When he did pay a visit to W. W. Story, the sculptor, it was greatly appreciated by his host. He listened in silence to his wife's entreaties that he would give up some of his work, go more often to London, and pay visits. Nothing happened. And yet in congenial company no one could be more delightful. He was probably right from his own point of view.

No doubt as time went on and Mrs. Gaskell's hands were domestically less tied, the four girls more independent, she became more occupied with social things, for like many women whose youth was cramped and who were plunged into the duties of motherhood early, she found enjoyment in getting free of her restrictions, in seeing interesting people and interesting places. She travelled a certain amount after her first visit to the Rhine country in 1841 with her husband, Heidelberg was visited in 1858 with her two girls ; there she made acquaintance with the Baron Bunsen (not the chemist) and others. She went also three times to France before " North and South " was published, accompanied by daughters and on one occasion by her husband. In Paris she stayed with Mrs. Salis Schwabe and became acquainted with Madame Mohl and the American Storys. The west coast of England and Wales she loved to visit. The many letters now preserved in Lord Brotherton's library give one a good idea of what her busy life was like. There was constant coming and going of visitors. Servants had to be shown their duties and tended when ill ; the girls were to be preserved from being made household drudges. It was the same life that most women were leading at the time. She writes as follows to her friend Miss Fox (whom she calls Tottie) whilst removing to the new house in 1850. It shows how all through the years the loss of her one boy was present to her mind :

*Oh dear, how I should like to come and see the
Exhibition and you. But, my dear, don't you see
there are beds to be taken down and curtains dyed and
carpets cleaned, and curtains chosen, and carpets
selected and cabbages planted in* our *garden—and that
I am the factotum della citta—and its Figaro quà,
Figaro là, all day long. . . . All idea of leaving home
till the removal is complete must be given up. . . .
I want to get associations about that home ; here there
is the precious perfume lingering of my darling's short
presence in this life—I wish I were with him in that
" light where we shall see light," for I am often sorely
puzzled here. But however I must not waste my strength
or my time about the never-ending sorrow. I think that
is one evil of this bustling life that one has never the time
calmly and bravely to face a great grief, and to view
it on every side so as to bring the harmony out of it.*

This is a typical housewifely letter to London
when domestic matters went badly and the char-
woman did not come :

*Oh dear, botheration take the house. Moreover we
can't get a bit of butter—our butter-woman won't come.
Please* bring *us some butter from London—really I
mean it. We can only make 4 lbs. a week at the* very
*outside, and with people in the house we shall make
less. Tell Hearn* [*the faithful servant*] *all her wits
are wanted in this desolate, butterless, servantless,
headless, washerwomanless, companyful household !*

In another letter to " Polly," who was set down
as superficial, and who has dared to give her opinion
on Free Trade and Protection, she is given a real
dressing down. She was told to read a paper in
the *Quarterly* on the subject of Free Trade, then

Mr. Cobden's speech, but first of all "we should read together Adam Smith on the 'Wealth of Nations,' not confusing ourselves as we read as to the limited meaning which he applies to the word 'wealth'. . . Have as many and as varied interests as you can ; but do not again give a decided opinion on a subject of which you at present know nothing." Poor Polly, the days of the emancipated young woman had not come as yet !

Of course Mrs. Gaskell loved her domesticities, and would not have liked any interference with them from husband or daughters. She adored the cow and the poultry she was now able to keep, and would not have been disencumbered of them for worlds. She was not too strong and thought the air of Manchester did not suit her, hence the frequent expeditions to North Wales of which she was so fond. Sometimes she writes : "I have not written one line of 'Margaret' [i.e. 'North and South '] for three weeks for headaches and dizziness." Silverdale, on Morecambe Bay, where she so often stayed, was a delightful resting-place. There she lived in a curious tower four stories high, with a sitting-room on the top, which meant a veritable refuge. She worked there before dawn, so glad was she to get a quiet spot to herself ; she wept over the sorrows of her heroines in peace, just as did Dickens over the sorrows of Little Nell, and as probably all other writers of pathetic fiction did also in those days of sentiment. Silverdale, of course, figures in many of her tales.

Now a new phase was about to open up in Mrs. Gaskell's life, for she was to come into contact with another famous woman of her time—one of very different surroundings but of even greater genius.

IT was during the latter years of Charlotte Brontë's life, 1850 to 1853, that there was any real friendship between these remarkable but very different women. It would never have been so notable a friendship in the eyes of the world had it not been for two things—the first and most important, of course, being that Mrs. Gaskell became the biographer of Charlotte Brontë ; the second that she wrote some exceptionally interesting and informing letters about her and her surroundings. As we have extra-ordinarily little first-hand information beyond Mrs. Gaskell's about a being in whom we must have the deepest interest, and about whom books upon books have been written, this has been a real godsend. Indeed without these letters we should have been in the dark as regards many personal matters that help us to understand an exceptional and baffling life. Therefore all admirers of the Brontës accord Mrs. Gaskell their heartfelt thanks.

Charlotte Brontë had a real and rather unexpected appreciation of her future biographer, for we should not from her antecedents have anticipated that the two women would have had much in common. The interest and attraction was, however, mutual. In 1849 Elizabeth Gaskell writes to Miss Winkworth : " Currer Bell (aha ! what will you give me for a secret ?) She's a she—that I will tell you—who has sent me 'Shirley.'" Earlier in the year, however, she had not realised her identity, for she says to the same correspondent : " Do you know Dr. Epps ? I think you do. Ask him to tell you who wrote ' Jane Eyre ' and ' Shirley.' *Do* tell me who wrote ' Jane Eyre.' " Mrs. Gaskell's admiration for " Shirley," published that year (1849), was great, and she had expressed her admiration to its author, who was six years her junior, at the same time sending her her own " Mary Barton " ; and in this way communication was established. But she did not wish to give away her knowledge, and says to the friend, to whom she signs herself " Shrew " : " You were rather provoking with your impatience about that d——d book."

This is another letter written to another friend, Miss Shaen, just a little later :

Dec. 1, 1849.

My dearest little Annie,

Oh dear ! this crowded, bustling, jolting world ! Well ! if health, taste and one's personal ideas-of-castles-in-the-air plans hold, I shall have a peaceful 3 months next summer. I hardly dare tell you how —it seems so visionary—but if we build in Victoria Park, i.e. if Mr. D. Darbishire builds for us, we shall be turned out of this house at midsummer and have no new house until September, so that 3 months we have a vision of spending at Silverdale.* . . . Have you heard that Harriet Martineau has sworn an actual friendship with the authoress of " Shirley " ? if not I'll tell you. She sent " Shirley " to Harriet Martineau. H. M. acknowledged it in a note directed to Currer Bell Esq. but inside written to a lady. *Then came an answer requesting a personal interview. This was*

———————
* A plan not realised.

towards, or about, last Saturday week and the time appointed was 6 o'clock on Thursday evening and the place appointed was at Mr. Richard Martineau's (married a Miss Needham) in Hyde Park Square, so Mr. and Mrs. R. Martineau and Harriet M. sat with early tea before them awaiting six o'clock and their mysterious visitor ; when lo and behold, as the clock struck, in walked a little, very little, bright-haired sprite, looking not above 15, very unsophisticated, neat and tidy ; she sat down and had tea with them, her name being still unknown ; she said to H. M. " What did you really think of ' Jane Eyre ' ? " H. M. " I thought it a first-rate book," whereupon the little sprite went red all over with pleasure. After tea, Mr. and Mrs. R. M. withdrew and left Sprite to a 2 hours tête-à-tête with H. M. to whom she revealed her name and the history of her life. Her father a Yorkshire clergyman who has never slept out of his house for 26 years ; she had lived a most retired life ; her first visit to London, never been in society, and many other particulars which H. M. is not at liberty to divulge any more than her name, which she keeps a profound secret ; but Thackeray does not. H. M. is charmed with her ; she is full of life and power, etc. etc., and H. M. hopes to be of great use to her. There ! that's all I know, but I think it is a pretty good deal, it's something to have seen somebody who has seen nominis umbra.

The two writers had not only known of each other before, but had even had some correspondence. The following letter from Miss Brontë is to William S. Williams, the literary adviser to Smith, Elder & Co., and is dated November, 1849 :

The letter you forwarded this morning was from

*Mrs. Gaskell, authoress of " Mary Barton " ; she said I was not to answer it, but I cannot help doing so. The note brought tears into my eyes. She is a good, she is a great woman. Proud am I that I can touch a chord of sympathy in souls so noble. In Mrs. Gaskell's nature it mournfully pleases me to fancy a remote affinity to my sister Emily.**

It was the greatest testimony to anyone that could be made by Miss Brontë to see a likeness to her beloved and admired sister. In this case the resemblance seemed so remote and incongruous that it is difficult to understand the statement, for the two women stood at poles apart. But the grief-stricken Charlotte seemed to read affinity in any-one in whom she found response to the deep feelings that surged in her breast. She even found it in so unlikely an individual as G. H. Lewes, a still more incongruous subject.

In any case Charlotte Brontë, living in her desolate home with few to talk to or sympathise with her, was drawn to the older woman, and the next year, 1850, they met face to face at Briery Close on the shores of Lake Windermere just above Lowood, then the residence of Sir James and Lady Kay-Shuttleworth. Mrs. Gaskell accepted an invitation to spend several days there, but her husband as usual remained at home " to prepare his sermons." He was not fond of country visiting or of being disturbed in his work. On August 25th Mrs. Gaskell wrote to Catherine Winkworth a letter which is so remarkable that it must be given almost in full :

* " The Brontës," by Clement Shorter, II, 86, 87.

Plymouth Grove.
Sunday Evng.
August 25th, 1850.

My dearest Katie,

If I don't write now I shall never. A fortnight ago I was in despair because I had so much to say to you I thought I should never get through it, and now, as you may suppose, I shall find I have more to do. Only I'll let you know I'm alive. And that on Thursday last I was as near as possible drinking tea with the Tennysons—and that I have been spending the week in the same house with Miss Brontë. Now is not this enough material for one letter, let alone my home events? Oh, how I wish you were here. I have so much to say I don't know where to begin. Wm. is in Birmingham preaching to-day. He stays over to-morrow. The two Greens are here; and Fanny Holland expected any day. That's all here I think. Last Monday came a note from Lady Kay-Shuttleworth asking Wm. and me to go to see them at a house called Briery Close they have taken just above Lowwood; and meeting Miss Brontë who was going to stay with them for 3 or 4 days. Wm. hesitated, but his Birmingham sermons kept him at home and I went on Tuesday afternoon. Dark when I got to Windermere station; a drive along the level road to Lowwood, then a regular clamber up a steep lane; then a stoppage at a pretty house, and then a pretty drawing-room much like the South End one, in which were Sir James and Lady K.-S., and a little lady in black silk gown, whom I could not see at first for the dazzle in the room; she came up and shook hands with me at once—I went up to unbonnet, etc., came down to tea. The little lady worked away and hardly spoke, but I had time for a good look at her. She is (as she calls *herself*) undeveloped ; *thin and more than half a head shorter than I, soft brown hair, not so dark as mine ; eyes (very good and expressive looking straight and open at you) of the same colour, a reddish face ; large mouth and many teeth gone ; altogether* plain ; *the forehead square, broad, and* rather *overhanging. She has a very sweet voice, rather hesitates in choosing her expressions, but when chosen they seem without an effort,* admirable *and* just *befitting the occasion. There is nothing overstrained but perfectly simple. Well, of course we went to bed ; and of course we got up again (I had the most lovely view from my bedroom over Windermere on to Esthwaite Langdale, etc.) Lady K.-S. was ill, so I made breakfast all the time I staid, and an old jolly Mr. Moseley, Inspector of Schools, came to breakfast, who abused our Mr. Newman soundly for having tried to acquire various branches of knowledge which " savoured of vanity and was a temptation of the D."—"* literal." *After breakfast we* 4 *went on the Lake ; and Miss B. and I agreed in thinking Mr. Moseley a good goose ; in liking Mr. Newman's " Soul," * in liking " Modern Painters," and the idea of the Seven Lamps ; and she told me about Father Newman's lectures in a very quiet, concise, graphic way. After dinner we went a drive to Coniston to call on the Tennysons, who are staying at Mr. Marshall's Hut Lodge—Sir James on the box, Miss B. and I inside, very cozy ; but alas it began to rain, so we had to turn back without our call being paid, which grieved me sorely and made me cross. I'm not going to worry you with as particular an account of every day ; simply to tell you bits about Miss Brontë.   She is more like Miss Fox † in*

* " The Soul," by Francis Newman.
† The mutual friend with whom Mrs. Gaskell constantly corresponded.

character and ways than anyone, if you can fancy Miss Fox to have gone through suffering enough to have taken out every spark of merriment and shy and silent from the habit of extreme intense solitude. Such a life as Miss B's I never heard of before. Lady K.-S. described her home to me as in a village of a few grey stone houses perched up on the north side of a bleak moor—looking over sweeps of bleak moors. There is a court of turf and a stone wall. (No flowers or shrubs will grow there) a straight walk, and you come to the parsonage door with a window on each side of it. The parsonage has never had a touch of paint or an article of new furniture for 30 years; never since Miss B's mother died. She was a "pretty young creature" brought from Penzance in Cornwall by the Irish Curate, who got this moorland living. Her friends disowned her at her marriage. She had 6 children as fast as could be; and what with that and the climate, and the strange half-mad husband she had chosen, she died at the end of 9 years. An old woman at Burnley who nursed her at last, says she used to lie crying in bed, and saying "Oh God, my poor children—oh God my poor children"! continually. Mr. Brontë vented his anger against things not persons; for instance, once in one of his wife's confinements something went wrong, so he got a saw and went and sawed up all the chairs in her bedroom, never answering her remonstrances or minding her tears. Another time he was vexed and took the hearth rug and tied it in a tight bundle and set in on fire in the grate, and sat before it with a leg on each hob, heaping on more coals till it was burnt, no one else being able to endure in the room because of the stifling smoke. All this Lady K.-S. told me.* The sitting-room at the

* The story appears to have been somewhat exaggerated by the woman.

Parsonage looks into the Churchyard, filled with graves. Mr. B. has never taken a meal with his children since his wife's death unless he invites them to tea—never to dinner. And he has only once left home since to come to Manchester to be operated upon by Mr. Wilson for cataract; at which time they lodged in Boundary St. Well! these 5 daughters and one son grew older—their father never taught the girls anything—only the servant taught them to read and write. But I suppose they laid their heads together, for at 12 Charlotte (this one) presented a request to the father that they might go to school; so they were sent to Cowan Bridge (the place where the Daughters of the Clergy were before they were removed to Castleton). There the two elder died in that fever. Miss B. says the pain she suffered from hunger was not to be told, and her two younger sisters laid the foundation of the consumption of which they are now dead. They all came home ill. But the poverty of home was very great (" at 19 I should have been thankful for an allowance of 1d. a week. I asked my father, but he said what did women want with money?"). So at 19 she advertised and got a teacher's place in a school—(where she did not say, only said it was preferable to the governess' place she got afterwards) but she saved up enough to pay for her journey to a school in Brussels. She had never been out of Yorkshire before; and was so frightened when she got to London—she took a cab, it was night, and drove down to the Tower Stairs and went to the Ostend Packet and they refused to take her in; but at last they did. She was in this school at Brussels two years without a holiday except one week with one of her Belgian schoolfellows. Then she came home and her sisters were ill, and her father going blind—so she thought she ought to stay at home. She tried to teach herself drawing and to be an artist but she could not —and yet her own health independently of the home calls upon her would not allow of her going out again as a governess. She had always wished to write and believed that she could ; at 16 she had sent some of her poems to Southey, and had " kind, stringent " answers from him. So she and her sisters tried. They kept their initials and took names that would do either for a man or a woman. They used to read to each other when they had written so much—their father never knew a word about it. He had never heard of " Jane Eyre " when, 3 months after its publication, she promised her sisters one day at dinner she would tell him before tea. So she marched into his study with a copy wrapped up and the reviews. She said (I think I can remember the exact words) : " Papa, I've been writing a book." " Have you, my dear ? " and he went on reading. " But, Papa, I want you to look at it." " I can't be troubled to read MS." " But it is printed." " I hope you have not been in- volving yourself in any such silly expense." " I think I shall gain money by it. May I read you some reviews." So she read them ; and then she asked him if he would read the book. He said she might leave it, and he would see. But he sent them an invita- tion to tea that night, and towards the end of tea he said, " Children, Charlotte has been writing a book— and I think it is a better one than I expected." He never spoke about it again till about a month ago and they never dared to tell him of the books her sisters wrote. Just in the success of " Jane Eyre " her sisters died of rapid consumption unattended by any doctor, why I don't know. But she says she will have none and that her death will be quite lonely ; having

*no friend or relation in the world to nurse her, and her
father dreading a sick room above all places. There seems
little doubt she herself is already tainted with consumption.*

*Now I shan't write any more till you write again
and tell me how to get a letter to Annie Shaen, kind of
paper to be used, etc., and how you and Emma are and
a quantity more I want to know.*

Yours very affectionate

E. C. Gaskell.

Miss Brontë's account of the same visit is as
follows : " Lady Shuttleworth never got out, being
confined to the house with a cold ; but fortunately
there was Mrs. Gaskell, the authoress of ' Mary
Barton,' who came to the Briery the day after
me. I was truly glad of her companionship. She
is a woman of the most genuine talent, of cheerful,
pleasing and cordial manners, and, I believe, of a
kind and good heart."*

And again to Mr. Williams : " The scenery was
exquisite—far beyond anything I saw in Scotland ;
but it did not give me half so much pleasure because
I saw it under less congenial auspices. Mr. Smith
and Sir J. K. Shuttleworth are two difficult people
with whom to travel. I need say nothing of the
former—you know him. The latter offers me his
friendship, and I do my best to be grateful for the
gift ; but he is a nature with which it is difficult to
assimilate—and where there is no assimilation, how
can there be real regard ? "†

In another letter she speaks of the fact of being in a
carriage spoiling everything. " I longed to slip out
unseen and to run away myself in amongst the hills
and dales."

* " The Brontës," by C. K. Shorter, II. 62.
† " Charlotte Brontë and her Circle," by Clement K. Shorter, p. 6.

However, in an earlier letter to her father she acknowledges that she enjoyed the visit to Ambleside exceedingly, and tells of Sir J. K. Shuttleworth having called several times and taken her out in his carriage. " He seems truly friendly," which was much for this shy and difficult woman to admit.

Mrs. Gaskell had been much struck by Miss Brontë's observation of nature, and specially of her careful examination of the shape of the clouds and signs of the heavens, which she " read as from a book " as regards the coming weather, saying that her friend had no idea what a companion the sky became to anyone living in solitude. Posterity has every reason to be grateful to Sir James Kay-Shuttleworth for having brought together these unlike women. The meeting had important consequences, consequences beyond what he could have foreseen. The Shuttleworths were in the habit of having regular "literary parties" which Sir James enjoyed, with visitors such as Matthew Arnold and Harriet Martineau. The drab-looking little spinster who had hardly ever left her own bleak home but for " situations " of one kind or another, must have drawn into her shell in the midst of this lively society of which she knew nothing, and been grateful to the minister's wife who held out so friendly a hand. It was wonderful to get her to come at all.

Soon after this visit there arrived to Mrs. Gaskell the gift of a little book—the poems of Currer, Ellis and Acton Bell, and this gift was followed by a letter, and the acquaintanceship was cemented. " The little books of rhymes was sent by way of fulfilling a rashly made promise ; and the promise was made to prevent you from throwing away four shillings in an injudicious purchase. I do not like my own share of the work nor care that it should be read : Ellis Bell's I think good and vigorous, and Acton's have the mint of truth and simplicity. Mine are chiefly juvenile productions, the restless effervescence of a mind that would not be still. In those days the sea too often ' wrought and was tempestuous ' and wind, sand, shingle—all turned up in the tumult. This visage is much too magniloquent for the subject, but you will pardon it."

One wonders how many times the four shillings would be multiplied in the price to-day for that copy of the poems !

She also says to her newly found friend : " Papa and I have just had tea ; he is sitting quietly in his room, and I in mine ; ' storms of rain ' are sweeping over the garden and churchyard ; as to the moors they are hidden in thick fog. Though alone I am not unhappy ; I have a thousand things to be thankful for, and, among the rest, that this morning I received a letter from you, and that this evening I have the privilege of answering it."*

The letter goes on to discuss an article in the *Westminster Review* on the position of women of which Miss Brontë on the whole approved.† She saw that men were beginning to regard the position of women in another light from that in which they used to do and to speak of it with a new candour that she admired. Women were advised that an amelioration of their lot depended on themselves—true advice as things turned out—but the writer of the letter believed that there were " evils—deep-rooted in the foundation of the social system—which no efforts of ours can touch ; of

---

* " The Brontës," by Clement K. Shorter, II, 163–4.
† This was probably the article by John Stuart Mill which caused a disagreeable correspondence later on between the writer and Mrs. Gaskell.

which we cannot complain ; of which it is advisable
not too often to think." Here her forecast, if it
were a forecast, was not perhaps so accurate.

Miss Brontë and her friend began to exchange
books. Wordsworth's " Prelude " was, for instance,
sent to Mrs. Gaskell, but the sender characteristically
says she would be glad to hear from her, but under-
lines the injunction that she is *never* to write unless
inclination prompts and leisure permits.

The three days spent with the Shuttleworths were
the beginning of a friendship between the two women
which lasted till Charlotte's death, though it was
possibly fostered on Mrs. Gaskell's side rather more
than on the other. Charlotte did not easily let
herself go—she had been used to keep her troubles—
deep enough indeed—to herself, and had a morbid
dread of letting them weigh upon others. In her
strange, isolated life she had but one or two real
friends, like Ellen Nussey, to whom she could un-
burden herself, and that sort of friend Mrs. Gaskell
never became. She feared in her proud self-
sufficiency to ask more of others than they were
ready to give, and Mrs. Gaskell was prosperous,
happy and successful, still beautiful as a woman ;
and the other was sensitive to what she considered
her poverty and plainness. Possibly this woman
was agreeable to her only from pity, she would argue
to herself. How could she really care for one who
lived a desolate life in the bleak sordidness of the
Haworth parsonage ? All the time the other was
pining for her friendship, did she only realise it.

Miss Brontë had been asked the year before to
accompany Mrs. Gaskell, who was paying a visit in the
South of England, but the plan seemed impossible
to accomplish. She says : " This I know, however,

very well—that if I *could* go and be with you for a
week or two in such a quiet south-country house,
and with such kind people as you describe, I should
like it very much. I find the proposal marvellously
to my taste ; it is the pleasantest, gentlest, sweetest
temptation possible ; but, delectable as it is, its
solicitations are by no means to be yielded to without
the sanction of reason, and therefore I desire for the
present to be silent, and to stand back till I have
been to Miss Martineau's, and returned home, and
considered well whether it is a scheme as right as
agreeable.''*

Next year, however, in the end of June, 1851, she
did accomplish the visit to Plymouth Grove on her
way home from London, where she had been staying
with her publishers, the Smiths. She writes this
letter to Mrs. George Smith, whose guest she had
been, after her return to Haworth :

Haworth, July 1st, 1851.
My dear Mrs. Smith,

*Once more I am at home where—I am thankful to
say—I found my father very well. The journey to
Manchester was a little hot and dusty—but otherwise
pleasant enough. The two stout gentlemen who filled
a portion of the carriage when I got in—quitted it at
Rugby—and two other ladies and myself had it to ourselves the rest of the way.*

*The visit to Mrs. Gaskell formed a cheering break in
the journey. She is a woman of many fine qualities
and deserves the epithet which I find is generally
applied to her—charming. Her family consists of
four little girls, all more or less pretty and intelligent ;
these scattered through the rooms of a somewhat spacious*

* '' The Brontës,'' by C. K. Shorter, Vol. II, p. 195.

*house, seem to fill it with liveliness and gaiety.
Haworth Parsonage is rather a contrast—yet even
Haworth Parsonage does not look gloomy in this bright
summer weather : it is somewhat still, but with the
windows open I can hear a bird or two singing on
certain thorn-trees in the garden. My father and the
servants think me looking better than when I left home,
and I certainly feel better myself for the change.*

*You are too much like your son to render it necessary
that I should say much about your kindness during my
visit. However, one cannot help (like Captain Cuttle)
making a note of these matters. Papa says I am to
thank you in his name and to offer you his respects,
which I do accordingly. With truest regards to all
your circle.*

Believe me, very sincerely yours,

C. Brontë.

To Mr. Smith she writes on the same day : " After
a month's voyaging I have cast anchor once more in
a rocky and lonely little cove, no doubt, but still
safe enough. The visit to Mrs. Gaskell on my way
home let me down easily ; though I only spent two
days with her, they were very pleasant. She lives
in a large, cheerful, airy house, quite out of the
Manchester smoke ; a garden surrounds it, and as in
this hot weather the windows were kept open, a
whispering of leaves and perfume of flowers always
pervaded the rooms. Mrs. Gaskell herself is a
woman of whose conversation and company I should
not soon tire. She seems to me kind, clever, animated, and unaffected ; her husband is a good and
kind man, too."*

As may be imagined Miss Brontë was none too

* " Life of Charlotte Brontë," Haworth edition, p. 539.

easy a visitor. This was the occasion on which she was asked if she preferred tea or coffee. " Tea " was the reply, " but please see that there is no green tea mixed with it, as I am never able to sleep after partaking of a cup of tea that has the least particle of green leaf." Mrs. Gaskell in vain recommended a mixture of green and black blended, which in fact was the tea she was making use of. Besides, it was too late to make a change, and the ordinary tea was used. Next morning the guest was asked how she had slept. There was a general smile when she said " Splendidly," and a similar tea was used to the end of the visit !

Soon afterwards Miss Brontë wrote to Mrs. Gaskell about the same visit, the sights she has seen in London, the books she has read, more particularly " The Saint's Tragedy," by Kingsley. She concludes : " Could you manage to convey a small kiss to that dear, but dangerous little person, Julia ? She surreptitiously possessed herself of a minute fraction of my heart, which has been missing ever since I saw her." Charlotte Brontë loved children, but was afraid of demanding from them what they were not willing to give her freely. When Mrs. Gaskell told the same little Julia to take her to some room in the house she shrunk back : " Do not *bid* her do anything for me," she characteristically said, " it has been so sweet hitherto to have her rendering her little kindnesses *spontaneously*." And in another letter to Mrs. Gaskell, who herself had the whole-hearted adoration of children to which Miss Brontë never could aspire : " Whenever I see Florence or Julia again, I shall feel like a fond but bashful suitor, who views at a distance the fair personage to whom, in his clownish awe, he dare not risk a near approach. Such is the clearest idea I can give you of my feeling towards children I like, but to whom I am a stranger—and to what children am I not a stranger ? "* That last expression is very sad, as is one in another letter about a wild flower sent by Mrs. Gaskell's children : " I prized the wild flower—not that I think the sender cares for me, she *does* not, and *cannot*, for she does not know me—but no matter." This intense sensitiveness was her bane in life. She could not accept what was offered simply as would another woman.

The second visit paid by Charlotte Brontë to Mrs. Gaskell was one of five days, from April 22nd, 1853, to the 27th, and this visit, Charlotte said, was " the very brightest and healthiest I have ever known for these years past." We can see the shy woman, full of sensibility, vanishing behind the curtains when a certain Mrs. Sidney Potter, " herself an author," and therefore worthy of better treatment, called to see her. She only reappeared from behind the curtains when the visitor departed ! Everything was done at Plymouth Grove that could be done by a kind hostess to make the visit pleasant. But Charlotte's shyness and reserve were hard to conquer, and whatever steps were taken to make her happy did not mitigate the discomfort of being in unwonted surroundings, and being subject to the constant incursions of the visitors who were always dropping in at Plymouth Grove. This was not the kind of life Charlotte Brontë was used to or cared for. Mrs. Gaskell tells in the Life how two guests had been singing Scottish ballads and how Miss Brontë had been so moved by the songs that from sitting quietly aside " the beautiful clear light came into her eyes ;

* " Life of Charlotte Brontë," Vol. II, pp. 227–228.

her lips quivered with emotion ; she forgot herself, rose, and crossed the room to the piano, when she asked eagerly for song after song." The sister singers* begged her to come to their home next morning when they would sing as long as ever she liked and she promised gladly. But alas, on reaching their house her courage failed, and while upbraiding herself for her timidity she walked up and down the street with her hostess and had to confess that she could not go in and meet yet another sister. This was difficult for her hostess to understand, but she had to submit and make the best apologies she could for her guest's non-appearance, dreading that anything else would bring on one of the headaches to which she was subject. Self-consciousness was surely seldom carried to such extremities ! Mrs. Gaskell ascribed it to Charlotte's intense sensitiveness to what she considered her ill-looks, which she conceived made any stranger who looked at her face careful not to let his eyes wander to that part of the room again. Of course the idea was preposterous, and in reality, without being good-looking, men were attracted to Miss Brontë and certainly she did not lack in proposals of marriage. Her hostess describes her " large grey eyes and silky brown hair " with admiration. Still, the Gaskells were disappointed when the men they asked to meet Miss Brontë found it impossible to get response from her in ordinary conventional conversation. It was only when they lighted on a subject in which she was specially interested, such as Thackeray's Lectures delivered in Manchester, that she warmed up and expressed herself with vigour. One thing Mrs. Gaskell had to avoid and that was the telling of eerie ghost stories

* The Misses Winkworth.

at night just before bed-time—a practice to which she was addicted. To this her guest at once demurred, as the story would undoubtedly mingle with her dreams and prevent her sleeping.

Then there was the invitation to a return visit to Haworth in June, 1854, to the place with " no attractions " as Charlotte describes it, the only resource being " not such a disagreeable one "—to walk on the moors. In the year before she had written : " When you take your leave of the domestic circle and turn your back on Plymouth Grove to come to Haworth, you must do so in the spirit which might sustain you in case you were setting out on a brief trip to the backwoods of America. Leaving behind your husband, children and civilisation, you must come out to barbarism, loneliness and liberty." The last word is significant. The other qualities counted as nothing without the liberty that those wonderful girls demanded—without it they were but as caged birds.

This visit had, however, to be postponed on account of an attack of influenza on Charlotte's part, accompanied by excruciating pain in the head. The letter written by Miss Brontë to Mrs. Gaskell shows more clearly than any other words can do the absolute gulf between the women. Miss Brontë for once expresses in words her real self.

Thank you for your letter ; it was as pleasant as a quiet chat, as welcome as spring showers, as reviving as a friend's visit ; in short it was very like a page of " Cranford." . . . A thought strikes me. Do you, who have so many friends—so large a circle of acquaintances—find it easy, when you sit down to write, to isolate yourself from all those ties, and their sweet

K

associations, so as to be your own woman, uninfluenced or swayed by the consciousness of how your work may affect their minds; what blame or what sympathy it may call forth? Does no luminous cloud ever come between you and the severe Truth, as you know it in your own secret and clear-seeing soul? In a word, are you ever tempted to make your characters more amenable than the life by the inclination to assimilate your thoughts to the thoughts of those who always feel *kindly, but sometimes fail to see justly? Don't answer the question; it is not intended to be answered.*

To be your *own woman* : only the greatest can be that. Emily Brontë was surely one of the few who reached the goal. How many men and what number of women can say that they are in possession of their own souls and are not swayed to and fro by the thoughts or actions of those around them—by those who feel kindly but sometimes fail to *see* justly. For real deep criticism of Mrs. Gaskell's work no criticism could be more scathing, kindly as it was expressed. Charlotte Brontë saw that her fellow-worker had great gifts, had within certain limitations a wonderful power of observation, had humour such as she had not, had honesty of purpose and conscientiousness in her work. But the world, the world of convention, the world of "hard Unitarianism" with all its splendid qualities, was pull, pulling her aside. Children always around her, a husband demanding attention as of right, Sunday scholars, neighbours, cooks, sewing maids, all dragging her away from herself. Elizabeth Gaskell was not unwitting of all this ; she was entirely sensible of it as her letters show, but how to escape ? Could she break with it all and scandalise the community, not to speak of her husband ? Could she leave her

happy, cheerful home—"leaving behind your husband, children and civilisation, you must come out
to barbarism, loneliness and liberty." Could she do
that ? She could not. It was impossible and unreasonable. Impossible, she used to say, to her
friend Miss Fox, for a woman with a home paramount to live an artist's life. Yet she knew well
what a refuge was that life—" the hidden world of
art when the daily cares press down on one." But
it was to her but a temporary refuge—not life itself,
and thus she missed the highest goal while accom-
plishing a great deal.

There was the solitary woman up in the dreary
moorlands doing it all with every ounce of strength
she had. She and her sisters sought no easy way.
" No coward souls were theirs." They faced misery,
pain, sickness with a courage that we can only
admire. We admire because the wonderful results
of their work have made us eternally grateful.

But we must not condemn those who could not
in the nature of things rise to such heights. Mrs.
Gaskell in her own sphere and her own way kept
a firm hold on herself. She writes, for instance,
to Charles Norton that she can *not* (it is not *will*
not) write as if she ever were to think of her readers
and what impression she was making on them.
And in " Mary Barton " and " Ruth " she faces
life fairly and squarely, or at least comes near doing
so. She had certain advantages lacking to her
contemporary novelist ; she had, and profited from,
that sense of humanity that living in a family gives,
and could understand certain important phases of
life to which the other was blind. If she had probed
to the depths of human knowledge with all its
horrors as well as its joys and sorrows, it might have

prevented her from having that meticulous power of observing the so-called obvious that the ordinary observer never sees.   There is the art that speaks of the soul and there is the other art that interprets the world of sight and hearing and that seldom reaches the inmost recesses of the spirit, and that yet tells us so much that we want to know about life as it presents itself to us.   Think what it would have meant if Jane Austen had faced up to the life of her time, the horrors of war, the miseries of the poor, the sufferings of the prisoners, the philosophy of her day—where would have been her power to delight us in health and soothe us in sickness ? What she does is to take our minds away from our troubles and to depict the comfortable, serene life of her own day with such marvellous accuracy and understanding that it lives for ever.   Its value is intrinsic and dependent on no external circum-stances—a lovely cameo indeed.   So evidently each one has to do his and her own tasks and not tackle those that do not belong to them.   We cannot have a more striking contrast than these two famous women of last century, Charlotte Brontë and Eliza-beth Gaskell, and it is particularly interesting to have them placed in conjunction one with the other.

CHARLOTTE BRONTË
From a drawing by George Richmond, R.A., in the National Portrait Gallery

CHAPTER
SIX

ELIZABETH GASKELL AND
CHARLOTTE BRONTË
VISIT TO HAWORTH AND
MISS BRONTË'S MARRIAGE

THERE is a letter from Mrs. Gaskell in the Life of Charlotte Brontë that tells of the one memorable visit during her lifetime to Haworth—a letter of great interest and value. The conversation between the two contrasting women is specially instructive. An even more full letter is, however, amongst the collection in Lord Brotherton's library, and has, I believe, not yet been published. It has been hastily written, but is full of vivid impressions newly made and jotted down as they occurred :

We turned up a narrow bye-lane near the church —past the curate's, the schools & skirting the pestiferous churchyard we arrived at the door into the Parsonage yard. In I went,—half blown back by the wild vehemence of the wind which swept along the narrow gravel walk—round the corner of the house into a small plot of grass enclosed within a low stone wall, over which the more ambitious grave-stones towered all round. There are two windows on each side the door & steps up to it. On these steps I encountered a ruddy tired-looking man of no great refinement,—but I had no time to think of him; in at the door into an exquisitely clean passage, to the left into a square parlour looking out on the grass plot, the tall headstones beyond, the tower end of the church, the village houses & the brown moors.

Miss Brontë gave me the kindest welcome, & the room looked the perfection of warmth, snugness & comfort, crimson predominating in the furniture, which did well with the bleak cold colours without. Every thing in her department has been new within the last few years; and every thing, furniture appointments &c. is admirable for its consistency. All simple, good, sufficient for every possible reasonable want, & of the most delicate & scrupulous cleanliness. She is so neat herself I got quite ashamed of any touches of untidiness—a chair out of its place,—work left on the table were all of them, I could see, annoyances to her habitual sense of order; not annoyances to her temper in the least; you understand the difference. There was her likeness by Richmond, given to her father by Messr. Smith & Elder, the later print of Thackeray, & a good likeness of the Duke of Wellington, hanging up. My room was above this parlour, & looking on the same view, which was really beautiful in certain lights, moon-light especially. Mr. Brontë lives almost entirely in the room opposite (right hand side) of the front door; behind his room is the kitchen, behind the parlour a store room kind of pantry. Mr. Brontë's bedroom is over his sitting room, Miss Brontë's over the kitchen. The servants over the pantry. Where the rest of the household slept when they were all one large family I can't imagine. The wind goes piping & wailing and sobbing round the square unsheltered house in a very strange unearthly way.

We dined—she and I together—Mr. Brontë having his dinner sent to him in his sitting room according to his invariable custom, (fancy it! and only they two left,) and then she told me that the man whom I met on the steps was a Mr. Francis Bennock, something Park, Black Heath, who had written the previous day

*to say he was coming to call on her on his way from
Hull where he had been reading a paper on currency.
His claim for coming to call on Miss Brontë was
"that he was a patron of Authors and literature—"
I hope he belongs to your Guild; Miss Brontë sent
to the address he gave to say she had rather not see
him, but he came all the same, captivated Mr. Brontë,
who would make his daughter come in; & abused us
both for "a couple of proud minxes" when we said
we would rather be without individual patronage if it
was to subject us to individual impertinence. (Oh,
please burn this letter as soon as you have read it.)
This Mr. Bennock produced a M.S. dedication of some
forthcoming work of Miss Mitford's to himself, as a
sort of portable certificate of his merits & it sounded
altogether very funny—but still a good natured person
evidently, & really doing a good deal of kindness I
have no doubt. Mrs. Toulmin of Crosland, & Mrs.
Charles Swain of our town were two authors to whom
he hoped to introduce Miss Brontë at some future
time. Mr. Brontë came in to tea—an honour to me
I believe. Before tea we had had a long delicious
walk right against the wind on Penistone Moor which
stretches directly behind the Parsonage going over the
hill in brown & purple sweeps and falling softly down
into a little upland valley through which a "beck"
ran, & beyond again was another great waving hill—
and in the dip of that might be seen another yet more
distant, & beyond that the said Lancashire came;
but the sinuous hills seemed to girdle the world like
the great Norse serpent, & for my part I don't know
if they don't stretch up to the North Pole. On the
Moors we met no one. Here and there in the gloom
of the distant hollows she pointed out a dark grey
dwelling—with Scotch firs growing near them often,—*

& told me such wild tales of the ungovernable families who lived or had lived therein that Wuthering Heights even seemed tame comparatively. Such dare-devil people,—men especially,—& women so stony & cruel in some of their feelings and so passionately fond in others. They are a queer people up there. Small landed proprietors, dwelling on one spot since Q. Eliz. —& lately adding marvellously to their incomes by using the water power of the becks in the woollen manufacture which had sprung up during the last 50 years :—uneducated—not strained by public opinion—for their equals in position are as bad as themselves, & the poor, besides being densely ignorant are all dependent on their employers. Miss Brontë does not what we should call " visit " with any of them. She goes to see the poor—teaches at the Schools most gently & constantly—but the richer sort of people despise her for her poverty,—& they would have nothing in common if they did meet. These people build grand houses, & live in the kitchens, own hundreds of thousands of pounds & yet bring up their sons with only just enough learning to qualify them for over-lookers during their father's lifetime & greedy grasping money-hunters after his death. Here and there from the high moorland summit we saw newly built churches, —which her Irish curates see after—every one of those being literal copies of different curates in the neigh-bourhood, whose amusement has been ever since to call each other by the names she gave them in Shirley.

In the evening Mr. Brontë went to his room and smoked a pipe,—a regular clay,—& we sat over the fire & talked—talked of long ago when that very same room was full of children ; & how one by one they had dropped off into the churchyard close to the windows. At ½ past 8 we went in to prayers,—soon after nine

*every one was in bed but we two ;—in general there
she sits quite alone thinking over the past ; for her
eyesight prevents her reading or writing by candle-
light, & knitting is but very mechanical & does not
keep the thoughts from wandering. Each day—I was
4 there—was the same in outward arrangement—
breakfast at 9, in Mr. Brontë's room—which we left
immediately after. What he does with himself through
the day I cannot imagine ! He is a tall fine looking
old man, with silver bristles all over his head ; nearly
blind ; speaking with a strong Scotch accent (he comes
from the North of Ireland), raised himself from the
ranks of a poor farmer's son—& was rather intimate
with Lord Palmerston at Cambridge, a pleasant
soothing reflection now, in his shut-out life. There
was not a sign of engraving, map, writing materials,
beyond a desk &c. no books but those contained on
two hanging shelves between the windows—his two
pipes, &c. a spittoon, if you know what that is. He
was very polite and agreeable to me ; paying rather
elaborate old-fashioned compliments, but I was sadly
afraid of him in my inmost soul ; for I caught a glare
of his stern eyes over his spectacles at Miss Brontë
once or twice which made me know my man ; and he
talked at her sometimes ; he is very fearless ; has taken
the part of the men against the masters,—& vice versa
just as he thought fit & right ; & is consequently much
respected & to be respected. But he ought never to have
married. He did not like children ; & they had six in
six years, and the consequent pinching & family disorder
—(which can't be helped), and noise &c. made him
shut himself up & want no companionship—nay be
positively annoyed by it. He won't let Miss Brontë
accompany him in his walks, although he is so nearly
blind ; goes out in defiance of her gentle attempts to*

restrain him, speaking as if she thought him in his second childhood; & comes home moaning & tired :— having lost his way. " Where is my strength gone ? " is his cry then. " I used to walk 40 miles a day," &c. There are little bits of picturesque affection about him —for his old dogs for instance—when very ill some years ago in Manchester, whither he had come to be operated upon for cataract, his wail was, " I shall never feel Keeper's paws on my knees again ! " Moreover to account for my fear—rather an admiring fear after all—of Mr. Brontë, please to take into account that though I like the beautiful glittering of bright flashing steel I don't fancy firearms at all, at all— and Miss Brontë never remembers her father dressing himself in the morning without putting a loaded pistol in his pocket, just as regularly as he puts on his watch. There was this little deadly pistol sitting down to breakfast with us, kneeling down to prayers at night to say nothing of a loaded gun hanging up on high, ready to pop off on the slightest emergency. Mr. Brontë has a great fancy for arms of all kinds. He begged Miss Brontë (Oh, I can't condense it more than I do, & yet here's my 4th sheet !) to go & see Prince Albert's armoury at Windsor ; & when he is unusually out of spirits she tells him over and over again of the different weapons &c. there. But all this time I wander from the course of our day, which is the course of her usual days. Breakfast over, the letters come ; not many, sometimes for days none at all. About 12 we went out to walk. At 2 we dined, about 4 we went out again ; at 6 we had tea ; by nine every one was in bed but ourselves. Monotonous enough in sound, but not a bit in reality. There are some people whose stock of facts & anecdotes are soon exhausted ; but Miss B. is none of these.

I'm sure. I am terribly afraid he won't let her go on being intimate with us heretics. I see she is, too, a little. However she is coming to us in May, and I must make the most of her then, and hope for the future. I fancy him very good, but very stern and bigoted ; but I dare say that is partly fancy. Still it arises from what she has told me. He sounds vehemently in love with her. And I like his having known her dead sisters and dead brother and all she has gone through of home trials, and being no person who has just fancied himself in love with her because he was dazzled by her genius. Mr. N. never knew till long after "Shirley" was published that she wrote books ; and came in, cold & disapproving one day, to ask her if the report he had heard at Keighley was true &c. Fancy him an Irish curate, loving her even then, reading that beginning of "Shirley"! However, with all his bigotry and sternness it must be charming to be loved with all the strength of his heart as she sounds to be. Mr. Shaen accuses me always of being " too much of a woman" in always wanting to obey somebody—but I am sure that Miss Brontë could never have borne not to be well-ruled and ordered—Well! I think I have got into a fiasco and I have hardly any right to go on discussing what she could or she could not do—but I mean that she would never have been happy but with an exacting, rigid, law-giving passionate man—only you see, I'm afraid one of his laws will be to shut us out, and so I am making a sort of selfish moan over it & have got out of temper I suppose with the very thing I have been wanting for her this six months past.

There follows a little about the writer's own work on " North and South," and of a character in it that never materialised :

Oh! I wrote to Mr. Dickens, and he says he is not going to have a strike—altogether his answer sets me at ease. I have half considered whether another character might not be introduced into " Margaret "—Mrs. Thornton, the mother, to have taken as a sort of humble companion & young housekeeper the orphan daughter of an old friend in humble, retired country life on the borders of Lancashire—& this girl to be in love with Mr. Thornton in a kind of passionate despairing way —but both jealous of Margaret, yet angry that she gives Mr. Thornton pain—I know the kind of wild wayward character that grows up in lonesome places, which has a sort of Southern capacity of hating & loving. She shd. not be what people call educated, *but with strong sense.*

I did so like your good long handsome note four or five days ago. I do so thank you for all your kindness. There! there are 2 sentences with " so " in them not followed by " as " as Mr. Gaskell says they ought to be. I will be so *much obliged to you* as *to be incapable of expressing my obligation but by saying that I am always*

Yours most truly,
E. C. Gaskell.

P.S.—Do you know what " petticoat-tails " are? Because it is rather a pretty derivation. Petticoat-tails are a sort of little cake they sell in Edinburgh, the receipt for which was said to have been brought to Scotland by one of Mary Stuart's French servants, petits gatelles.

Mr. Gaskell is pleased about the lectures* I am sure, though he does not say anything except pitying Mr. Chapman. I will do my best to make things smooth & rapid at this end.

She writes likewise to John Forster : " Mr. Nicholls returned to Haworth to be curate to the father (himself only a perpetual curate under the Vicar of Bradford with £250 a year *pour tout potage*, out of which he pays Mr. Nicholls' salary). They are all three, father, daughter and husband, to live together. She says her father now seems so anxious to make up for former injustice and is so kind that at times she could cry that she has not been able more to gratify his natural pride."

Charlotte Brontë had had several offers of marriage including that of Mr. Nicholls, the favoured suitor, who was passionately attached to her. But her father at first was adamant, he " did not approve of marriage " and Mr. Nicholls was sent away to his deep distress. As it turned out, however, the same father who thought first and foremost of himself sorely missed the presence of the faithful curate, and the marriage was finally arranged for June 29th, 1854. Mrs. Gaskell was of course a sympathetic and helpful friend. There was another—a third visit—to Plymouth Grove early in May while the bride was making her necessary purchases, which were but scant.

Mrs. Gaskell writes in the following month this (incomplete) letter to the same correspondent. It is concerned not only with Miss Brontë's affairs but also with her own :

I troubled you with my groans, my dear Mr. Forster, so now you see I am going to send you my reliefs— selfish the first is. I don't believe Miss Brontë will soon become bigoted, or ever lose her true love for me —but I do fear a little for her happiness just because he is narrow and she is not. Good, true, pure &

L

affectionate he is, but he is also narrow, and she can never be so. That's gladness the first. Secondly I have worried Mr. Gaskell, by assuring him he shall have no peace or comfort at home, into going away. He has fixed to go away next Monday, & looks better already with the prospect of a change, in which he now indulges himself. He will form no plans, but bachelorige off comfortably guided by the wind of his own daily will; but he faintly purposes to be in London & at the opening of the Crystal Palace. You cannot think what a relief this is to me. *All last week I was* stupid *with anxiety, & the utter want of power to influence him. Now if, as I said, we were not a full household till the 20th and longer, I could fly & I could run and I could write M. Hale,* which Mrs. Shaw† has put me in spirits by liking, much to my surprise ; and she, trained in German criticism is a far surer judge than you, grunting and groaning whom she does not like. She says it is good—but out of proportion to the length of the planned story written or published—and so cramfull of possible interest that she thinks another character would make it too much. She finds faults, but not disheartening ones, only still I feel it to be flat and grey. . . .*

Evidently this was why the other character was given up.

In the life of Catherine Winkworth there is a very interesting account of a conversation with Miss Brontë while she was staying with the Gaskells in the spring of 1854 : " Lily "‡ greeted me in a brilliant manner. Mr. Gaskell's proofs of his

* Margaret Hale the name first proposed for the book.
† An American friend.
‡ Mrs. Gaskell.

"Lancashire Lectures" had come in all right and put her in excellent spirits; so she drew me in directly to the room whispering : " Say something about her marriage." I began, " I was very glad to hear something Mrs. Gaskell told me about you." " What was it ? " " That you are not going to be alone any more. . . . It will be a great happiness for you to have someone to care for, and make happy." " Yes, and it is a great thing to be the first object with anyone." " And you must be very sure of Mr. Nicholls : he has known you and wished for this so long, I hear." " Yes, he has more than once refused preferment since he left my father, because he knew he never could marry me unless he could return to Haworth ; he knew I could not leave my father." She stopped, and then went on : " But, Katie, it has cost me a good deal to come to this . . . I cannot conceal from myself that he is *not* intellectual ; there are many places into which he would not follow me intellectually. . . . I do believe Mr. Nicholls is as reliable as you say or I would not marry him." " You are not acting in a hurry." " That is true, and indeed I am quite satisfied with my decision ; still—" here Lily came in. " Still such a character would be far less amusing and interesting than a more impulsive and fickle one ; it might be dull ! " " Yes, indeed," said Lily. " For a day's companion, yes," I said, " but not for a life's . . . such a character would have the advantage that one might do the fickleness required oneself, which would be a relief sometimes." "Oh Katie, if *I* had ever said such a wicked thing," cried Lily, and then Miss Brontë—" Oh, there is truth in it ; so much that I don't think I could ever have been so candid."

" Lily " was called away and the two began to talk about the future husband. " He is a Puseyite and very stiff ; I fear it will stand in the way of intercourse with some of my friends. But I shall always be the same in my heart towards them, I shall never let him make me a bigot. . . . I think if he could come to know Mr. Gaskell it would change his feeling." Then the bride-to-be began to question Miss Winkworth about her brother-in-law, whether her sister was sincerely happy in her married life, whether her husband was selfish in small things, whether he took his share in small economies, and what doubts and fears her sister had before she married. When " Lily " returned she said she felt greatly comforted.

There was then a talk with Mrs. Gaskell about Charlotte's prospects and an account of all her troubles and how she had six letters before she answered Mr. Nicholls, and how at last her father felt he missed him. Miss Winkworth says : " If only he is not altogether far too narrow for her, one can fancy her much more really happy with such a man than with one who might have made her more in love, and I am sure she will be really good to him. But I *guess* the true love was Paul Emanuel after all, and he is dead ; but I don't know, and don't think Lily knows." There she had got beyond the confidences of a friend into regions unknown. The Héger letters published long years afterwards throw some light on the subject.

Miss Brontë had arranged to do some papering and painting at the Parsonage, convert a small flagged passage-room used for stores into a study for the husband. He of course had to have a study : such was never thought of for Charlotte herself ;

her " parlour " was the public room—the parlour for breakfast and everything else. All her thoughts were for her father and husband-to-be. How her friend must have longed with her peculiarly feminine gifts of housekeeping and her love of doing things in order, to have helped the poor little bride who seemed to have so little to look forward to that was joyous! What pleasure it would have given her to choose her frocks and find comfortable chairs and a convenient writing desk. But that was not to be. There was but a modest replenishing of her wardrobe and only three days were spent with the Gaskells before she went to Leeds to carry out her purchases. " All her life was but labour and pain ; and she never threw down the burden for the sake of present pleasure," as a friend of early days says of her. So that her preparations were " neither expensive nor extensive," as Mrs. Gaskell tells us.

Charlotte went home, where she was busy stitching, as she writes to Mrs. Gaskell. " The little new room is got into order, and the green and white curtains are up ; they exactly suit the papering, and look neat and clean enough." But she was anxious about Mr. Nicholls who was suffering from some rheumatic affection and had been ill even when she was with the Gaskells. As usual she took a gloomy view of the future that she had so much reason to dread. " I fear—I fear ; but if he be doomed to suffer, so much the more will he need care and help. Well, come what may, God help and strengthen both him and me ! " Mr. Brontë had a slight illness also and the unselfish but anxious woman had all the weight of both anxieties on her shoulders. As to the wedding, she says : " Mr. Nicholls is a kind, considerate fellow. With all his

masculine faults, he enters into my wishes about
having the thing done quietly, in a way that makes
me grateful ; and if nobody interferes and spoils his
arrangement, he will manage it so that not a soul in
Haworth shall be aware of the day." That was all
the consolation—poor consolation it seemed—that
remained.

The consequence of all this secrecy was that
Mrs. Gaskell was not invited to the wedding, which
took place on June 29th, 1854. She can hardly but
have felt disappointed. When all was ready and
every arrangement made for Mr. Brontë's comfort
during his daughter's absence on her honeymoon,
the wedding dress laid out, the inconceivably
selfish father, who had made his daughter sacrifice
her life to him and also treated her still as a wayward child, suddenly announced that he was not
going to church to give away his daughter. No
male was left to do so, and as the only way out one
of the two female friends who were present had to
fill the father's place.

Mrs. Gaskell was invited to visit the newly-married
pair afterwards, but she did not go at the time to her
lasting regret, for no opportunity was given later. The
next visit was soon after Mrs. Nicholls's death.

The events following Mrs. Nicholls's marriage were
pathetic. At last with her narrow-minded but truly
affectionate husband she seemed to have found
something like happiness, though of a mild kind.
There is a very interesting letter to Miss Winkworth
describing the trip taken to Ireland, Killarney and
Glengarriff by the Gap of Dunloe. This letter to
Catherine Winkworth tells of an accident to Mrs.
Nicholls which one fancies may have had some
connection with her untimely death.

Dear Katie,

It was at a little wild spot on the south-west coast of Ireland that your letter reached me ; I did not at first recognise the handwriting, and when I saw the signature and afterwards read the full and interesting communication, I was touched ; you are very good, Katie, very thoughtful for others.

Yes ! I am married. A month ago this very day (July 27th) I changed my name. The same day we went to Conway ; stayed a few days in Wales ; then crossed from Holyhead to Dublin. After a short sojourn in the capital we went to the coast. Such a wild rock-bound coast ; with such an ocean view as I had not yet seen, and such battling of waves with rocks as I had never imagined !

My husband is not a poet or a poetical man, and one of my grand doubts before marriage was about " congenial tastes " and so on. The first morning we went out on the cliffs and saw the Atlantic coming in, all white foam, I did not know whether I should get leave or time to take the matter in my own way. I did not want to talk, but I did want to look and be silent. Having hinted a petition, license was not refused ; covered with a rug to keep off the spray, I was allowed to sit where I chose, and he only interrupted me when he thought I crept too near the edge of the cliff. So far, he is always good in his way, and this protection which does not interfere or pretend, is, I believe, a thousand times better than any half sort of pseudo-sympathy. I will try with God's help to be as indulgent to him whenever indulgence is needed.

We have been to Killarney. I will not describe it a bit. We saw and went through the Gap of Dunloe. A sudden glimpse of a very grim phantom came on us in the Gap. The guide had warned me to alight from *my horse, as the path was now very broken and dangerous ; I did not feel afraid and declined.   We passed the dangerous part, the horse trembled in every limb and slipped once but did not fall.   Soon after, she started and was unruly for a minute ; however I kept my seat, my husband went to her head and led her. Suddenly, without any apparent cause, she seemed to go mad—reared, plunged ;—I was thrown on the stones right under her.   My husband did not see that I had fallen—he still held on ; I saw and felt her kick, plunge, trample round me.   I had my thoughts about the moment—its consequences, my husband, my father. When my plight was seen, the struggling creature was let loose, and she sprang over me.   I was lifted off the stones, neither bruised by the fall nor touched by the mare's hoofs !   Of course the only feeling left was gratitude for more sakes than my own.*

I can write no more at present ; only that under the circumstances I can't see that Mrs. Gaskell is one whit in error.*   Mr. Dickens may, I think, have been somewhat too exacting, but if she found or thought her honour pledged, she does well to redeem it to the best of her ability—as she will—and I have no doubt it will be worthily done.

I go home soon : good-bye, dear Katie, I direct this to Plymouth Grove, not being sure of your address.

C. B. Nicholls.

In 1855 Mrs. Gaskell on her part was evidently feeling ill owing to a fall.   She writes from Plymouth Grove on New Year's Day, 1855, to Catherine Winkworth :

Thanks for your note ; and best and kindest wishes

---

* Respecting the writing of a contribution to a magazine about which there had been trouble.

for you at the New Year; " best wishes" leave happiness *in the hands of God, to come or not at His good pleasure. I think " best wishes" means to me a deeper sense of His being above all in His great peace and wisdom, and yet loving me with an individual love, tenderer than my mother's. Oh Katie, that fall has made me ill—a constant feeling of coming faintness which never comes and has done with it. . . .*

Miss Brontë's letter is very nice; I wish she'd write to me—should I to her? Last time I wrote it was a sort of explanation of my way of looking at her Church (the Establishment) and religion; intended for her husband's benefit. She has never answered it. I'm glad she likes " North and South"—I did not think Margaret *was so* over *good. What would Miss B. say to Florence Nightingale I can't imagine! for there is intellect such as I never came in contact with before in woman!—only two in men—great beauty, and of her holy goodness, who is fit to speak?*

Possibly it was difficult for Charlotte Brontë— now Mrs. Nicholls, though Mrs. Gaskell disregards the fact—to get into a discussion with a Dissenter on a subject so delicate, as far as her husband was concerned, as religion. In any case it was not very long before the end of her life.

IT was soon after this that the end came, just when the newly-married wife was hoping to have a child. Whether or no the fall in Ireland had to do with the event we cannot tell.

Following on her death there were of course all sorts of tales current about the woman who had become so famous within the last few years—about her strange life and the life of her sisters. Old Mr. Brontë became convinced—one hardly knows how for he was leading such a detached life cut off from the world—that a Biography of his daughter should be written. Mr. Nicholls, to whom, although he loved her as a wife, the literary side of her character hardly counted, was violently opposed to this. The very fact that Mrs. Gaskell as a Dissenter might be asked to undertake the work may have influenced him. But Charlotte's good friend, Ellen Nussey, seems to have been a wise intermediary and persuaded him (after the publication of an article in *Sharpe's Magazine* of which he disapproved) to allow Mrs. Gaskell to undertake the " just and honourable defence " of one of whom many false tales had got abroad. Fortunately, and quite comprehensibly, Mrs. Gaskell had very favourably impressed Mr. Brontë on the occasion of her one visit, and hence he asked her to be responsible for the writing of the Life. The favourable impression made on him was never lost, which was really marvellous considering that she wrote very frankly of his relations to his children. The truth is, Elizabeth Gaskell seemed to suit him. She was probably the sort of woman whom he imagined would have made his life a happy one.

It was really a momentous decision and the only, or about the only, good mark that we can give the selfish old man is in its regard. He became secretly proud of his daughter when he saw that she had become distinguished in the eyes of the world, expecting her distinction to rebound somehow on himself, and not remembering that he had lived his own life utterly regardless of the well-being, physical and intellectual, of his children. Mr. Nicholls' objections were transparent. He loved his wife, but he had no idea of the world's claim upon her and why should his privacy be invaded? One sometimes wonders whether he would have liked her called by her legal name in the Life about to be written; whereas no one in those days would have had a conception of who was meant if Charlotte Nicholls were spoken of. Our sympathies are with him in some ways, and one's gratitude goes out to him for certain, though short-lived, happiness. His limitations were no fault of his.*

The question occurs, if Charlotte Brontë had been told that her Life, and, in a minor sense, the lives of her sisters, had to be written, whom would she have chosen as biographer? Her two closest friends had no literary gifts, though Ellen Nussey was ready with her help; and outside them she had few for whom she really cared in a personal sense. Perhaps Mrs.

* Mr. Nicholls was the original from which Mr. Macarthey, the curate in " Shirley," was taken.

Gaskell was as near the ideal biographer as any that could be found, though in this case one has the feeling that a man might have had more understanding of that "Titan-like" being, Emily Brontë, who seemed to have all the will force and intellectual power of the male, combined with the more subtle qualities of the woman, curbed and cramped as they might be by the conditions of her existence. Her genius it was not given to such a one as Mrs. Gaskell fully to understand. Emily to her "did not always create a pleasant impression." Indeed, we understand that, for it took a generation to appreciate her as she deserved to be appreciated, and the appreciation has come largely from the other sex. But then the Life was not to be that of Emily, but of Charlotte Brontë, and here a woman biographer had certain advantages over a man. Unlike Emily, Charlotte was thoroughly a woman ; she had the passions of a woman—inhibited as they usually were ; she had the woman's deference to authority, and was prepared to allow that authority to exist. Hers was no rebel soul as was her sister's. She understood that side ; she was acutely sensitive to injustice ; but she, woman-like, was full of sensibility, and therefore a woman might understand her character as well as or better than a man. There was not, it is true, much resemblance between the two women concerned— none in external conditions and very little in their tastes and outlook. But after all this was not necessary, and there was a profound admiration of the younger woman on the part of the elder ; there were gifts on her part which were very valuable— gifts of description, gifts of style, gifts given by popularity with the public already attained. So that Mr. Brontë did one of the wisest acts in a far from wise life in writing to ask Mrs. Gaskell to undertake this task. Perhaps his daughter, if she felt the work had to be done perforce, would have said amen, since she could not have suggested a better.

The Life, as we all know now, was a wonderful success. It has been praised in an exaggerated manner. It was said to have had a greater sale than Boswell's Life of Johnson or Lockhart's Life of Scott. This is difficult to believe. George Eliot " cried over it " and " felt the better of it," both of which people did in those days, even the serious George Eliot and George Lewes. It was indeed a book to weep over—a tragedy such as would make the hardest heart melt—to read of sister after sister going to their death stoically and uncomplainingly after lives of suffering and sorrow. Going in their youth unmourned, except by one another, leaving immortal work behind them, but unrecognised. It was only Charlotte who attained to public appreciation in her lifetime and had a glimmer of joy towards the end ; and that was like a light to be quickly extinguished.

A great task had been put into Elizabeth Gaskell's hands and she, used to allow her fancy to play un-trammelled in ghost story and adventures, felt it hard to be " fettered by truth," though one would have said in this case truth was as little fettering as in any. There certainly was scope for the liveliest imagination in the work. She took on her task with a tremendous sense of responsibility. She " weighed every line with her whole power and heart," and she deserves much from posterity for what she did, and for collecting information which could never have been found again. Mr. Brontë was satisfied, and as

for Mr. Nicholls, let us hope that he did do what
Sir James Kay-Shuttleworth hoped he would do—
rejoice that his wife would be known as " a Christian
heroine who could bear her cross." He did not say
what that cross was formed of—that might have
been difficult and personal.

When we read the book, what strikes us most is
the simplicity with which the tale is told. Mrs.
Gaskell at her best had the gift of style—what she
wrote had distinction—but here she seems as if she
lost herself in her subject and wished simply and
almost reverently to tell all she could about women
greater than herself. It was interesting to see how
the work grew upon her. At first with some reason
she thought that she had not material for her work—
what was there to tell about so uneventful a life ?
Mr. Brontë is said cynically to have observed, " Well,
madam, if there is not enough, surely you can easily
invent something "ᵢ! He himself probably thought
" there was nothing to tell "—why should there be ?
He knew so little and had cared hardly at all. Of
course as things went on there was more than enough
to tell, but one of the attractions of the book is its
shortness ; it is in this respect a model, and in
another that the writer was content to be a Boswell
without his loquaciousness, and to tell her story in
forgetfulness of herself. Then she knew the life and
the country and could realise the interior as no man
could have done, for after all it was mostly a sort of
Dutch interior she had to draw, with a bleak wind-
swept exterior such as she must often have seen and
had in her weirder stories tried to delineate. The per-
sonalities seemed to draw themselves by their words
and actions ; it was only those still living on whom
she dared not fully exercise her pen. She must often

have longed to do so, but she burned her fingers badly when she attempted the task.

The occasion of the writing of the book was one of the few on which Mr. Gaskell gave a helping hand, though he is said in other cases to have given some assistance over Lancastrian dialect when required. He went with his wife to the "Black Bull" at Haworth—how Mr. Nicholls must have hated it— and did what he could to collect information. This was in the end of July, 1855, four months after Charlotte's death, and in a month the information was gathered together. It was no easy task, for the two clergymen terrified the would-be biographer. However, she boldly saw the servants and parishioners and drove around picking up her facts. Ellen Nussey, who lived at Birstall, was of the greatest help, and she had mercifully preserved her letters from Charlotte: in a less degree Miss Wooler, Charlotte's kind schoolmistress, also gave her assistance. Then a journey was made to the Clergy Daughters' School, now removed and well conducted, as well as to the original "Lowood"—then to London to see Mr. W. S. Williams, of the firm of Smith, Elder & Co., Charlotte Brontë's publishers and helpful friends. Mrs. Gaskell also went to Brussels, where Charlotte was first pupil and then teacher, but had a cold reception from Mme. Héger, the head, who indeed refused to see her, though her husband received her kindly enough. It is a dangerous thing to have a genius taken to the intimacy of your home, and in this case there were two—young women hyper-sensitive, over-observant, and feeling everything with an acuteness that made to the ordinary woman accustomed to the rough and tumble of life, mountains out of mole-hills. Mrs. Gaskell was probably aware of all this, but she was also aware that geniuses are not to be measured by ordinary standards and she did not so measure them.

Mrs. Gaskell writes to Miss Nussey a full account of her work and her troubles in 1856—her difficulties at Brussels, etc. " In fact," she wrote, " I think I have been everywhere where she ever lived except the two little pieces of private governess-ship. I still want one or two things to complete my materials, and I am very doubtful if I can get them—at any rate, I think they will necessitate my going to Haworth again—and I am literally *afraid* of that."

Then she explains that M. Héger asked her to try to see his letters to Charlotte, but she doubted whether Mr. Nicholls had not destroyed them. She also found that Mr. Nicholls would object to her seeing the manuscript of " The Professor." It seemed to be that Mr. Brontë's own consent or opinion on such matters had very little weight with Mr. Nicholls. Mr. Smith, the publisher, had apparently been concerned about what was said of Mr. Brontë in view especially of the possible strictures of reviewers. One cannot but wonder how more critical matters, such as those connected with Branwell, passed muster.

Anyhow, Mrs. Gaskell did her best to be truthful, and not to take the views either of the Dissenters of Haworth who were full of criticism of the queer *ménage* at the Parsonage, or that of the respectable people of Manchester ; but in her efforts after truth she made a bad mistake against which her husband, who had a well-balanced and legal type of mind, might well have warned her. Perhaps, like Miss Nussey, he did not really read her proofs, but was content to collect minor information. He is always represented as overwhelmed with his own work for the public weal and his wife's probably came second.

Branwell Brontë was, of course, the black sheep of the family. He was private tutor to the children of a woman with whom his sister Anne was governess, and who was stigmatised as having led him altogether astray. " The wretched woman," it was said, " not only survives, but passes about in the gay circles of London Society as a vivacious, well-dressed, flourishing widow," and by revealing the misery and early death of her partner in guilt, Mrs. Gaskell trusts that there might be awakened in her some feelings of repentance. There was a good deal more about her shocking conduct during the lifetime of her bedridden husband, and though the lady's name was not mentioned, she was easily recognised. To publish all this in a manner that made clear the identity of the lady was, of course, quite unpardonable, more especially if it were not absolutely certain, and the matter was very naturally taken up by a firm of solicitors who acted on her behalf. The end was that in May, 1857, the solicitors on Mr. and Mrs. Gaskell's side retracted every statement contained in the book imputing to " a widowed lady referred to, but not named therein, any breach of her conjugal, of her maternal, or of her social duties " and particularly the imputation of guilty intercourse between the two—that is between Branwell and herself. Mrs. Gaskell is said to wish to express her deep regret that she made the statement on information given her. The lady's solicitors accepted the apology fully, which was rather wonderful considering that the matter had been dealt with in the strongest manner and in several different places in the book. There may have been letters found in Branwell's

M

pocket after his death which made the lady anxious, though the old servant denied it, but to say, " He died—she lives still—in May Fair. . . . Now let us read, not merely of the suffering of her guilty accomplice, but of the misery she caused to innocent victims, whose premature deaths may, in part, be laid at her door "—to say all this was to invite retaliation. What seems strange now, is that though the objectionable matter was deleted this did not occur till both the early editions had nearly run through their courses.

The reason of the delay was in part that after reading the proofs Mrs. Gaskell, with her two elder daughters and her great friend Miss Catherine Winkworth, went off to Rome. They actually started on the day of the publication of the book, but it took eight days to reach their destination. This was in February, 1857. There they had a delightful time, saw much of W. W. Story, the American sculptor, and became acquainted with the Brownings. They returned in time to see a great Art Exhibition at Manchester, but when they arrived at home they learned that though the book had from a publishing point of view been a great success and had reached a second edition, a storm of criticism was impending.

Mr. Brontë was only concerned about what he considered as certain inaccuracies regarding the feeding of his children and would not have troubled very much. Miss Nussey says he laughed over the statements made about himself. But Mr. Nicholls was not so easily satisfied, for he does not appear in the book as the most sympathetic of husbands, and the servants were furious about being called wasteful. Consequently Mr. Brontë had to write a

certificate of character (which has been preserved)
declaring that they were not wasteful but kind and
honest. The village people had certain other comprehensible objections to the description given of
them, and a reference to a girl who had been seduced
was unfortunate. All this was nothing to the final
matters, first the apology that had to be made to
the lady spoken of above,* and secondly to the very
difficult question of the school at Cowan Bridge
attended by the Brontë sisters, which had been
conducted by the Rev. W. Carus-Wilson, well known
and highly respected in Evangelical circles, and
which was believed to be in all respects what it
ought to have been. The relatives of Mr. Carus-
Wilson threatened an action at law, and there was
much correspondence over the matter, followed by a
pamphlet by Mr. Wilson's son-in-law, the Rev. H.
Shepheard, incumbent of Casterton, entitled " A
Vindication of the Clergy Daughters' School and of
the Rev. W. Carus-Wilson from the Remarks in
' The Life of Charlotte Brontë.' "

It was indeed, as she said, " a veritable hornet's
nest " into which Mrs. Gaskell had returned. Her
unfortunate husband, who ought doubtless to have
foreseen what would happen, had found it necessary
to deal with the matter of the Branwell controversy
even before her return. He found, of course, what
was likely considering Branwell's character, that
statements that had been accepted as facts were
fabrications. Later investigation confirmed this.
Charlotte's sister Anne, who was governess at

* The lady, whose name has been published, was the wife of a
clergyman and is said by Mrs. Gaskell to have the blood of
honourable families mixed in her veins, and " underneath her roof
there have sat those whose names are held saintlike for their good
deeds."

Thorpe Green, where Branwell was tutor, probably believed all her brother's tales unquestioningly, and so did the others. Thus they were repeated to Mrs. Gaskell as facts. All unsold copies of the first two editions were withdrawn and alterations made in the subsequent editions. The " seduced " girl was now said to have been " betrayed " and so this matter was eventually put out of the way. As to the question of the school, Mrs. Gaskell felt on surer ground, and she showed great courage in holding to her statements. This for a rather specially sensitive woman of her nature was a real achievement. In May of 1857, Mr. Shepheard, now the Secretary of the School, wrote a long letter to *The Times* declaring that there was not a word of truth in the allegations, and that the promulgator of the falsehoods had received her information about the food being bad and insufficient and the treatment being so neglectful that illness broke out, from poisoned sources. " The Clergy Daughters' School is a public institution, open to public inspection," its defender writes, " and all who desire to know the truth are invited, as the best possible test, to visit the school itself ; their horrors of starvation will be pleasantly dissipated by a burst of merriment from 100 round and rosy-cheeked girls, and their better feelings, I trust, raised in thankfulness to Him ' from whom all good comes and just works do proceed ' while they gaze upon the fruits of Mr. Carus-Wilson's faithful labours, and hear of the love and veneration felt for one whose name will be remembered with gratitude by children's children long after his calumniators are forgotten." No " spiritual pride " or " love of power " or " want of tenderness " had been seen in him by other pupils, and so on. A reply appeared a few days later, pointing out that Mr. Shepheard greatly exaggerated the criticism made by Mrs. Gaskell, that her accusations were not as serious as was made out, and that she had not omitted to mention many redeeming features in the conduct of the teachers. Of course, the real trouble was that no one had a doubt about Casterton being identical with Lowood in " Jane Eyre," and already Yorkshire had a bad name for boys' schools (and girls' schools in a less degree) and Dickens was doing his best in " Nicholas Nickleby " and elsewhere to bring about their reformation by depicting their mismanagement, so that people were ready to believe the worst. The school could not have been good ; it was cheap, and Mr. Brontë was no doubt glad to get rid of the responsibility of nurturing his delicate, motherless daughters who had the faculty of taking every disease that was going ; the younger one when she went to school had just recovered from measles and whooping-cough combined, and it must all have worried the selfish parent. The children were all hyper-sensitive, born of a delicate mother as so many children of genius are, and what to a normal healthy child might have been nothing, was hell to them.

Mrs. Gaskell's pluck carried her successfully through, and she would make no alteration in her account of the school, but the whole thing was a trial to her and she seems to have felt unequal to great literary exertion for the next two years. On the other hand she was supported by the wealth of praise that was showered on the book. It is supposed that the worry was the cause of her desire that her own life should not be written, though this has been likewise ascribed to her being influenced by Thackeray's very explicit desire in regard to his life. She did not, however, feel discouraged from biographical writing in itself, for she had it in mind to write a life of her much admired Madame de Sévigné. Indeed, she was well equipped for such work, for she was not afraid of speaking her mind, besides being gifted with the power of letting her subject have the chance of making her own character known. In this case the biography, without being a great book or a classic in one sense—i.e. in making known to us the depth of the Brontës' minds or the dæmonic element in their natures, the range of their intellect or the greatness of their philosophy of life—yet gives us a true and faithful account of them in their setting : certainly a very vivid impression of their strange lives and surroundings and home conditions. It is that perception of small things as well as large, that acute power of observation, and that still more unusual power of putting that observation into words that express what is seen, that makes Elizabeth Gaskell's writing so pleasing to us. There is no wonder that she admired Mme. de Sévigné for she had not a little of the same kind of gift as she. And in applying that gift she had a marvellous subject—the writing of a biography that was also a romance. " A Romance it is," as Miss Flora Masson says, " this true, sad, intimate, unequalled story of another woman's life."

As to her critics, and they were many, she put on a bold front whatever she may have felt. Sometimes she had the courage to brave those " cautious dunces," as she calls them, so slow in finding merit. On certain occasions she tries to justify herself. Harriet Martineau had been very critical and evidently felt she ought to have been consulted. She writes to Miss Winkworth in an unpublished letter : " Mrs. Gaskell's readiness to do justice in all the particulars in which I have any concern is everything that could be wished. It is only a pity that in a matter which she ' could not remember ' she did not ask me a question. It seems now necessary for C. B.'s sake, to give a fuller explanation than would otherwise have served ; and a third edition never can set right the mistakes caused by a first." Mrs. Gaskell had sent her Mr. Brontë's letter on the publication of the Life, but it did not meet with Miss Martineau's approval. She says in her usual vigorous language : " The old monster ! Anything so appalling as one sentence in it* I am sure I never saw come from a human hand. Beautiful as the book is in many ways, I do mourn that Mrs. G. ever came in the way of that awful family." " She tells me of the Carus-Wilson threat, but I don't apprehend any harm from that quarter." " I am very sorry to hear from you that Mrs. G. did not see the letters to Branwell B. It aggravates the case, we think, that she had not seen the letters she speaks of. My own impression is that if she had, she would have found something very unlike what she concluded from C. B.'s account. She takes for granted in her letter to me that B. B.'s affair caused the deaths of both his sisters ; but C. B. never gave the least hint of the affair to me. She simply said her brother died of his vices."†

The letter from Mr. Brontë to which Miss Martineau refers is as follows :

I thank you for the books you have sent me containing

* Probably the reference to Branwell Brontë which is indeed rather strange in coming from a father. In a letter to Mrs. Gaskell he said that this was the part of the book he liked best !
† Letter to Miss Winkworth.

*the Memoir of my daughter.   I have perused them with
a degree of pleasure and pain which can only be known
to myself.   As you will have the opinion of abler
critics than myself I shall not say much in the way of
criticism.   I shall only make a few remarks in unison
with the feelings of my heart.   With a tenacity of purpose unusual with me, in all cases of importance, I
was fully determined that the biography of my daughter
should, if possible, be written by one not unworthy of
the undertaking.   My mind first turned to you, and
you kindly acceded to my wishes.   Had you refused,
I would have applied to the next best, and so on ; and
had all applications failed, as the last resource, though
about eighty years of age and feeble, and unfit for the
task, I would myself have written a short though
inadequate memoir, rather have left all to selfish, hostile,
or ignorant scribblers.   But the work is now done,
and done rightly, as I wished it to be, and on its com-
pletion has afforded me more satisfaction than I have
felt during many years of a life in which has been
accomplished the saying that " man is born to trouble,
as the sparks fly upwards."   You have not only given
a picture of my dear wife, and all my dear children,
and such a picture, too, and so full of truth and life.
The picture of my brilliant and unhappy son is a
masterpiece.   Indeed, all the pictures in the work
have vigorous, truthful and delicate touches in them,
which could have been executed only by a skilful female
hand.   There are a few trifling mistakes which, should
it be decreed necessary, may be corrected in the second
edition.**

W. R. Greg was always one of Mrs. Gaskell's most
trenchant critics, and he did not allow her to escape

* " Life of Charlotte Brontë," Haworth edition, p. xxviii.

his lash over her Biography of Charlotte Brontë. Mrs. Gaskell, he declared, appeared to have learned the art of the novel-writer so well that she cannot discharge from her palette the colours that she used in the pages of " Mary Barton " and " Ruth." Thus the accusation made—and made by others besides Greg—is that the author romanced in her biography in order to obtain effect. Now there was a slight justification for this assertion. Mrs. Gaskell visualised her subject and her surroundings and, as she had reason to know, she was apt to take unreliable statements for reliable ; to forget how when facts are stated in black and white they must first be checked. For instance, she ought not to have made certain statements in regard to the will of the supposed injured husband and its bearing on his widow, without taking the elementary step of getting a copy of the will from Somerset House, and so on. But though she showed some lack of worldly wisdom here, she did it not maliciously, but in order to justify his sisters in their attitude towards the erring Branwell, who was certainly blameworthy, but who was believed to be sinned against as well as sinning ; and this formed part of the picture she had clearly in her mind. The picture on the whole was a just one : there might have been some exaggerations about Mr. Brontë's conduct to his wife, but then he never said this was so, and from the letters that have been discovered later it would not seem so. People do not now conceive biography to consist of a bald relation of facts ; this gives no real idea of the individual who is portrayed any more than a bare list of events tells us about history in its real meaning. There is no " simplicity of daylight " in the relation of human beings. They are extraordinarily complex and have to be interpreted by understanding minds. The old pompous criticism, like that of W. R. Greg, which warns against setting up a pillory in Paternoster Row, and tells us that it is " the duty of literary criticism to expose and discover " such methods, only amuses us now, though doubtless it gave real pain at the time.

This is a letter from Mr. Gaskell to Miss Nussey soon after the book was published : " I hope your copy of the Life, and the one for Miss Wooler came safe. All the notices that I have seen have been favourable, and some of the best exceedingly so. I have had a considerable number of letters, too, from distinguished men expressing high approval. Mr. Brontë, I am happy to say, is pleased, and I can only hope that Mr. Nicholls will (as Sir J. K. Shuttleworth says) ' learn to rejoice that his wife will be known as a Christian heroine, who could bear her cross with the firmness of a martyr saint.' "

To Ellen Nussey Mrs. Gaskell writes in 1853, telling her of Mr. Brontë's request to her to write his daughter's Life. " Both he and Mr. Nicholls agreed to this. Mr. Brontë, not perceiving the whole extent of the great interest in her personal history felt by strangers, but desiring above all things that her life should be written and written by me. His last words were, ' No quaking, Mrs. Gaskell, no drawing back.' "

Mr. Nicholls was really far more aware of the kind of matter people would look for and his feelings were against the Life being written, but he yielded to Mr. Brontë's " impetuous wish " and brought about a dozen letters from his wife's receptacles, mainly to her sister Emily. He advised Mr. Gaskell to apply to Miss Nussey for help, which she immediately did, making plans for meeting.

Mr. W. S. Williams's letters, sent at once to the biographer, were very useful. She writes : " I like the series better than any other excepting one "— no doubt those to Emily—and goes on, " How beautifully she writes about her wanderings on the moor after her sister's death ! "*

The portrait in the beginning of the book was apparently flattered in the view of those who knew the subject best. An old friend and schoolfellow, Mary Taylor, writes from abroad : " I had rather the mouth and eyes had been nearer together, and shown the veritable square face and large disproportionate nose." The facts of the life she said were given with accuracy, " a true picture of a melancholy life," and marvels that reviewers should not see the harm in such a woman living her life " in a walking nightmare of poverty and self-suppression." It is a striking fact that this woman, next to Ellen Nussey, Charlotte's greatest friend, should think that the conditions as stated were not as gloomy as the truth.

This letter to Emily Shaen in September, 1856, describes a visit to Haworth with Sir James Kay-Shuttleworth and her views about publishing Miss Brontë's posthumous work :

I was so sorry when I got your note last night, darling, that I had not written the day after I got home ; that is not I could not have written, but I could have made one of the girls do it, but I wanted so very much to write to you myself, and that literally

* Clement Shorter's privately printed Letters on C. Brontë and Mrs. Gaskell.

was impossible till I did. I am writing my last letters to-day ; to-morrow I set to and fag away at " Miss Brontë " again, you see in general you hear (or I like to feel you do) all sorts of things about me and us from Katie and Susanna*, so that I always feel you are " au courant," and now it seems as if I had such a great deal to say to you. I think I had better begin about Miss B. You would hear before you left Alderley that I had been to Haworth with Sir J. P. K. S. He had not the slightest delicacy or scruple; and asked for an immense number of things, literally taking no refusal. Hence we carried away with us a whole heap of those minute writings of which William showed you one or two at Alderley : the beginning (only about twenty pages) of a new novel which she had written at the end of 1854 before marriage, and I dare say when she was anxious enough. This fragment was excessively interesting : a child left at a school by a rich flashy man, who pretended to be her father, the schoolmistress's deference to the rich child, her mysterious reserved character evidently painfully conscious of the imposition ; the non-payment of bills ; the inquiry—no such person to be found, and just when the child implored mercy and confessed her complicity to the worldly and indignant schoolmistress the story stops—for ever. Besides these things we carried off the " Professor "—that first novel, rejected by all the publishers. This Sir James took away with him intending to read it first and then forward to me. He wrote to me before he forwarded it, praising it extremely —saying it would add to her reputation—objecting to certain coarse and objectionable phrases—but offering to revise and expunge and make the necessary alterations, and begging me to forward his letter to Mr.

* Winkworth.

Smith. I dreaded lest the " Professor" should involve anything with M. Héger—I had heard her say it related to her Brussels life, and I thought if he were again brought before the public what would he think of me ? I believed him to be too good to publish those letters, but I felt that his friends might really with some justice urge him to do so. So I waited the arrival of the " Prof." (by Mrs. Gaskell at Dumbleton) with great anxiety. It does relate to the school; but not to M. Héger, and Madame, or Madame Beck, is only slightly introduced; and on that ground there could be no objection to publishing it. I don't think it will add to her reputation, the interest will arise from its being the work of so remarkable a mind. It is an autobiography—of a man, the English Professor at a Brussels school—there are one or two remarkable portraits, the most charming woman she ever drew, and a glimpse of that woman as a mother—very lovely, otherwise little or no story; and disfigured by more coarseness and profanity in quoting texts of scripture disagreeably than in any of her other works. However I had nothing to do except to be a medium,—so I sent Sir J. P. K. S.'s letter on to Mr. Nicholls, and told him I was going to send a copy of it to Mr. Smith if he had no objection; that I did not think so highly of the book as Sir J. P. K. S. although I thought that great public interest would be felt in it, that I thought that she herself having prepared it for the Press, Sir J. P. K. S. ought not to interfere with it—as, although to my mind there certainly were several things that had better be expunged; yet that he (Mr. N.) was, it seemed to me, the right person to do it. I did not*

* Mr. C. Shorter says Mr. Nicholls would not let Mrs. Gaskell edit and change the " Professor." He was apparently mistaken in this.—" Charlotte Brontë and Her Circle," p. 465.

know what Mr. N. would say to this, as he certainly is under obligation to Sir James for the offer of a living, but I don't know if you remember some of the passages I copied out in her letters relating to Sir J. and there were others I did not—*all making me feel she would have especially disliked* him *to meddle with her writings. However Mr. N. quite agreed with me and wrote to Sir James declining his proposal, saying privately to me that he feared Sir J. would be hurt (he Sir J. evidently wants to appear to the world in intimate connexion with her) but that knowing his wife's opinion on the subject, he could not allow any such revisal, but that he would himself look over the " Professor" and judge as well as he could with relation to the passages Sir J. and I had objected to, so there it rests with Mr. Nicholls to whom the MS of the " Prof." was returned a fortnight ago. With regard to Mr. Smith of course he jumped at the idea; whatever sum I fixed on as the price should be cheerfully paid—(I declined the responsibility—but said I thought it ought to be paid for like her other works in proportion to the length). Would I edit it? (No! for several reasons). When would the Life be ready? Michaelmas? The time of publishing the " Professor" would have to be guided by that. All I could say in reply was that I would make haste but that it could not be ready by Michaelmas possibly. Since then (about 10 days ago) I have heard nothing either from Mr. Smith or from Mr. Nicholls. Now as to the Life. Among that heap of minute writing I found quantities of fragments, very short but very graphic, written when she was about 12, giving glimpses of her life at that time, all of which I had to decipher and interweave with what I had already written—in fact I had to re-write about 40 pages. They give a much pleasanter*

though hardly less queer *notion of the old father.
Moreover Mrs. Woodsworth sent me a letter of Branwell's to Mr. W.; and altogether it was dreary work,
looking over, correcting, interweaving etc. etc. etc. and
besides that I* wrote 120 new *pages while we were
absent on our holiday, which was no holiday to me—
I used to go up at Dumbleton and Boughton to my
room directly after I'd done breakfast and come down
to lunch at ½ past 1, up again and write without allowing any temptation to carry me off till 5 or past;
having just a run or a walk before 7 o'clock dinner.
I got through an immense deal; but I found head and
health suffering—I could not sleep for thinking of it.
So at Broad Leas (the Ewarts) I only wrote till lunch;
and since then not at all, I have been too busy since
I came home. I enjoyed Broad Leas far the most
of any visit, perhaps owing to my not having the sick
wearied feeling of being overworked; and Mr. Gaskell
being very jolly; and delicious downs (Salisbury
Plain) get-at-able in one afternoon, drives, great sweeps
of green turf, like emerald billows stretching off into
the blue sky miles and miles away,—with here and
there a " barrow " of some ancient Briton, and Wans-
dyke, and Silbury Hill, and the great circle of Avebury
all to be seen, while the horses went noisily over the
thick soft velvety grass high up over blue misty plains
and villages in nests of trees, and church spires which
did not reach nearly up to where we were in our beautiful free air and primitive world. . . . Mr. Gaskell is
going off with Mr. James (Unit. minister of Bristol,
his last year's Swiss travelling companion) to the
Lakes on Friday next for 10 days. It is now Monday
morning—this letter has been written under all sorts
of difficulties, and now I'm treading on my precious
Brontë time.*

The accusation of having written coarse and objectionable phrases as criticised by Sir James Kay-Shuttleworth would have shocked their author, who, Mrs. Gaskell tells us, when such were discussed in regard to other writers, said with great earnestness to her and Sir James : " I think God will take from me whatever power of invention and expression I may have before He lets me become blind to the sense of what is fitting or unfitting to be said ! " Mrs. Gaskell, however, with her exaggerated sense of propriety, could not wholly exonerate her from the accusation, but put it down to the company in which she had perforce to live : the brother Branwell included : " Circumstances forced her to touch pitch, as it was, and by it her hand was for a moment defiled."*

Of this, the last visit, Mrs. Gaskell writes to Catherine Winkworth : " It was a most peaceful visit. Both Mr. Brontë and Mr. Nicholls cried sadly. I like Mr. Nicholls. We left very late and got to Shipton that night very tired." A later letter to Emily Winkworth, now Mrs. Shaen, from Mrs. Gaskell's daughter, tells about a visit made by her to Haworth with her mother. She gives a different account of Mr. Nicholls.

My dearest Emily,
Thank you so very much for your kind little letter, which reached me this morning. I did not think you would ever write to me again ; at any rate not kindly,— for I fancied you would blame me as much as I did myself for my stupidity in giving you so much trouble in mining amongst your books for La Question Romaine. Mama and I are both as fat and well now as possible ;

* " Life of Charlotte Brontë."

and I only hope that she may keep the strength she has gained here during the winter. . . . We came here on Monday. It is such a pleasant little place, and the landlady is such a good, sweet creature, who tries in all sorts of ways to make us comfortable, and to pet us. We have a large sitting-room, an old-fashioned " parlour " quite—with a low ceiling of carved wood ; a window-seat crowded with pots of flowers, and real china basins of pot-pourri : a canary : a look-out on to a luxuriant little garden scenting the room with lavender ; a sofa at right angles to the bright fire, and many pleasant quaint etceteras—and Mrs. Middle-brook, having been cook at the Hall, does send us up such dainty appetising 4 o'clock dinners, and teas with proper Yorkshire cakes. You can't think what good this is doing Mama. But what I want really to tell you about, is a visit which Mama and I paid to old Mr. Brontë to-day. We were talking about him on Thursday, and I was expressing a great wish to see him, out of which conversation sprung a plan for my going alone to call on him—Mama saying that she fancied he would not like to see her ; because so many reviews, letters in newspapers, etc., which she knew had reached him, had dwelt on the way in which, while pretending to have been his daughter's friend, she had held up his character to ridicule, etc. etc. But, however, at length it seemed better that she'd go too ; to brave his displeasure if there were any, and to please him by the attention if there were none. So she wrote on Thursday evening to ask him if we might go. This she did, thinking that then, if he really had any objection to seeing her, it would give him the opportunity of preventing our visit. However, this morning there came a few tremulous, feeble lines to say he should be glad to see us ; and we scuttled through our breakfast

N

and caught the 8.40 train, which took us to Keighley, and then we got a fly that brought us to Haworth by about 11.15. " Martha," such a blooming, bright, clean young woman, gave us a hearty welcome; and took us into the parlour (Miss B's sitting-room), where we waited for about ¼ of an hour; when she came to fetch us to Mr. B.—Mama had no idea that he was confined to bed, as he is now—we were taken into his bedroom; where everything was delicately clean and white, and there he was sitting propped up in bed in a clean nightgown, with a clean towel laid just for his hands to play upon—looking Oh! very different from the stiff scarred face above the white walls of cravat in the photograph—he had a short soft white growth of beard on his chin; and such a gentle, quiet, sweet, half-pitiful expression on his mouth, a good deal of soft white hair, and spectacles on. He shook hands with us, and we sat down, and then said how glad he was to see Mama,—and she said how she had hesitated about coming,—feeling as if he might now have unpleasant associations with her—which never seemed to have entered into his head—then he asked her how, since he last saw her, she had passed through this weary and varied world—in a sort of half grandiloquent style—and then interrupting himself he said, " but first tell me how is that young lady, whose friend went to the Massacres in India ? " I thought he meant the Ewarts, or something, and was quite surprised (besides other things) when Mama pointed to me, and said I was here, and then he prosecuted his inquiries about the engagement, and its breaking off;* and then turned round and told me that he hoped I would forget the past; and would hope—that we ought all to live

---

* Miss Meta Gaskell's engagement to an officer, which was broken off.

on hope.—Then he told Mama how many, many applica-
tions he had for bits of Miss B's hand-writing,—how
he had to cut up her letters into strips of a line each.—
He talked of her as simply "Charlotte" without any
hesitation—He said to Mama—"As I told you in
my first letter, the Memoir is a book which will hand
your name down to posterity," and that there was only
one fault he had to find with it; might he speak out
openly before me? Mama told him he might, and
we both sat expecting some allusion to the Lady S. part
—but what he said was that the statement that he had
not allowed his children to have meat till they were
(a certain age) had been quoted by either Mr. Carus
Wilson, or his defenders, as more likely to have been
the cause of their delicacy than the fare they subse-
quently had at Cowan's Bridge. Now—this statement
was a mistake. His children had always been allowed
meat; but he said he had chosen not to defend himself
at the expense of proving Mama inaccurate: and so
giving a handle to those who accused her of mis-state-
ments—I wish I could remember more of what he said.
He very soon turned the conversation to politics: asked
Mama whether she thought the English ought to inter-
fere in Italian affairs at present, or wait till the Italians
asked for help; and seemed very much pleased when
she said she thought we ought to hold back for the
present, "You see we agree in politics as in everything
else." He had been very much pleased with Thackeray's
notice in the Cornhill—he thought it showed "heart,
but Thackeray was an odd man, a very odd man."
He alluded to his own "eccentricity" with a certain
pride; and his "independence," too, of other people's
opinion; not but what he valued the opinion of good
people—Mama said: "Yes—I was just telling my
daughter as we came up the hill, that I thought you

*had always done what you thought right."—" And so
I have," he said, " and I appeal to God." There was
something very solemn in the way he said it ; and in
him altogether—None of the sternness I had fancied—
Mama said something about our not staying too long
to tire him and that we were going, for me to make a
sketch ; And he said, " There are certain circumstances,
you see," looking very knowing, " which make it
desirable that when you leave in 5 minutes or so, we
should shake hands—and I give your daughter free
leave to make a sketch, or do anything outside the
house. Do you understand Latin ? Mrs. Gaskell
does at any rate, well,* verbum sap., *a word to the wise,"
and then he chuckled very much ; the gist of it was,
as Mama saw, and I guessed, that he feared Mr.
Nicholls' return from the school—and we were to be
safely out of the house before that. Mama is telling
Mr. Shaen all about the sexton. Just before leaving
Haworth we went to call on John Greenwood ; and
whilst Mama was talking to him, his wife volunteered
to me how she disliked Mr. N., as they all seemed to
do—(The sexton said, " Aye, Mester Brontë and Mr.
Nicholls live together still* ever near *but* ever separate,"*
and he told us how when the fresh monument was put
up in the church, Mr. N. made him take the old tablet-
stone, and with a hammer break it into small pieces,
which he then bade, and saw, him bury 4 ft. deep in
the garden : for fear any one should get hold of a piece
for a relic). Well—Mrs. Greenwood had a puny,
precocious little lad clinging to her dress, about 1½ years
old—so of course I asked its name, and she said
" Brontë, Miss, Eh, Mr. Nicholls was angry a' that.
He heard they were going to give it the name ; and
said in Mr. B's hearing that he wouldn't christen the
child, whereupon Mr. B. sent word by Martha of his*

*determination to the Greenwoods, to spare them the
annoyance of a direct refusal, so they kept the child
unchristened till it was 6 months old when it became
so ailing that they thought it wouldn't live ; and Mr. B.
hearing of this, sent for it (as far as I understand) to
his own bedroom (it is a year since his health began to
fail) and christened it there ; having the Register-book
for baptisms, and writing down its name with his own
hand.   It was years since he had christened a child.
Of course the next baby Mr. N. condescended to christen,
he went to write its name down, and there saw Mr. B's
registration of the christening of little Brontë Greenwood.   Mrs. G. said that there and then he strode
straight back to the Parsonage, and up into Mr. B's
bedroom ; and " So I see you have christened your
namesake."   And Mr. B. got out of it by saying that
he had done it to save Mr. N. from the terrible scrape
in which he would have found himself, had the child
died unchristened, etc.   But this is a specimen of Mr.
N's sullen, obstinate rooted objection to any reverence
being paid to Miss B. one might almost say, at any rate to
people caring to remember her as an authoress . . ."*

This final letter gives a more favourable account
of Patrick Brontë, though it is rather sad to read
of the relations between the two bereaved men.
Mr. Clement Shorter gives a much more agreeable
account of Mr. Nicholls as he was in later life and
after his retiral to Ireland. The truth of Miss
Gaskell's account of this visit is borne out by Mrs.
Gaskell's own account of it to Mr. Williams in the
same year, 1860. She says : " Mr. Nicholls seems
to keep him [Mr. Brontë] *in terrorem*. He is more
unpopular in this village than ever and seems to
have even a greater aversion than formerly to any

strangers visiting his wife's grave; or, indeed, to any reverence paid to her memory even by those who knew and loved her for her own sake," and then describes the visit much as above.* Mr. Nicholls had been offered the living of Padiham, near Gawthorpe, by Sir James Kay-Shuttleworth but could not accept it because it would involve leaving Mr. Brontë. After his wife's death he finally retired to King's County where he lived and farmed till his death in 1906 at the age of ninety. It is related by Mr. Shorter who saw him (as did Mr. Reginald Smith) that he read everything published regarding his wife but uttered not a word. For that one respects him.

But whatever Mr. Nicholls's character really was, it had its strange side, for he was clearly an exacting husband. Soon after her marriage his wife writes to Ellen Nussey to say that Mr. Nicholls had told her that " she must give him a plain pledge to burn all her letters, or he will read every line I write and elect himself censor of our correspondence." This promise was no joke but a serious matter and the pledge was to be written " on a separate piece of paper in a legible hand."† Even in those days this seemed the action of a man hardly responsible for his actions but perhaps it was less so than one imagines.

* " The Brontës Life and Letters," C. Shorter, p. 293.
† *Ibid.*

Old Nurse's Story "—was a really remarkable piece of work. It was written in 1852 for the Christmas number of *Household Words*. Many people write detective stories and tales of strange adventures with success, but few succeed with the supernatural. We can all believe in murders and robberies, for we hear of them every day, but when it comes to asking us to credit tales of ghosts and fairies—when we leave, what we call the rational for the irrational—it is a very different matter. The writer of such tales must necessarily engender an atmosphere of eeriness and get the readers to be so immersed in this that they are ready to give credit for the time being to tales wholly incredible. Now Elizabeth Gaskell had just this power. She was able to make us feel the desolation of the great house at the foot of the Cumberland Fells with trees all around, their branches broken and dragging against the walls when the wind blew, and the little garden scooped out of the thick dark wood, so overshadowed that few were the flowers that would grow in it. Then the story tells of how the organ was heard—the old Lord—long since dead—playing it—the mysterious " other " little girl who appeared in the snow to the real child who was the nurse's care and joy. How the " other " child drew little Rosamund after her in the snow—the " evil child " who had the tragic history ; how this poor child cried and beat against the windows to get in but had to be kept off—the terrible fact was that she and her mother had been driven from the house by the fierce Lord on just such a night, so that the poor woman was found in the snow crazy, with a dead child in her arms. The end of the story, the dramatic appearance of the ghost of the old Lord driving before him his daughter and her child with crutch uplifted, ready to strike —the dreadful sequel—brought this really wonderful ghost story to an artistic conclusion.   Anyone who, like the present writer, has heard that tale read aloud on a Christmas night with lights low and the wind howling outside can bear witness that it is a marvellously successful effort towards making real to us the unseen and invisible !

Dickens wished to make some alterations in the story, the ending of which he thought " terrific," as indeed it was, but its author was firm in her rejections of his suggestions.   In the end, in spite of his criticisms, he allowed that it was a very fine short story, " nobly told and wonderfully arranged."

Mrs. Gaskell doubtless enjoyed writing such stories and feeling that she was causing our flesh to creep !   She had that almost mischievous joy in her art that gives it a unique character.   But she knew all the time that it was a *tour de force* and perhaps she thought of it as a blessed relief from the conventional everyday existence led by the wife of a reputable Manchester citizen, living in a comfortable home with a flourishing young family around her and all the usual domestic duties to attend to.   When she visited Oxford in 1860 she talked of ghosts to Augustus Hare and would indeed have liked to have taken part in a debate on the subject which was to be held at the Union !   One cannot but believe that she really believed in her ghosts—the ghosts that were so much more attractive than those of later days who became mixed up with melodeons and tambourines.

The same year, 1852, there came " The Shah's English Gardener," a short paper in *Household Words* again—really the account of an interview with a gardener in Stafford who had once been in the service of the Shah of Persia.

Next year appeared the "Cumberland Sheep-shearers" which narrates a visit to the annual sheep-shearing amongst the Cumberland Fells, followed by "Morton Hall." This is a strange story—not, indeed, a ghost story, but one that deals with the passing of the old family and the coming in of the new, and the scene is laid in the neighbourhood of Drumble, that is, of course, Manchester. There is a pathetic account of how the young squire, who had squandered his money, returned to starve proudly with his sister, until at last she died of hunger and he was afterwards found dead on the moors, and then there is a further tale of their successors. The whole plot—if plot it may be called —is not well devised and the reader gets confused even in the short space that is taken up in narrating the events recorded. Mrs. Gaskell had an unfortunate way of going on with a story and not letting it rest at its proper conclusion. This was probably encouraged by the serial form in which she found herself compelled to write and which has perforce to conform to order. In this case she had to fill two numbers of *Household Words*, and consequently there are two not very clearly connected lines of narrative.

"My French Master," which came later in the same year, is a very charming account of a French *émigré* who gave lessons in his own language to the writer. She describes (and this is reminiscent of experiences of her youth) how M. de Chalabre " wore a wig, delicately powdered, frizzed and tied in a queue behind " ; his politeness was such that " we had always a feeling that he would catch cold, and

that he was doing us too great an honour, and that
he did not know how old or rather how young we
were, until one day we saw him (far away from our
house) hand a country woman over a stile with the
same kind of dainty, courteous politeness, lifting her
basket of eggs over first ; and then, taking up the
silk-lined lapel of his coat, he spread it on the palm
of his hand for her to rest her fingers upon, instead
of which, she took his small white hand in her plump,
vigorous grip, and leant her full weight upon him.
He carried her basket for her as their roads lay
together ; and from that time we were less shy in
receiving his courtesies, perceiving that he considered them a deference due to our sex, however
old or young, or rich or poor." This little story has
the stamp of truth and carries the reader back to
the old days of a schoolgirl at Knutsford. For as
has been said, Elizabeth Stevenson had had the
benefit of receiving lessons from a French master,
M. Rogier, for whose instruction she was for ever
grateful. He made her love the literature and
'anguage of France and it is he, with his firmness
and gentleness, his aversion to dirty boots, and his
search for rare plants, who is depicted in her story.
It was in the garden of her aunt's house that she
was sometimes allowed to have her lessons. Indeed,
this M. Rogier was a famous character in Knutsford,
for like so many of his countrymen at that time
when French dancing was an art, he taught dancing
as well as language, and then he had the honour of
instructing none less than William Pitt, who was
visiting in the neighbourhood. He is said to have
remarked (and if this were serious it shows that a
sense of humour was not one of his characteristics) : " There was nothing whatever in Pitt's

dancing to indicate what a great man he would become ! "*

It was perhaps the turn given to Mrs. Gaskell's thoughts by her French master that interested her in the story of the Huguenots. Anyhow, she wrote an account of them for *Household Words*, that may have seemed a little serious for a periodical publication but was just the record of all that the writer knew or had heard about these people when refugees in England. The " Squire's Story," published the same year, is very different, for it is rather an entertaining, if not entirely convincing, story of how a man named Higgins, a professional robber and even murderer, managed to live for years in an attractive house in Derbyshire, to join the local hunt, and to be so much esteemed in the neighbourhood that he eventually married the squire's daughter, without allowing it to be discovered how he made his living during his frequent absences from home. Finally, seven years after his marriage a dreadful murder, with robbery, was committed at Bath, and the truth came out that Higgins was the murderer. The story is like that of the famous Claude Duval who " collected his rents on the highway like many another ' gentleman ' of the day," but who, at last, was convicted of murder and was hanged at Derby in 1775. As a matter of fact, Higgins, who was executed at Carmarthen in 1767, resided at Knutsford, where he was married and lived as a married man for at least eight years, being all the while received in the best society. So that there was considerable basis, in fact, for a story which is told at length in Henry Green's

* " Mrs. Gaskell's Haunts, Homes and Stories," by Mrs. Ellis H. Chadwick, p. 22.

" Knutsford, its Traditions and History."* De Quincey gives a florid account of the matter in his Autobiography, but the actual facts are strange enough to inspire many writers of fiction. Mrs. Gaskell tells the tale excellently; it is made perfectly clear and entrancing, and, best test of all, one would like it to be longer than it is. Certainly the writer had the art of narrating a good short story well when she had no moral to point, and allowed a gentle sense of humour to have its play.

In 1854, the same magazine, *Household Words*, had various brief contributions, " Bran," " Company Manners," which has Madame de Sablé as its text, and next year " Modern Greek Songs," an account of Fauriel's " Chants Populaires de la Grèce Moderne," and in 1855 a very weird account of the strange " Accursed Race "; this deals with the persecution of a people supposed to have descended from lepers—the Cagots by name. This was just the sort of unusual history that appealed to Mrs. Gaskell —the history of a strange race that dwelt in that part of France which extended from the valleys of the Pyrenees to Lower Brittany. These poor people were subject to the most cruel treatment owing to the prejudice against them. Though not necessarily lepers, they were kept apart and made to use a lepers' door in church when allowed to attend the services at all.

Then comes " Half a Life-Time Ago " and " The Poor Clare."

All the time that she wrote these short tales, there was a constant output of editions of Mrs. Gaskell's various works—Tauchnitz editions and French editions of " Mary Barton "; " Cranford " appeared in

* Second edition, 1887.

German in 1857, and " Ruth " in French (translated by Mme. Cornelie de Witt) in 1856. The Life of Charlotte Brontë was published in 1857, and it ran through four editions in two years in England, besides being also published in America ; republication of the novels seemed also to have been incited by its means. Not content with her own work, Mrs. Gaskell edited " The Lamplighter," by Maria S. Cummins, a book that had a great vogue at the time. The short stories she seemed always ready to produce ; she also managed on one occasion to escape from *Household Words* to *Harper's Magazine*, and there bring out* " The Doom of the Griffiths," in the same year in which she published " The Half-Brothers." As a matter of fact, " An Accursed Race," " Half a Life-Time Ago," " The Poor Clare " and " The Half-Brothers " were all included in what was called " Round the Sofa," which was issued in 1859 along with the stories entitled " My Lady Ludlow," and " The Doom of the Griffiths." The stories are introduced by an account of the writer's visit to Edinburgh before her marriage, when she was living in " dull lodgings with only poor, grave Miss Duncan for my companion," and forced by the decorum of the streets of that impressive town " to tie up my bonnet strings neatly and put on my shawl with some regard to straightness." The long winter evenings were worst in the grey, drab rooms, and it is made to appear that a certain Mrs. Dawson invited the lonely girl to her Monday evenings, when the stories were read aloud. The suggestion is that these were the rather famous " evenings " given by Mrs. Fletcher, who was a well-known Edinburgh hostess, but as a matter of fact Mrs.

* In 1858.

Fletcher's parties really took place in the days of Elizabeth Gaskell's parents' residence there, and not during her own stay. Mrs. Fletcher, in her Autobiography, tells of her pleasure in making acquaintance with the daughter of the parents she knew in old Edinburgh days, and the idea of hanging her stories round the gatherings of Edinburgh celebrities doubtless occurred to Mrs. Gaskell from her knowledge of her parents' experiences. It is to be feared that the celebrities of that day and place would hardly appreciate the somewhat long-drawn-out " My Lady Ludlow."

This was really the first of the " Round the Sofa " series, which wandered along through many numbers of *Household Words*. The title was given because the centre of attraction was the sister of a famous surgeon (under whose care the narrator was supposed to be) who was confined to the sofa but who was the admiration of young and old. She was, it was explained, not Scottish but Lancashire born, and she was induced to tell her story on condition that others promised to contribute their experiences or narratives at a future time.

" Lady Ludlow " would have made a first-rate story if it had been perfected and not allowed to wander afield. The characters are well drawn. The Lady herself—the old aristocrat of former days—is absolutely true to life ; the way in which she brought up the " young gentlewomen " whom she educated, her views on education and the place of the Church ; her treatment of the advanced young clergyman who wished to establish Sunday schools ; the manner in which she prevented herself from listening to his revolutionary arguments by erecting glazed windows round her pew which could on necessity be closed, is all told excellently. Her description of how the clergyman was politely but firmly dismissed when he dared to quote the authority of the Bishop against that of the Lady of the Manor is delightful : " I could only rise and curtsy, and curtly dismiss him. It is one of the few cases when abruptness is desirable." The old maid, Miss Galindo, is also as good as her name foretells. The part which deals with the great lady's appreciation of scents, the delicate perfection of which must be cultivated for generations, is most entertaining : " My dear, remember that you try if you can smell the scent of dying strawberry-leaves in the next autumn. You have some of Ursula Hanbury's blood in you and that gives you a chance."

The story goes off at a tangent into an entirely unconnected one about a French boy, Clément de Créquy, and then into all sorts of other devious ways, and what was long enough to print as a book in America resulted. But the pity is that we have not a second " Cranford " instead. There is a superabundance of good material, if only the part about the life at Hanbury Court and Miss Galindo and her devotion to an illegitimate child— the child of a man she had formerly loved—had been worked out. Miss Galindo knew the condemnation her action would bring upon her head, for Lady Ludlow " neither saw nor heard, nor was in any way cognisant of the existence of those who had no legal right to exist at all." The long story reminds one, as Mrs. Gaskell's so often do, of the stories children rely upon the good-natured grown-up to tell—stories that must carry on the same people from day to day and yet provide a varied series of events.

" An Accursed Race," which has been mentioned,
was supposed to be reprinted in a paper put
together by Mr. Dawson for " The Philosophical
Society." It was submitted to with some demur,
but found to be more interesting than anticipated.
" The Doom of the Griffiths " was said to be delivered by Miss Duncan, the dull friend, and read
in a " high-pitched, ill-assured voice." It is a
terrible and heart-rending tale of horror. How the
dull Miss Duncan managed to get through it in her
high-pitched voice one wonders—still more how the
audience supported it. Murder follows murder, and
the writer seems to enjoy it : " I fancied, perhaps,
I could do something to give a little pleasure," she
murmured ! It was followed by " Half a Life-Time
Ago," another most melancholy tale about a West-
morland woman who chose to tend an idiot boy
confided to her by his dying mother, when this was
the alternative to marriage. The poor invalid, Miss
Dawson, must have had bad nights after her Monday
receptions.

The next of the series was contributed by an
Italian writer and called " The Poor Clare," another
of the strange " curse " stories, and this is, perhaps,
one of the strangest. It is difficult to think how
the story of the terrible dual personality and the
evil spirit that could only be exorcised through the
life of poverty and death by starvation which was
the lot of the member of Poor Clares, could have
been conceived by the author. It was one of the
tales of terror and violence that appealed so strongly
to Mrs. Gaskell.

The last part of this curious symposium was
simply an account of how a despised half-brother
and his dog had saved the narrator's life.

Of the short papers or stories published in 1858, there were " The Manchester Marriage," a touching story of domestic life of a periodical kind, and " Right at Last," about a young woman who against her guardian's wish married a doctor of unknown parentage and discovered him to be the son of a noted forger ; and how she pluckily got him to face the situation and prosecute a blackmailing servant. " The Crooked Branch " (or " The Ghost in the Garden Room ") came next year, not in *Household Words*, but in *All the Year Round*, for now the first Dickens periodical had been given up.   This is an account of a spoilt boy brought up on a Yorkshire farm, who goes to the bad and ends in leading a robbery in his father's house.   It is quite well told, though in a simple way.   " Lois, the Witch " was quite different, for it is a story of Salem witchcraft.   The tale is of an English girl who goes to join her uncle at Salem and becomes suspected of sorcery and is finally executed as a witch.   It must have cost the writer a good deal of trouble to discover the facts, and she describes the life with great skill and sympathy, making the feelings of the people, overborne as they were by terror and religious mania, comprehensible ;   the stern puritan spirit of the pastors is well depicted by one who understood their point of view.   Of course, it brings Hawthorne to our minds ;   there is just the atmosphere of charm, half mysterious and half religious, that we have in Hawthorne's tales, and doubtless they had been read in the minister's home in Manchester.

After this time there were not many more journalistic efforts :   " Curious if True " was a sort of fairy-tale dream, printed in the *Cornhill Magazine* ;

" The Grey Woman " showed that Mrs. Gaskell's
powers of depicting the terrible were not exhausted,
though in 1861, when it appeared, she was over fifty
years of age.   It is a really exciting " shocker."
The adventures of a German woman married to a so-
called French nobleman, found to be one of a gang
of " chauffeurs," a name now innocent, but then
given to bandits.   The escape from his clutches
with the aid of a faithful maid is a thrilling adventure—there is all the orthodox machinery ; the
old castle, the murderers detected in their nefarious
work by the would-be victim concealed beneath a
table, the hairbreadth escape and the loft in the
inn—nothing is omitted.   What joy it must have
given the author to write it all from the comfortable
surroundings of a Manchester villa !

Mrs. Thackeray Ritchie tells us of Mrs. Gaskell's
love of telling ghost stories—" of Scotch ghosts,
historical ghosts, spirited ghosts with faded uniforms,
and nice old powdered queues."   She describes a wonderful summer evening at the George Smiths' house
at Hampstead when Mrs. Gaskell went on telling
stories as her listeners asked for them—legends of
smugglers as well as of ghosts ; adventures, too, and
stories with weather in them, wild snowstorms,
rising and dying away.   Leslie Stephen came down
and joined them with Mr. Thurston Holland, Mrs.
Gaskell's son-in-law-to-be, and gradually the talk
became general and the story-telling came to an
end.   Then, again, Augustus Hare, in the " Story
of His Life," gives a detailed account of a ghost
story he heard from Mrs. Gaskell at Oxford, in which
she herself took part.   The spirit of the wife of a
carter who had been found dead in the streets of
London haunted his home, and he could not sleep

because he saw her weeping figure beside his bed. Mrs. Gaskell went to see him, but the door was locked. Whilst some of the party went to the back of the house to try another door, those in front saw through a latticed window, a woman who walked from one side of the house to the other. When the rest of the party returned, renewed efforts were made to enter the house but they could not do so, and it was ascertained that no living person was within the house. It is not always that the narrator of ghost stories has herself the luck to see one!

" Six Weeks at Heppenheim " is a sentimental story in true German romantic style of a maiden who marries her master. For once there was no tragedy in it. It was published in the *Cornhill Magazine* in 1862, three years before the writer's death. There were one or two other papers of no particular importance written about this time, such as " Crowley Castle," an account of the Camorra in Italy (societies of robbers were always of interest to Mrs. Gaskell), but most of the articles of any importance have been mentioned (if we omit some verses, which are of little account) except one quite long story published by Smith, Elder in 1863, and entitled " A Dark Night's Work." It is a tragic tale describing a prosperous attorney, who, in anger with his partner, strikes a blow which causes his death. The body is buried in the shrubbery and not discovered till long after, when an old servant is tried for the murder, and the daughter of the lawyer has to obtain his reprieve by going to the judge (her former lover) and telling him the true story. The tale gives the effect of being hastily written, and is not on a level with Mrs. Gaskell's other work. It is evident how the level of her work varied according to the conditions under which it was produced. A short story called " The Cage at Cranford," published in *All the Year Round*, is a chapter of misunderstandings regarding a " cage," i.e. a crinoline sent to Miss Pole in lieu of a dwelling for her parrot. But it is not worthy of the predecessor whose name it bears.

Now that the short stories and journalistic efforts of Elizabeth Gaskell have been described, it is worth while also to consider why they are never likely to be popular again. They are often enough well told, and the plots are elaborately planned, though the planning does not always convince the reader. But there is usually a feeling of hurry, as if the printers' devil was waiting to seize the manuscript thus giving the author no chance of developing her theme. There was hurry really, because the stories were written in scraps of time—in the intervals between visiting the cook and supervising the children's lessons. And yet why did Mrs. Gaskell write thus when she could do first-rate work by giving herself a chance ? First of all, there is no doubt that there was a journalistic strain in Elizabeth Gaskell and that she was pleased to think she could gain a few guineas by very little effort of brain. The guineas were useful ; they were not essential, but they gave a sense of power, and helped to make the girls well dressed and happy and the house attractive to visitors. But I think there was something more. Elizabeth Gaskell, from the time she was little Elizabeth Stevenson, had a vivid imagination. She longed to get outside a very conventional and rather humdrum existence. She revelled in the mysterious and dreadful, and yet her thought-out novels had to be of the world she knew, and she excelled in domestic comedy. The way out of her commonplace existence was to accept Dickens's offer to write for his magazine. She got tired of this, and indeed tried to escape from it, and to publish in America. Some of her later work was done for the *Cornhill Magazine*, published by Smith & Elder, which required a different type of work from that of Dickens's " Christmas Tales." And yet these others probably gave her the greatest pleasure.

In December, 1863, Mrs. Gaskell published a short article in *Macmillan's Magazine* about Robert Gould Shaw, the son of a friend met while staying in Paris with the Mohls in 1855. It is a touching story of a young man who lost his life in the American Civil War fighting with the Abolitionists. He left a crack regiment to live with and train coloured people—the " niggers " who were going to fight for the freedom of their brothers in the South—and with his " niggers " he died.

DESPITE the troubles connected with its publication, the Biography that made its author's reputation almost as much as " Cranford," caused letters of appreciation to pour in. Indeed, the sales were, in those days, phenomenal for this type of literature, and what is interesting to us is that the popularity of the book has continued ever since, and that it is still read as the standard Life of one respecting whom quantities of literature have been lavished. This is doubtless owing to the fact that the book was written while the events were fresh in the writer's mind, and these were related with a simplicity that bore evidence of truth. " You have had a delicate and great work to do, and you have done it admirably," said Kingsley, and others were equally laudatory.

From 1858–60 there was a sort of lull in Mrs. Gaskell's production. Only short stories like " Round the Sofa," " My Lady Ludlow " and " The Doom of the Griffiths " were published in 1858–59. In the latter year, however, a summer holiday was taken by the Gaskells, not on the West coast as usual, but on the East, in a house facing the sea at Whitby. Any new scene suggested some new effort, and in this case Elizabeth Gaskell was impelled to work out a story which did not appear till 1863 and which was called " Sylvia's Lovers." All the district near Whitby was changing fast under the influence

of Mr. Hudson, the railway king, and the Developers
of the day. But though that was so, there were,
on the other hand, certain advantages from a
novelist's point of view which made up for the new
influx of population and the sophistication it
brought with it. The country was still full of
tales of smugglers' days, of press-gangs and riots.
So that there was just the sort of material Mrs.
Gaskell delighted in for her adventure stories ready
to her hand. This was, she decided, to be a real
tale of love and daring—no contemplative work of
calm existence like " Cranford " ; nor was it again
to be a tale with any special moral in view, as was
" Mary Barton." It was to be a straightforward
story like some of the shorter tales she had written
before, but more carefully developed and, above all,
accurate in all its details. It was a big piece of
work to undertake, and for some reason it had a
special dedication to Mr. Gaskell—a Victorian
dedication " to my dear husband by her who best
knows his value," with a truly Victorian quotation
from Tennyson appended. Was it in recompense
for her husband's very real help during the time of
trial following on the publication of the Life ? Or
perhaps it was due to a feeling that something was
owing that had never been rendered to one in whom
she had real pride, though perhaps of rather a
distant kind, and that this was an important piece of
work worth his acceptance ? As to this we cannot
say.

The tale necessitated a good deal of historic knowledge, and Mrs. Gaskell had never been in the habit
of delving for knowledge of an antiquarian or
historical kind, yet there is nothing of the gazetteer
or local guide-book about the volume. The writer

as we have seen, was well educated, as women brought up in intelligent circles were in those days. She had probably read more classical works in English literature than many of the High School girls of the present time. But research was foreign to her ; and in this case she had to research, to seek out records from the British Museum and Admiralty, local history and records of trials at York and Hull. She took pains about this, and made some corrections in the second edition of the book, owing to having discovered some error in the legal procedure as recounted in the trial she describes. The human element was, of course, most useful of all, and this was got from old inhabitants whose memories went back sixty or seventy years. It is always supposed that this book derived a good deal from the Brontës, and especially from " Wuthering Heights," and it is pretty certain from internal evidence that it did so. Without being at all as forceful as that titanic book, it has a good deal of its bleak, northern atmosphere ; and both the men and the women described have some of those elemental qualities that make one feel that tragedy is inherent in the plot. There is not much comedy ; it is curious that Mrs. Gaskell, who perceived the implicit funniness of life more than anyone—to whom the life of a little town was one continuous comedy—seemed to lose her sense of fun in many, if not all, of her longer novels. There are amusing characters, of course, and much humour of a quiet sort, but for the most part the serious element predominates. Certainly it is so in " Sylvia's Lovers." " It is the saddest story I have ever written," the author says herself, and some of the others were sad enough.

The tale is concerned with the press-gang days in the end of the eighteenth century—the terrible time when no young fisherman was safe from being impressed into the navy, and when all sorts of tragic happenings occurred in connection with the press-gang fights which preceded the mutiny at Spithead and the Nore in 1797. At that time, that is to say about 1793, after comparative peace, the war had just broken out against France, and the warships had to be manned by hook or by crook. Hence the coast was divided up into sections or districts, each controlled by naval officers whose business it was to carry out His Majesty's orders, and each was supplied with a " rendezvous " as house of call. At Whitby there was a riot in 1793, when the rendezvous was destroyed, and the ringleader was executed. No one felt safe, not even those by law exempt, for even landsmen might happen to be impressed. The heroine of this story is a farmer's daughter named Sylvia Robson, who comes into the little town with her goods for sale at market, and happens to see the exciting event of the arrival of the Greenland whalers ; and then, while purchasing a cloak in the main street of the town, suddenly hears the shocking news that the press-gang is out. Indeed, there had already been a fight at sea and one man was killed, while another, Charley Kinraid, the specksioneer, who becomes Sylvia's lover, was so badly injured that he was left for dead. There was wild indignation of course, since, though eligible men of seafaring habits between the ages of eighteen and fifty-six were liable to impressment, certain fishermen, like these Greenland whalers, were exempt, and they had just returned from months of hardship in the North Sea.

Philip Hepburn, the rival lover, is a staid draper's assistant with good prospects before him, who naturally cannot understand Sylvia's infatuation for Kinraid. Finally Kinraid is once more laid hold of in a remote spot, overcome by his adversaries and carried off, wounded but alive. Philip was witness of the fight, was given a message to Sylvia, but persuaded himself that his rival would never return, kept the knowledge of what had happened from Sylvia, and they marry. Then, of course, Kinraid returns, and Sylvia cannot forgive her husband for his deception. The latter enlists as a soldier, and saves Kinraid's life abroad, and returns a broken man. There is a final reconciliation between husband and wife, such as was essential in every novel of this period. The endings of novels is a study in itself. We have an example in " Enoch Arden," and in hundreds of stories like it, of the tragic ending which satisfied the sense of justice in combination with teaching the lesson of forgiveness and morality, without which mere justice was accounted insufficient. It was one far from the modern " that's that " or " there's nothing more to tell," but tending away from the old " and they lived happily ever after," which was, in a yet earlier generation, so satisfying to the easygoing reader. The worst is that the ending in Mrs. Gaskell's case was almost necessarily artificial as well as heart-rending :

" ' My wife ! Sylvia ! Once more forgive me all ! '

" ' Oh wicked me ! forgive me—me, Philip ! ' she answered. Then he spoke and said :

" ' Lord, forgive us our trespasses.'

" ' As we forgive each other.' "

He then dies, and Sylvia likewise dies shortly

afterwards. This is apt to suggest the melodrama of the films, and, indeed, both this story and some of the shorter tales seem well adapted to the new engine of dramatic representation.

But the story as a whole is well planned and related. Sylvia's waywardness is attractive ; and so is the account of the town of Monkshaven, with the smugglers, and coast-guardsmen doing their best to protect the King's interests. " Still sea-wrack was a good manure, and there was no law against carrying it up in great osier baskets for the purpose of litter, and many a secret thing was lodged in hidden crevices in the rocks till the farmer sent trusty people down to the shore for a good supply of sand and seaweed for his land." One of these farmers was Sylvia's father, and within the farm-house " fletches of ham and hands " (i.e. shoulders of cured pork, the legs or hams being sold, as fetching a better price) " abounded ; and for any visitor who could stay, neither cream nor finest wheaten flour was wanting for ' turf-cakes ' and ' singing hinnies,' with which it is the delight of the northern housewives to regale the honoured guest, as he sips the high-priced tea, sweetened with dainty sugar." Then the very masculine master of the house is well described ; he who kept his womenkind in their places and, though incapacitated by rheumatism from going outside, would not demean himself by asking questions about any event occurring in the town. " He had a strong notion of being a kind of domestic Jupiter." " ' Women's well enough i' their way, but a man may have too much on 'em. Now there's me, leg-fast these four days, and a'll make for to say to yo', a'd rather a deal ha' been loading dung i' t' wettest weather ; an' a reckon it's

th' being wi' naught but women as tires me so ;
they talk so foolish, it gets int' t' bones like.' "

Mrs. Gaskell is entirely at home with all these
country folk, and the tale of the first visit of the
press-gang and the fight that ensued is recounted
by a travelling tailor with wonderful vividness in
the vernacular of the district, which she took pains
to acquire. Mrs. Gaskell loved the sea, and liked
to think that she had the blood of the Vikings in
her, so that she enjoyed all this narration. Kester,
the farm servant, almost rivals some of Scott's
inimitable serving-men. Sylvia had been much
beholden to him and offered to spare waistcoat
fronts out of the stuff bought for her new red cloak.
" ' Na, lass,' said he, deliberately, after a pause.
' A could na' bear to see thee wi' thy cloak scrimpit.
A should be a'most as much hurt i' my mind to see
thee i' a pinched cloak as if old Moll's tail here were
docked too short,' " showing, by taking a wisp of
straw and rubbing down the old horse, hissing the
while, that the conversation was at an end.

The Vicar of Monkshaven is one of the few clergymen of the Established Church described in Mrs.
Gaskell's novels. There was, of course, the Rev.
Mr. Hale in " North and South," but then he
speedily left the Church and became a Dissenter.
The Vicar was a " kindly, peaceable old man, hating
strife and troubled waters above everything. He
was a vehement Tory in theory, as became his cloth
in these days. He had two bugbears to fear—the
French and the Dissenters. It was difficult to say
of which he had the worst opinion, and the most
intense dread. Perhaps he hated the Dissenters
most, because they came more in contact with him
than the French ; besides, the French had the

excuse of being Papists, while the Dissenters might have belonged to the Church of England if they had not been utterly depraved." But it appeared that not only would he dine with a follower of Wesley, since " Wesley was an Oxford man, and that makes him a gentleman," but he was also an ordained minister of the Church of England, and " that grace can never depart from him." And his breadth of view even went to sending broth and vegetables to a rabid recusant dissenter. He had a hard task indeed to preach on the death of a man, the son of his gardener, who had been killed while breaking the law of the land. His sympathies were all on the side of the lad and his father ; so that, his conscience smiting him the while, he hastily mumbled over a sermon that " might have done as well for a baby cut off in a convulsive-fit " ! The whole scene is described with much the same intimate knowledge as is shown by another non-churchwoman, George Eliot, in her " Clerical Tales " ; but then she was brought up in the Church, and hence with an understanding that was denied to her fellow-author.

Mrs. Gaskell had learned much since she wrote her earlier tales. There is in " Sylvia's Lovers " the similar truthful observation of minute objects and behaviour that there is in " Cranford " ; it is of a kind that a man hardly ever attains to. Trollope with his sure touch in regard to clerical life, did not venture into the same region of intimate domestic life. Sylvia's lessons in writing, under the eye of her devoted but pedantic admirer Philip, is, for example, delightfully described. " If ever I write thee a letter," she concludes, " it shall just be full of nothing but ' Abednego ! Abednego !

P

Abednego ! ' ''   And when her mother urged her to learn to write in order to get a position in life, she exclaimed : " I'd do a deal to please yo', Mammy ; but weary befa' riches and land, if folk that has 'em is to write ' Abednegos ' by the score, and to get hard words int' their brains, till they work like barm, and end wi' cracking 'em ! "

The two Quaker brothers, John and Jeremiah Foster, who carried on the draper's and grocer's shop in which Philip served, as scrupulously as their father had done before them, are delightful characters. They had no objection to smuggling, of course ; everyone in Monkshaven smuggled who could, and the excise officer and his wife were not unfriendly. Mrs. Gaskell certainly managed to get the atmosphere of this north country and, in its own way, serious and God-fearing smuggling town, and she has an almost masculine power of describing a riot such as that owing to which Sylvia's father was hung at York—a power which had been shown in her description of the riot in " North and South." She had, indeed, the art of choosing her words and making her story " go," so that in reading it we are carried on perforce. It is of course direct story-telling, with nothing of the modern suggestiveness, but that was so with most of the stories of the day. The interesting thing about this book is that it showed that the writer had made a clear advance on her former work, and that she was able to develop a plot with skill, and describe characters of a different kind from those with which she had hitherto dealt. Perhaps it also shows that if she had been given more time and opportunity for work she might have done even greater things. It is a difficult business making an end to a novel, and in this some of the best novelists have failed. We think of " The Mill on the Floss," and wish the last of the three volumes had been unwritten, and this novel has a certain resemblance to it. The mean actions of Philip, with all his high professions, make one feel he was " no gentleman " any more than was George Eliot's Stephen. The defence of the last part of the novel is said to be that it had to be spun out to make the orthodox three volumes of the day ; anyhow, it loses the truthfulness of the earlier portion of the book. Mrs. Gaskell probably felt this herself, and endeavoured to remedy it in future work ; for though her last considerable novel was not completed, its ending was both inevitable and convincing.

Mrs. Chadwick has taken great pains in identifying the scenes and persons of this novel. The scenes, houses in the town, farms and church can, or could be, identified easily enough. And so, indeed, could many of the characters. It is an art to be able to take reality, or what we call reality, and transform it through the artist's hands. The art may really be to see the truth through the appearance. All artists in prose, poetry or painting, naturally do this in their various degrees, even the very idealistic ones, like—to take an extreme instance —Blake and some of our moderns, whose portraits seem far removed from actuality. But then again, there are those who, like Scott, are always looking out for live figures and actual speeches that they may make use of them, and yet who are none the less artistic ; for theirs is no photographic presentation —it is moulded and formed by the artist's hand. And it gives us honest pleasure to see how Mrs. Gaskell did this in her writings, not always succeeding, but

usually doing so. Every bit of her " experience "
was made use of, and she was always looking out
for more. It is a marvel to those not gifted in this
way to see how far what seems slight knowledge of
the world can be made to go.

It was men who interested Mrs. Gaskell more
than nature. We do not have many descriptions
of the landscape, for instance—there are hardly
any in " Cranford," though we know the inhabitants
by heart. In " Sylvia's Lovers " we have more
about nature than anywhere else, but when we
examine the descriptions they are mostly, as has
been pointed out, about nature as it materially affects
man, about crops and farms and the sea, and taken
in relation to those who work in them. These
descriptions are wonderfully vivid, however, and
more real than many of the vague writings of the
romantic school. Mrs. Gaskell loved Romance, but
she was not a true Romantic ; she belonged to the
Realists despite her adventures into Romanticism
in some of her shorter tales. To her life was as it
seemed, and as she saw it in her everyday life or
pictured it in the not very far away past. The
smugglers and traders of Whitby gave her capital
material.

The book was much criticised on the ground that
the conduct of the principal actors, wife and husband
equally, violates probability. The passion and its
effects were said to be unrestrained, and the exaggeration in the last part when the husband returns and
craves forgiveness, it was said, rose to the point
of absurdity. R. H. Hutton, of the *Spectator*,
attacked the book on these grounds, and there is
some justice in his criticism. But the way in
which the nature of the surroundings is described,

and the manner in which it shows how these affect the characters, give it a character of its own and a very attractive one at that.

Du Maurier, when reading " Sylvia's Lovers " with a view to illustrating it, talked the matter over with Charles Keene, and he, having made some sketches of Whitby the year before, offered to lend them to Du Maurier because they seemed to resemble the place described by Mrs. Gaskell. They did not know till later that Whitby and Monkshaven were one and the same place. " George du Maurier," Mrs. Ritchie tells us, " used to read the book with delight and loved the name of Sylvia. He used to speak of the story, I remember, with a sort of pride, as if it belonged to him, just as he himself belonged to Monkshaven, where he, too, worked and played. He used to point out the Fosters' shop and the road Sylvia took when tripping from the farm to buy her red duffle cloak."

At the very same time that Mrs. Gaskell was at Whitby gathering impressions preparatory to writing "Sylvia's Lovers," Hawthorne was on the same coast at Redcar, only ten miles off, and engaged in finishing " Transformation," the subject of which Mrs. Gaskell sketches in writing to her friend Mrs. Story in Rome. She tells of the outbreak of the faun nature, the animal, in the strange hero, which moves him at a given moment to the commission of a murder : " For all of which, somehow, you like Donatello the better ! " She was proud of her knowledge of the statue of Cleopatra (by Story) commemorated in " Transformation " : " I feel funnily like Quin, who, when George III made his first speech before Parliament after his accession, said, ' I taught the boy to read ! '—for I came in crowing over my having seen the thing even in the clay and describing more fully what everyone is talking about. I can't say, unluckily, 'I taught the boy to imagine beauty.'"

Mrs. Gaskell's work was clearly not of the ephemeral kind that arises like the gourd which bursts forth to fade away. On the contrary, her first work was by no means her best. She learned to write with the skill and beauty of her later years, after the first burst of passion that brought forth " Mary Barton." But much as we admire " Cranford," written in 1851, we can hardly claim for it a higher place than the beautiful idyll, " Cousin Phillis," which was written in 1863. Sir Arthur Quiller-Couch points out the fact that the whole of Elizabeth Gaskell's activity as an author came within eighteen years—from 1848 to 1865, the central years of last century—that she lived through the typical times of Victorian literature and yet kept the even tenor of her way uninfluenced by one writer or the other. She knew her limitations and never tried to go beyond them, but she also, in her quiet, unassuming way, worked hard to express herself and the best ideals of her age in language that the later ages will find it hard to copy.

" Cousin Phillis " is the story of a young man named Paul Manning, who is sent to live in a little town near which the modern railway system was developing, and he is thus brought into contact with Mr. Holdsworth, the managing engineer. His work took him into a difficult bit of country where the line had to be laid over moor and bog, and he discovered that near where he was working a relative, named Ebenezer Holman, was Independent minister and likewise a farmer. The Holmans had

one precious daughter named Phillis. Rather un-
willingly the boy made their acquaintance, as
directed by his father. Holman was a man who
spent Saturday and Sunday writing his sermons and
visiting his flock, while at five in the morning on
Monday he would be at the plough. His was just
the sort of character that Mrs. Gaskell loved to
draw, and she had an original for the minister-
farmer in her own father.

There is a delightful account of how Paul goes
forth with his pretty cousin to find her father
working in the fields and how the busy farmer
suddenly put on his coat, changed his tone and said,
" Now I will give out the psalm ' Come all harmoni-
ous tongues ' to be sung to Mount Ephraim tune " ;
lifting up his spade to beat time while the two
labourers and Phillis followed him in song. This
ended the day's work.

The boy finds that this strange farmer stops to
gaze at the sunset, and quotes Virgil, which the girl
understands, for she has been taught by him ; and
he discovered her name written in classical books
in his room. He comforted himself by thinking
he could show that he knew something better
than that dead-and-gone language, and was inclined
to boast of his father who " invented Manning's
patent winch." But he found to his surprise that
the minister had been studying mechanics and even
asked him to recommend an easy book on dynamics.

As always, Mrs. Gaskell excels in the character of
a dissenting minister, and this one is to her heart.
There is an impressive account of the family prayers :
after a long and rather desultory impromptu suppli-
cation, the minister proceeded to include in his
petitions the animals—the cattle—and then, before

anyone had risen from their knees (indeed before Betty was well awake, for she made a nightly practice of having a sound nap during prayers, her weary head lying on her stalwart arms), the minister, still kneeling in their midst, but with his eyes wide open, and his arms dropped by his side, spoke to the elder man, who turned round still kneeling, to attend. " John, didst see that Daisy had her warm mash to-night ; for we must not neglect the means, John—two quarts of gruel, a spoonful of ginger, and a gill of beer—the poor beast needs it, and I fear it slipped out of my mind to tell thee ; and here was I asking a blessing and neglecting the means, which is a mockery."

A really interesting part of this story from the historical point of view is that regarding Paul Manning's father, the engineer of whom the boy was so proud, and who had many jokes about one of the gentlemen apprentices who used to set about his smith's work in washleather gloves for fear of spoiling his hands. The knowledge of the nature and properties of materials must, he said, come through the fingers. He was, in fact, drawn from James Nasmyth, the well-known engineer and inventor, who was the son of Alexander Nasmyth, the artist. James Nasmyth, who invented the steam hammer and many other mechanical instruments, served first in Maudsley's engineering works in London, where he lived on ten shillings a week ; then he moved to Manchester, where he took as partner a Mr. Holbrook Gaskell of Liverpool, one of the Gaskell family. The great Bridgewater Foundry was at that time controlled by Nasmyth and Gaskell, and the Nasmyths became friends of the novelist and her husband. In Miss Shaen's

"Memorials of Two Sisters" she tells how her aunt, Catherine Winkworth, met Mr. Nasmyth at the Gaskells' house and how she went to the foundry at Patricroft with him. He was in the habit of illustrating his remarks by diagrams drawn on the wall with his sooty finger.* In the story we read : "After tea, I heard an irrepressible exclamation from Cousin Holman—' Whatever is the man about !' And on looking round, I saw my father taking a straight burning stick out of the fire, and, after waiting for a minute, and examining the charred end to see if it was fitted for his purpose, he went to the hard wood dresser, scoured to the last pitch of whiteness and cleanliness, and began drawing with the stick—the best substitute for chalk or charcoal within his reach, for his pocket-book pencil was not strong or bold enough for his purpose." With this diagram he began to explain his new model of a turnip-cutting machine to the minister, for though he had admired his cattle, he had been very critical of his machinery. Poor Mrs. Holman was, meantime, while pretending to be interested in the drawing, secretly trying on an outside mark, to see how it would come off and leave her dresser as clean as it was before !

Paul himself is a clever portrayal of an honest, awkward youth with whom one yet perforce sympathises. The description of Paul's father was that of many capable working men of the day.

"My father, in his decent but unfashionable Sunday clothes, his plain, sensible face, full of hard lines—the marks of toil or thought—his hands blackened beyond the power of soap and water by

* Mrs. Gaskell visited him at his home in Penshurst in Kent.

years of labour in the foundry, speaking a strong Northern dialect."

This type of character appealed to Mrs. Gaskell. In " North and South " the steam hammer and its wonders are also described by Mr. Thornton, the millowner, who was proud of the skill and invention of a townsman of his own, and who felt assured that there was material still to carry on the work of compelling material power to yield to science. Nasmyth in his later days was taken as the original of the employer who paid good wages and himself took part in the practical work. Being likewise an astronomer, at night he used to view the heavens through a telescope, made by himself and placed in his garden ; thus he got the credit of being a " ghostly apparition " !

Paul introduced to the simple, happy family his employer in the engineering enterprise they were engaged on, and though he was a friend of his father's and to all appearances an excellent man, the tragedy of Phillis began. Mr. Holman liked him though " there was a want of seriousness in him." " It is like dram-drinking. I listen to him till I forget my duties, and am carried off my feet. Last Sabbath evening he led us away into talk on profane subjects ill-befitting the day." But Phillis had begun to love him. Then suddenly he announced that he was going to Canada, where he had had an advantageous offer to take charge of a Canadian railroad which was in making. He promised to return, but alas, his promises were false, and he found another love in a French Canadian girl.

Such is the story—not an uncommon one—but it is told with a touching simplicity mingled with real

humour. Betty, the servant who puts Paul in his
place in case he followed after Holdsworth's foot-
steps, sets forth his duty thus :

" It's a caution to a man how he goes about
beguiling.   Some men do it as easy and innocent
as cooing doves.   Don't you be none of 'em, my lad.
Not that you've got the gifts to do it, either ; you're
no great shakes t' look at, neither for figure nor yet
for face, and it would need be a deaf adder to be
taken wi' your words, though there be no great
harm in 'em."   As the writer says, a lad of nineteen
or twenty is not flattered by such an outspoken
opinion even from the " oldest and ugliest of her
sex."   The ending is where the writer once more
fails.   It is the conventional one of brain fever
which, after causing the most acute anxiety to all
around (and the Job's comforters in the form of
fellow ministers who wished Mr. Holman to " lay
bare his heart " and set an example of resignation,
are faithfully described), ends in a " deep sleep,"
then supposed to be the specific for all ills of a
feverish sort, and the patient, if, like Phillis, suffering from an illness brought on by thwarted love,
usually woke up better in mind and body.   Blunt-
spoken Betty gave the best advice : " ' Now,
Phillis,' said she, coming up to the sofa, ' we ha'
done a' we can for you, and th' doctors has done a'
they can for you, and I think the Lord has done
a' He can for you, and more than you deserve, too,
if you don't do something for yourself.   If I were
you, I'd rise up and snuff the moon, sooner than
break your father's and your mother's heart wi'
watching and waiting till it pleases you to fight
your own way back to cheerfulness.   There, I never
favoured long preachings, and I've said my say.' "

LETTER-WRITING is one of the arts—possibly not very numerous—in which women may claim to excel, if the type of letter is clearly defined. It is not every sort of letter a woman can write well. The brief note which conveys information along with the touch of distinction that causes it to be called a letter, is done better by the sex which accustoms itself to be concise and clear, if indeed, in addition it possesses what we call literary attributes. But, as a rule, the other sort of letter—the one that meanders through all sorts of divergent paths, and yet manages to convey its message along with every kind of relevant and irrelevant matter—the letter we love to get, partly because of its unexpectedness—is the letter of a woman. No doubt some men—many men— write delightful letters of the other sort, as Cowper did, and Walpole did, but they are the exception. They are generally best at writing diaries and journals, where you want a grasp of the relations of the events of the day to those of the age. Women excel at bringing into their work the personal and individual touch.

Now Elizabeth Gaskell was not a model letter-writer : she had not great matter to relate nor any marvellous gifts of expression in recording what she had to say, but she could express herself admirably. She had the invaluable sense of humour that counts for so much in letter-writing, and which itself makes her letters worth reading. Her correspondents were many, but much of her correspondence was of a domestic kind and, of course, only some has been preserved : probably no one kept her letters until she became recognised as an author. Would many of Jane Carlyle's letters have seen the light had she not come into notice as the wife of a famous man ? Letters worth preserving are supposed to bring us into touch with what we consider to be outside the commonplace, and consequently some of the best letters may be consigned to the waste-paper basket, or else be resting in the receptacles of some of our " commonplace " friends.

Of the Gaskell letters preserved in later days a number are business ones addressed to Mr. John Forster, of Chapman & Hall's firm, who was Mrs. Gaskell's constant " reader " and indulgent critic. He appreciated her work from the early days when it first came before his notice. Miss Brontë begged her to desert Chapman for her publishers, Smith and Elder, with her valued friend Mr. Williams as literary adviser, but until the Biography appeared that was not possible. Forster was, of course, in touch with many literary men of the day, and Mrs. Gaskell turned to him when she was in difficulty or anxious to approach literary people outside her orbit. For instance, she had become intensely interested in a certain Samuel Bamford, one of the typical Radical countrymen of the day who frequented Mechanics' Institutes, and very likely Mr. Gaskell's lectures. Tennyson was rather improbably the object of Bamford's special admiration, and the idea occurred to Mrs. Gaskell of getting the great man himself to present to him his poems. This is the letter to Mr. Forster :

Oct., 1849.

Now I want to ask for your kind offices, and I don't know how to begin. I think I must commit a plagiarism on a " Tea and Coffee " circular lying before me. " Emboldened by past favours, Mrs. Gaskell ventures to solicit a continuation of future kind attention to the "—the next word is merits, and I am not sure if that would quite do. So you must suppose the prettiest apology in the world made, and also the most earnest real *request made that you won't scruple to say no ; plump* no, *if you would rather have nothing to do with the matter. And now to begin. You know Tennyson, don't you ? Miss Fox said you did, and you know who Samuel Bamford is, don't you ? A great, gaunt, stalwart Lancashire man, formerly hand-loom weaver, author of " Life of a Radical," etc.—age nearly* 70, *and living in that state which is exactly " decent poverty " with his neat little apple-faced wife ; they have lost their only child. Bamford is the* most *hearty (and it's saying a good deal) admirer of Tennyson I know. I dislike recitations exceedingly, but he repeats some of Tennyson's poems, in so soft, and yet so simple a manner, utterly forgetting that any one is by, in delight in the music and the exquisite thoughts, that one can't help liking to hear him. He does not care one jot whether people like hearing him or not, in his own intense enjoyment. Then once I saw him blaze up when some one in an argumentative moral and utilitarian spirit " wondered what Tennyson had done for his pension." He had been " minding his manners " till then, but this was too much ; so he first choked, and then broke out into beautiful broad Lancashire, and then as that hardly served to carry him high enough, he took to Bible language till his adversary fairly stood rebuked. One more thing—he*

*says when he lies awake at night, as in his old age
he often does, and gets sadly thinking of the days that
are gone when his child was alive, he soothes himself
by repeating T's poems. I asked him the other day
if he had got them of his own ;—" No," he said, rather
mournfully ;—" he had been long looking out for a
second-hand copy,—but somehow they had not got into
the old book-shops, and 14s. (or 18s. which are they?)
was too much for a poor man like him to give—" and
then he brightened up, and said, " Thank God, he had
a good memory, and whenever he got into a house
where there were Tennyson's poems he learnt as many
as he could off by heart ; so he thought he knew better
than twelve "—and he began " Œnone," and then the
" Sleeping Beauty." Now I wonder if you catch a
glimpse of what I want. I thought at first of giving
him the Poems this Xmas ; but then I remembered
with what beautiful composure and boldness you asked
Mr. Stone for those two engravings, and I thought
you were not likely, (at all, at all,) to have grown either
shy, or ill-natured ; and so I thought you would
perhaps ask Tennyson if he would give Bamford a
copy from himself ; which would be glorious for the
old man.—Dear ! how he would triumph. He would
set off, I dare say next Christmas, wrapped in his
plaid, and come looming down upon him to thank
him some foggy Jany. morning. If you would rather
not do it, pray never mind, and take no notice of my
request. I do so dislike refusing myself, that I would
much rather spare you the pain, as I know you would
do it, if you thought it right or proper.*

* * * * *

One is glad to know that the scheme worked out
happily and Mrs. Gaskell was able herself to convey
to Bamford the treasured volume.

The next letter is to a sister-in-law, Eliza Gaskell,
who was also a constant correspondent. It casts
some light on the domestic affairs of the family and
their manner of life, and describes the original home
in Rumford Street which was soon to be exchanged for
the more commodious Plymouth Grove.

1849.

*We dined at the Darbishire's last night, and talked
so much about you, my dear—that I am seized with a
crave to write to you to-day ; although you don't write
to me. I don't exactly know anything I have to say,
but I am looking forward to your coming with great
pleasure and you are to be so good as not to cheat me.
I wonder if you ever see Mr. Newman's papers on
Hungary or if you are to ;—Kossuth is coming here
to visit a friend of ours, so I mean to see him by hook
or by crook. . . . We are all just now in a state of
great curiosity about the Mrs. Froude Mr. F. is
bringing home on Saturday ; it is a very romantic
story ; she was going into a convent when he went away
from Oxford, took refuge in her brother(s ?)-in-law's
(where should the " s " come ?) Mr. Kingsley's ; but
instead of a nunnery she has chosen a marriage—still
she is a strict Puseyite, confesses to a priest etc. etc.
. . . It always seems of no use beginning on long
subjects in a letter ; but we will have some famous
" contes " when you come. I don't think you know
what a conte is, do you now ? . . . I always feel very
full of something to the exclusion of almost everything
else ; and just now houses haunt me. . . . Are you
prepared for a garret, rather like Campbell's rainbow,
" a happy spirit to delight mid way twixt earth and
heaven " ; with no fireplace, only a great cistern,
which however we lock up for fear of our friends
committing suicide. Are you prepared for a cold*

*clammy atmosphere, a town with no grass or beauty
in it, a house full of cold draughts, and mysterious
puffs of icy air? Are you prepared for four girls
in and out continually, interrupting the most interesting
conversation with enquiries respecting lessons, work,
etc. :—If these delights thy mind can move, come live
with me and be my love. I like the house very much,
though I acknowledge we have out-grown it ; you shall
have a bottle of hot water in bed, and blankets ad
libitum, and we keep glorious fires. The girls are very
nice ones though I say it that should not say it, and I
do think that you will like them all in their separate
ways, so please write soon and fix your time for coming.*

Then in 1850 there is a letter to a great friend
whose name has appeared before and who is always
addressed as Tottie (Mrs. Gaskell signed herself as
Gaskell or simply as G.). She was the daughter of
Mr. W. J. Fox, who was a well-known Unitarian
divine (though later on disowned by the body) and
who was a well-known writer and politician, and
for many years represented Oldham in Parliament.
He owned the *Monthly Repositary,* and was in touch
with many literary people. His daughter was remarkably intelligent. It tells of that early visit to the
Kay-Shuttleworths that had such momentous results
in beginning the friendship with Charlotte Brontë.

Tuesday Aug. 1850.
My dearest Tottie,
   *So you are come home again I conclude by the speed
with which I received my i.e.* your *Examiner. Some
charming angel took a fancy for some time to send me
the Athenæum ; always round by Silverdale, but
this week said anonymous angel has dropped it ;
more's the pity—I am obliged to lie down on the sofa*

Q

constantly which I think addles my brains for I feel
very stupid; but I did too much last week in the way
of motion. Thank you, dearest, for your last letter.
Wm. is at Birmingham; he was preaching there last
Sunday; and is staying for some days. It is funny
how we never go from home together. He is so anxious
about the children; he says he is never easy if we are
both away; it takes away all his pleasure, so first he
went to an Edinburgh scientific association, and prowled
about Scotland, then last week quite unexpectedly Lady
Kay-Shuttleworth wanted us to come and meet Miss
Brontë, and William could not go—and then the people
he is with at Birmingham wanted us to go; and he
said he shd. not be happy if I went; so we are like
Adam and Eve in the weather glass. I wish, my dear,
you were here. It would be a charming beguiling of
my sofa imprisonment. I am very happy nevertheless
making flannel petticoats; and reading Modern
painters. Miss Brontë is a nice person. Like you,
Tottie, without your merriment; poor thing, she can
hardly smile she has led such a hard cruel (if one may
dare say so), life. She is quiet, sensible, unaffected,
with high noble aims. Lady K.-S. was confined to
one room so she and I had much of our day to ourselves with the exception of some lectures on art, and
" bringing ourselves down to a lower level," and " the
beauty of expediency," from that eminently practical
man Sir James, who has never indulged in the exercise
of any talent which could not bring him a tangible
and speedy return. However he was very kind; and
really took trouble in giving us, Miss Brontë especially,
good advice; which she received with calm resignation.
She is sterling and true; and if she is a little bitter
she checks herself, and speaks kindly and hopefully
of things and people directly; the wonder to me is

how she can have kept heart and power alive in her life of desolation. I made her give me an account of the " Editorial party,"—Do you know who " Annie and Ellen Green" are? two country friends of our girls aged 14 and 15. They are come here for a month's music-mastering: and the air is redolent of DO RE MI &c. I have been writing a story for Xmas; a very foolish engagement of mine—which I am angry with myself for taking but I promised it and have done it. I have got an " In Memoriam" of my own, it is a pleasure to me to have what I like so earnestly of my own. Do you know I was as near as possible seeing Tennyson. He and Mrs. are staying at Coniston, and Sir James, Miss B. and I were on the Lake there, when we heard it; and Sir James knows him; and said he would go and call; and then looked up at the sky and thought it was going to rain, so he didn't. I held my peace, and bit my lips. All the world at the Lakes was full of the " Prelude," have you read it? Miss Brontë has promised that Mr. Smith (& Elder) shall lend it to me. Certainly Manchester is a behindhand place for books. Susanna Winkworth is going to BONN not Rome. She is to live in the house of Professor Brand and study German life. She makes me write and ask questions of Mr. Forster, to which he answers by changing the words of my remarks on the question and passing them off as his own; so we don't get on; and yet I am astonished at my own wisdom, when it comes back to me dressed up grand. Now do write to me. The post coming is the great event of my day.

Yours very affectly.
Gaskell.

The following letter refers to G. F. Watts's picture of

the " Good Samaritan, " which was finally purchased for Manchester.

Tuesday, Jan. 24, 1850.

On Saturday I heard from Mr. Tom Taylor to this effect. A Mr. Watts (who is he, answer me that Master Brook) an artist inspired by the record of Mr. Wright's (whom Mr. Taylor will call Mr. Hill) good deeds, has painted a picture for the Academy Exhibition of the Good Samaritan, under which is to be an inscription relating to Mr. Wright—now Mr. T. Taylor says some people in London desirous of honouring Mr. W. and encouraging the application of art to such high purposes are desirous of purchasing this picture and presenting it to some Manchester charity and he wants some detailed acct. of Mr. W. and to know if there would be any response in Manchester to this plan. I have got Mr. Schwabe, the Bishop, and Dr. Bell all pretty well interested, and have copied out prison reports, by way of statistical information as to Mr. Wright. Then Miss Maggie Bell has sent me MS. novel to look over,—she is a nice person, and I know I once wanted help sorely, or else I am so busy what with making mourning, etc. . . . I must write again soon to you darling, for this is not satisfactory, and tell me about Mr. Watts, no one here knows either him or Mr. Tom Taylor even by name. I think Mr. Schwabe confused the latter up with Jeremy Taylor! Now write and tell me about Mr. Watts. Mr. Cobden will be here the end of this week, and I want to work him up, but must know about Mr. Watts. William's best love. We long for you back, the little ones ask after you—Children dear, was it yesterday— (call once more) that she went away.

Yr. truly affecy.

E. C. Gaskell.

It seems strange that Mrs. Gaskell did not know more of " a Mr. Watts," for G. F. Watts was well known by the time he gave expression to his longing to improve the condition of humanity by painting the picture of " The Good Samaritan," as expression of the admiration he had for the philanthropy of Thomas Wright of Manchester. To that city he presented the work, but his intention might not have been known at the time Mrs. Gaskell wrote.

Oddly enough, there was a movement to have a portrait of Mrs. Gaskell painted by Watts later on, but the scheme did not mature, though he was anxious to undertake the work.

Another letter to " Tottie " tells about the new home to which a move was to be made, and regarding which its future owner had all the qualms of one who was about to make a considerable advance in social comfort at a time at which there was still much poverty and suffering even although the worst of the misery of the " hungry forties " was past. It was indeed a serious question for a minister and his wife, since £150 in those days was a large rent in Manchester, and a large house meant more expense in every way. But the minister himself was clear about it and so was young " Meta," her daughter. Mrs. Gaskell's own inclinations were all for a pleasant home life with plenty of company. So that the big house and the pleasanter neighbourhood carried the day.

About 1850

My dearest Tottie,

I was going to have written a letter to myself, and sent it to you to fill up, only your most welcome letter this morning put a stop to that. I am so glad always to hear from you, and should be more gladder to see you, dear little lady. And we've got a house. Yes! we really have. And if I had neither conscience nor prudence I should be delighted, for it certainly is a beauty. It is not very far from here, in Plymouth Grove—do you remember our plodding out that last Saty. in snow to go and see houses? and looked at 2, one inhabited by a Jewish Mrs. Abram and old clothes. Well, it's nearly opposite to the first we looked at (not the old clothes one). I shall make Meta draw you a plan. You must come and see us in it, dearest Tottie, and try and make me see " the wrong the better cause," and that it is right to spend so much ourselves on so purely selfish a thing as a house is, while so many are wanting—that's the haunting thought to me ; at least to one of my " Mes," for I have a great number, and that's the plague. One of my mes is, I do believe, a true Christian—(only people call her socialist and communist), another of my mes is a wife and mother, and highly delighted at the delight of everyone else in the house, Meta and William most especially who are in full ecstasy. Now that's my " social " self I suppose. Then again I've another self with a full taste for beauty and convenience wh. is pleased on its own account. How am I to reconcile all these warring members ? I try to drown myself (my first self) by saying it's Wm. who is to decide on all these things, and his feeling it right ought to be my rule. And so it is—only that does not quite do. Well! I must try and make the house give as much pleasure to others as I can and make it as little a selfish thing as I can. My dear! it's £150 a year, and I dare say we shall be ruined ; and I've already asked after the ventilation of the new Borough Gaol, and bespoken Mr. Wright to visit us—The said good Mr. Wright drank tea here

last night, and said " By Jingo" with great unction,
when very much animated, much to William's amuse-
ment, not to say delight. (We have a greenhouse at
the new house—to be; which delights the girls; we
shall remove in about 6 weeks).

The next letter was written just before the move,
to Miss Shaen, who lived at Crix, near Chelmsford,
and whose brother was to marry one of the Winkworth sisters, who were perhaps the closest of all
the Gaskells' friends. Crix was often visited and it
counted for much in the Gaskell social life. This
letter shows what a wound the death of little Willie,
the one baby boy, had left. It is in keeping with
the ways of the time that this, the bitterest sorrow
in the mother's life, and possibly in the father's,
was never spoken of. In silence they bore their
pain apart. Death was a great divider.

Home. April 24, 1851.
Knowing Crix ways and customs I felt pretty sure
I should have a budget this evening : we were sitting
at tea in the drawing room when Hannah entered.
Wm. seized the letters saying he was sure they were
for him *; but perceiving that yours and Mrs. Shaen's*
were for me, he said this *is Louey's and this I* know
is for me. You see he thought all that sitting by her
at the piano had not been without due effect. . . .
I have just been up to our room. There is a fire
in it, and a smell of baking, and oddly enough the
feelings and recollections of 3 years ago came over me
so strongly—when I used to sit up in the room so often
in the evenings reading by the fire, and watching my
darling darling *Willie, who now sleeps sounder still*
in the dull, dreary chapel-yard at Warrington. That
wound will never heal on earth, although hardly any

one knows how it has changed me. I wish you had seen my little fellow, dearest dear Annie. I can give you no idea what a darling he was—so affectionate and reasonable *a baby I never saw. . . . Read " Jane Eyre," it is an uncommon book. I don't know if I like or dislike it. I take the opposite side to the person I am talking with always in order to hear some convincing arguments to clear up my opinions. Tell me what Crix thinks—everybody's opinions. Mary Holland has just received " Notes from Books " from her friend Henry Taylor and said she liked them as well as " Friends in Council." I have copied Lizzie Lindsay—such a pretty old Irish air with words by Lady Balfour* which must be sung very* naïvely*; it is pathetic and must not be made fun of, only you can't keep from smiling, on the making a compliment and spoiling it (??) . . . Lizzie Lindsay is a glorious specimen of man monarchy ? The poor Glasgow burgher's daughter is wooed by an unknown suitor and naturally asks who he is, whereupon he makes answer " Oh Leezie lass ! ye maun ken little— Sin that ye dinna ken me," and tells her he is Lord Ronald Macdonald ; whereupon she drops a curtsey and says " thank ye Sir " ;—never mind ! it is a very pretty* naïve *little thing, and we can't always be high flown and moral in our stories. If you like you may adapt a sentence out of Mary Wolstonecraft to this air.*

Dec. 1851.

To " Tottie."

I've a deal to say more than mortal can get through in the ¼ *of an hour I have before me, and now it's Sunday and I've the comfort of sitting down to write to you in a new gown, and blue ribbons all spick and*

* Usually stated to be a " Traditional Ballad."

span for Xmas—and cheap in the bargain. " Elegant economy " as we say in Cranford—There now I dare say you think I've gone crazy but I'm not ; but I've written a couple of tales about Cranford in " Household Words," so you must allow me to quote from myself. . . .

It was a bustling, worrying life that the untiring housewife had to live, and it was fortunate that her sense of fun carried her more or less happily through. Perhaps " Ruth " might have been a more competent book, especially in the not very satisfactory conclusion, had there been time and quiet to work it out.

1852 . . .

> *Dr. Davy's,*
> *Lesketh How,*
> *Near Ambleside.*

. . . . .

. . . Well, I'm here ! How I came, I don't seem to know, for of all the weary, killing wearing out bustles in this life that of the last week passed all belief. Thackeray's lectures, two dinners, one concert card party at home, killing a pig, my week at the school which took me into town from 9 till 12 every morning —company in the house, Isabella leaving, Wm. too busy to be agreeable to my unfortunate visitors, (Mr. and Mrs. Wedgwood, Dot and Jane, their servant, Annie and Ellen Green, closely packed !) so I had to do double duty and talk æsthetically (I dare say) all the time I was thinking of pickle for pork, and with a Ruskinian face and tongue I talked away with a heart like Martha's. And at last when Meta's and my cab came to take us to the station not before the house cleared, they smashed into " Ruth " in grand style. I have not much hope of her now this year, for I've

been frightened off my nest again. Mr. Chapman wrote a polite invitation to me to come and see the Duke's funeral from his shop window (a sight I should dearly have liked,) and, also, that civility being furnished, informed me that Mr. Forster had given him the MS. of " Ruth " and that the first 2 vols. were printed; all complete news to me ! But I set to on the trumpet sound thereof, and was writing away vigorously at " Ruth" when the Wedgwoods, etc. came : and I was sorry, very sorry, to give it up, my heart being so full of it, in a way which I can't bring back. That's that. . . .

The mercy was that there was an occasional escape to the Lake District and also to beloved Knutsford, where were the Holland cousins and where good resolutions could be formed for future conduct.

Nov. 1851.
To Miss Ann Shaen.

I am so much better for Knutsford—partly air, partly quiet and partly being by myself a good piece of every day which is I am sure so essential to my health that I am going to persevere and enforce it here. I don't mean to have odd poppers-in, in an evening unless I have visitors in the house. I mean to be out all calling time with the children, and I mean to get all my society duties done by great large parties where many people always entertain each other. Then I am going to confine my letter writing to Thursdays, when I always write to Ma in singing lesson time—no—now he's coming on Monday—and scrabble in as many letters as I can after that one is done. So don't you approve of these rules for my life ;—I don't mean with regard to writing anything like a book, but solely for my own health and mind. Strange is it not that people's lives apparently suit them so little. Here is a note from Miss Brontë oppressed by the monotony and solitude of her life. She has seen no one but her Father since 3rd of July last. Here is Mary Holland and Louy at Knutsford absolutely ill for want of being more by themselves—each wishing that she could be alone in the evenings. Well !—the world's a puzzle. . . .

She—Susanna—has sent over to-day to ask if she may sit with me, but I, possessed with my love of solitude—or rather my sense of its necessity, savagely declined.

In the end of 1852 " Ruth " was finished, and there was anxiety about Miss Brontë's health.

Tuesday, Dec. 20th, 1852.

. . . And " Ruth " is done—utterly off my mind and gone up to the printers—that's all I know about it. . . . (You'll get a " Ruth " one of these days " from the author.") . . . Miss Brontë has been ill—very ill I'm afraid, but I only heard of it yesterday morning thro' the Shaens, who had asked her there, and she gave that as her excuse or reason for not coming to them. I wrote to her directly—though I don't know that that did much good—only one felt how lonely and out of the world she must be, poor creature. I've a great mind to go and see her uninvited some day. I cd. (that's to say if I'd the money to stay at the Inn so as not to be in Mr. Brontë's road). However, I don't mean to stir from home this long time when I get back, but write, write, write, I really do mean to do something good and virtuous.

It cannot be said that Mrs. Gaskell was devoid of courage—she showed plenty over " Cowan-Bridge

School " and even over " Mary Barton." But the strictures on " Ruth " were just the kind that hurt her to the quick. Had she been what was then called unwomanly or unladylike ? Had she glossed over immorality and given reason to the enemy to blaspheme ? It is only those who knew what walls of " inhibition " were built round women's lives at that time who could realise the unnecessary pain these underwent over the smallest attempt to break them down. Did a woman say a kind word or do a kind deed to a " fallen " sister, she was almost torn asunder by those who professed the doctrine of pity and forgiveness. And it was just in circles such as the Gaskells moved in that these standards were most rigidly upheld, even though they belonged to the broader section of the community. Breadth of doctrine did not mean breadth in view so far as the social proprieties were concerned.

1853.

My dearest Tottie,
    I have been so ill; I do believe it has been a " Ruth " fever. The beginning of last week my own private opinion was that I should never get better. I was so utterly weak after it, but I have picked up and this cold weather braces me—I suppose you abominate it. I should never have left your last letter unanswered so long if it was not for that—but oh! I was so poorly ! And cd. not get over the hard things people said of " Ruth." I mean I was just in that feverish way when I could not get them out of my head by thinking of anything else but dreamt about them and all that. I think I must be an improper woman without knowing it, I do so manage to shock people. Now should you have burnt the last vol. of " Ruth " as so

very *bad*? *even if you had been a very anxious father of a family*? *Yet two men have; and a third has forbidden his wife to read it; they sit next to us in Chapel and you can't think how " improper " I feel under their eyes. However some people like it—Mr. A. W. Darbishire for one. However I won't bother you or myself any more about it. . . . We have capital accounts from Meta* and Marianne does famously with the children; especially as her only two dances as yet have come on a* Friday *allowing her a good long sleep on Saturday morning when the children have no lessons. . . . Send me some London news—the world here is very flat, and my heart is very flat. Good-bye my own dear Tottie.*

The next letter, addressed to Miss Fox, is more cheerful. It was probably " North and South " that was on the stocks.

P. Grove,
Dec. 24, 1854.

My dearest Tottie,
Oh what a shameful time it is since I've written to you! and what a shame of me not to write, for yr. last letter was such a nice one, though it's been stinging me with reproaches these two months past, but I believe I've been so nearly dazed and crazed with this c—, d— be h— to it, story as can be. I've been sick of writing, and everything connected with literature or improvement of the mind; to say nothing of deep hatred of my species about whom I was obliged to write as if I loved 'em. Moreover I have had to write so hard that I have spoilt my hand, and forgotten all my spelling. Seriously it has been a terrible weight

* Who went to Miss Martineau's school. Marianne was teaching the little sisters.

on me and has made me have some of the most felling headaches I ever had in my life, so having growled my growl I'll go on to something else. We are all well that's the first unspeakable comfort. . . . Altogether everything looks very sad this Xmas. The war accounts make one's blood run cold at the rotting away of those noble glorious men. What is Mr. Fox about to allow it? Mr. Macready has been here; yes! actually staying here from Saty. noon, about 2 o'clock, to Monday morning. It was very pleasant after I had got over my fear of him; but it was Mr. Gaskell's busy days, and so I had him to myself, and I was afraid, at first, I confess, more especially as we could not muster up anybody worthy of meeting him. Mr. Fairbairn away. Mr. Scott came to dinner on Monday and that was nice! said Mr. Scott has been very ill almost ever since, diarrhœa and these sort of things, and Owen's College is falling off on account of the badness of the times. I expect rather *to go to Paris with Meta in February; i.e. last year a Madame Mohl (English in spite of her name) whom I have known a little for many years asked me to go three times; and three times it had to be given up. Now she peremptorily commands us to come in February; so if all goes on well and my wretched story is done, I think we shall go and escape the reviews, hang 'em. Now my vision is this—what do you think of coming back with me when I come back —say* 1st *half of March—but I'm not sure of dates. We do so want to have you here a bit; and Manchester is not damp (because its east-windy) in the Spring—& we should so like it! all seems so uncertain I don't like to plan decidedly for even a month beforehand— but will you try and turn events towards the fulfilment of this plan. About Wm. Arnold? yes!* I just

*know him. First he and his wife, out of their lieu-
tenant's pay in India sent me £10 for the poor of
Manchester,—I wrote to thank and we corresponded
once or twice till he came to England on acct. of ill
health. I fancy Oakfield is a very literal piece of his
own life, except that he recovered instead of dying
on returning home. This year I just met his sister
in the street, leaning on the arm of such a handsome
beautiful elegant young man,—quite different to an
Arnold ; but this was Wm. Arnold, as his sister told
me. He did not catch my name, and I was in a
hurry ; and I don't think I ever heard him speak.
He was then afraid of having to return to India at
the end of his 3 years' absence, as no employment
in England had turned up, but the very next week, I
believe, Lady Byron employed him to be tutor to one
of Lady Lovelace's boys ; and so there he is dear,
leading this young king at Bonn. How is Amelia
Green getting on with her music ? I wrote and
ordered a Dorking cock—lo behold ! they sent me a
pen, a cock and two hens, price £3. 12. 6. I cried my
eyes out, for I had been so trying to be saving, (given
up* The Times just at the most interesting time !) and
they would not take them back.*

To Mrs. Jameson, author of " Sacred and Profane
Art," who appreciated, although she criticised, her
friend's work :

*Plymouth Grove,
March 7th, (1853)*

*I meant, and I meant * to thank you for your
letter, and if I could, without telling you what had
become of it ; for every day I have been hoping it
would be restored to me. Oh dear ! Do you know*

* *Sic.*

it is lost ! along with several other valued and comforting letters about Ruth ; while every letter of reprobation and blame comes to me straight as an arrow, the precious little packet I sent to a dear friend in London for her pleasure and sympathy was lost at the Post Office. We have made enquiries at both ends, and they give us hopes that it may be restored but meanwhile I can not any longer delay writing my thanks of the kind words (that told of kind thoughts,) in your letter. I should have often found it a comfort and a pleasure to read it again,—a comfort and a pleasure because I am sure you understand what I aimed at,— from any one who sympathises in that aim I can bear a great deal of personal fault-finding. Not that you did anything of the kind, Mrs. Jameson. I never spoke much on the subject of the book before ; and I am surprised to find how very many people—good kind people—and women infinitely more than men, really and earnestly disapprove of what I have said and express that disapproval at considerable pain to themselves, rather than allow a " demoralising laxity " to go unchecked. Three or four men have written to approve, some—one or two at least high in literature —and two, with testimony as valuable as fathers of families,—grave thoughtful practical men. I think I have put the small edge of the wedge in, if only I have made people talk and discuss the subject a little more than they did.

The next letter gives a woman's view of art as a pursuit for women immersed in home duties :

Tuesday, a week ago.

To Miss Fox (" Tottie ")
    Here is Mr. Broinett giving his lesson,* and I am
* To her girls.

playing Dragon; so while I dragonize, (I wish you could hear O Salutaris Hostia *they are now singing) I shall write to you. I have a great deal to say; only I don't know if I can ever get the leisure to think and say it out. One thing I must say is that your letters do give me so much pleasure, I look them over and wonder what it is that pleases me so much and I can't make out. . . . And now I could say so much about the Munich plan; and what follows in your letter about home duties and individual life; it is just my puzzle; and I don't think I can get nearer to a solution than you have done. But if you were here we cd. talk about it so well. Oh! that you were here! I don't like the idea of your being a whole six months away from call; but that is selfish and not to be taken into consideration. One thing is pretty clear,* Women *must give up living an artist's life, if home duties are to be paramount. It is different with men, whose home duties are so small a part of their life. However we are talking of women. I am sure it is healthy for them to have the refuge of the hidden world of Art to shelter themselves in when too much pressed upon by daily small Lilliputian arrows of peddling cares; it keeps them from being morbid as you say; and takes them into the land where King Arthur lies hidden, and soothes them with its peace. I have felt this in writing,—I see others feel it in music, you in painting, so assuredly a blending of the two is desirable. (Home duties and the development of the Individual I mean), which you will say it takes no Solomon to tell you, but the difficulty is where and when to make one set of duties subserve and give place to the other. I have no doubt that the cultivation of each tends to keep the other in a healthy state,—my grammar is all at sixes and sevens I have no doubt, but never mind if you*

R

can pick out my meaning. I think a great deal of what you have said.

Thursday.

I've been reading over yr. note, and believe I've only been repeating in different language what you said. If Self is to be the end of exertions, those exertions are unholy, there is no doubt of that—and that is part of the danger in cultivating the Individual life; but I do believe we have all some appointed work to do, wh. no one else can do so well; Wh. is our work; what we have to do in advancing the Kingdom of God; and that first we must find out what we are sent into the world to do, and define it and make it clear to ourselves, (that's the hard part) and then forget ourselves in our work, and our work is the End we ought to strive to bring about. I never can either talk or write clearly so I'll ee'n leave it alone. Hearn* has been nearly 3 weeks away nursing her mother who is dying, so we are rather at sixes and sevens upstairs. The little ones come down upon us like the Goths on Rome; making inroads and onslaughts into all our plans. I was very nearly going to the Cobdens' for 6 days or so last week—but did not. I have sent such a number of charming people to see Mr. Watts, he must think I have a glorious circle of friends.

G . . .

This letter is an answer to a request to sign a petition for a Married Woman's Property Bill, regarding which Mrs. Gaskell was none too enthusiastic, though she gave her signature :

---

* Hearn was for very many years a most faithful and valued maid, and regarded as one of the family.

Xmas 1856. *Plymouth Grove,*
Monday.

My dearest Tottie,
  You ask for the petition back again without loss of time, so I send it you although to-day certainly I shan't be able to write a long letter, I don't think it is very definite, and pointed ; *or that it will do much good,— for the Turnkey's objection (vide " Little Dorrit ") " but if they wish to come over her, how then can you legally tie it up " &c. will be a stronger difficulty than they can legislate for : a husband can coax, wheedle, beat or tyrannize his wife out of something and no law whatever will help this that I can see. (Mr. Gaskell begs Mr. Fox to draw up a bill for the protection of* husbands *against wives who will spend all their earnings.) However our sex is badly enough used and legislated* against, *there's no doubt of* that—*so though I don't see the definite end proposed by these petitions I'll sign. I could say a great deal more, but have my own heart chock-full of private troubles and sorrows just now—a very little more and this letter would go to you wet with my tears. However it's no use maundering—and* perhaps *some day long hence, if you'll remind me of Xmas and New Year 1856 I may tell you a sad little story which only concerns me indirectly. I will write you a very long letter soon.*
    Yours very affect.
      E. Gaskell.

During 1858 a visit was paid to London and much society seen. Mrs. Shaen wished Mrs. Gaskell to come to meet Mazzini, but she wrote from Hyde Park Gardens : " I should so like to come, and above all things to know a little of Mazzini, but there is a great dinner-party here, made for me—Macaulay,

Hallam, Sir Francis Palgrave, and Lord Campbell—I don't *think* I can get away *before* 10, and then it is 3 miles to go—but I'll leave it a little open, please, for all that."

Later she says : " Another great dinner to-night, dinners being Lady C's visiting; she declines all evening parties." Lady C. would not hear of her going into lodgings. " I go to dine at the Monckton Milnes on Tuesday, to the Dukeries* on Thursday, and must get in a day for Mr. Carlyle."

To a friend in London.

About 1859.

I ought not to write to you, wherefore I do, you naughty, lazy, abominable woman ! you bid me write directly and I do, as directly as man can do and then please, when do you answer me ? I am so glad you are returned to a Christian country—I wish Sir John Franklin were—your whereabouts of late days have been as much unknown to me as his. Dear and I have such a deal to say ! Do you know I think we're going to keep a cow, and I'm sure we're going to keep a pig, because our pig stye is building and I find my proper vocation is farming ; and Frank is gone poor fellow ! and going to live at Southport and we've got a new man James by name ; and I've got a new cook instead of Mary, who is to be married " by Master " in February and said new cook is coming in January, and her name is Isabella Postlethwaite of Legberthwaite in Tilburthwaite, you may guess her habitat from that ; and we have got a Bessy instead of a Maria, and a Margaret instead of Margaret, all changes against my will at the time, but improvements I think. What do you think of Kossuth is he

* She visited the Duke of Devonshire at Chatsworth.

not a WONDERFUL *man for cleverness. His speech was real eloquence, I never heard anyone speak before that I could analyze as it went along, and* think *what caused the effect, but when he spoke I could only feel ; —and yet I am not quite* sure *about him, that's to say I am* quite *sure about his end being a noble one, but I think it has so possessed him that I am not quite* out *and out sure that he would stick at* any *means, it's not for me to be poking into and judging. . . . I wish you could see Lucy Holland's water colour drawings ; I wonder if you would think them* good. *They are very pretty at any rate and Meta has been copying some. . . . And oh ! Fanny and I have had a split about Libbie Marsh, which that wretched man at Liverpool was going on republishing ad infinitum and I stepped in and objected as gently as I cd., and I am afraid Fanny is hurt. I am* very *sorry ; but I showed my letter to Wm., and he says it was quite a gentle proper letter. Do* you *hear any of her plans from any one ? Susanna W. keeps Wm. busy at work correcting her proofs,* for my dear ! Niebuhr is on the point of appearing before the public ! and poor Mary Barton gets more snubbed than ever as a " light and transitory " work. I have offered myself to the " Critic " as a writer. I did it in a state of rage at that Marples man at Liverpool, and Chapman and I swore I would penny-a-line and have nothing to do with publishers never no more ; so my critics generously offered me 7s. a column. (I never saw the paper but I heard it was a respectable dullard) and I counted up and I think its about 3d. a line, so I think I shall do well. Wm. is very mad about it, and calls me names which are not pretty for a husband to call a wife " great goose " etc. . . . Tell me some literary gossip,*

* She was translating " Niebuhr."

for though I've turned farmer, I've a little sympathy yet left for " book-sellers' hacks." . . . How are the Dickens ? wretch that he is to go and write MY *story of the lady haunted by the face ; I shall have nothing to talk about now at dull parties. . . . Our cow is such a pet. Half Alderney, quarter Ayrshire, quarter Holderness. . . . We've got a mangle and we're washing at home, and we do it so beautifully.*

Judging from the preceding, there was a slight jealousy of Susanna Winkworth, the one of the sisters who translated " Niebuhr," and perhaps thought rather highly of her work. Or perhaps Mr. Gaskell, the serious minded, did so, and seemed to overlook the authoress at his side. Then there was the trouble over Magazine writing.

To " Tottie."

All day long I've been talking to Meta and spudding up dandelions, and now I've half a hundred letters to write, having sent the girl to bed. Oh dear ! My dear little Tottie your note gave me a heartache going to bed the last thing at night, and when I wakened this morning I knew *there was some bad news, though I could not remember* what. *My dearest Tottie I was so tired and ill last week I dare say I wrote roughly and " nakedly "—and I did not tell you* half *what pleasure we should all have in your visit with us at Silverdale, or you* would *have come. When I gave up Bonn with many sighs because W. was so against it, I made a paction 'twixt us two that you* should *come to Silverdale and now, love,* do *come, the money could not be spent in any way to give us* all *more pleasure. We have perhaps been foolish in talking of your coming as a certainty and hence the little ones too talk so of your coming. I would paint a picture of the Corn Law League (do you remember my indigna-tion against Herbert over the schoolroom fire ?) to get you to come ;* can *man say more ? Oh ! Mrs. Fox will settle herself, and if it is a little later it does not signify—and Charlotte will I know be on our side. Do let me help you to clear away difficulties. Leave it open if you like, but try. I'm afraid I burnt your note about F. B. and Mr. Fox only yesterday morning —clearing off before Meta came. How well the lassie looks ! and so full of politics and water colours. Such a pleasure to have her again. She has flown out upon us laughing at* her acct *of the Corsican brothers, which was irresistible though it was meant to be solemn. She has been* very *happy with you and has been* very *gay compared to what she will be here, but I did not want* gaiety *for her at all ; only " en-largement of ideas," as Mr. L. wd. say, wh. I think she has got in this absence from home. She shocks me by saying you told her Mrs. Ruskin was separated from her husband—is it true ? Dear Tottie I return to the burden. Do come with us to Silverdale. As for our going up it is all in the clouds, may be, may not be,—x x x I am turning such a farmer—I bodily curry the cow and carry her her pail of licking. You don't know what licking is ? not you. And with a spud under my arm I reckon I represent the agri-cultural interest Tottie ! you don't know how* beautiful *Silverdale is and a tower of our own ! think of that ! its a sort of country you never saw before. I'll answer for it. I dare say we shall never go there again— and I for one, don't expect to live till another summer, when you so coolly talk of coming—Do come,—think of it ! difficulties vanish in thinking with me ; or perhaps the thinking is the greater difficulty. I am not half thanking you enough for all your kindness to Meta—but I* do *thank you. I have so much to say too, that can never come in in writing, an employment I hate more and more. Now I can't write more to-night I am sorely tired, not being strong. Thursday.*

But her beloved correspondent " Tottie " suddenly settled to take to herself a husband, a Mr. Bridell, and became in consequence Mrs. Bridell-Fox. The event appears to have been sudden.

This is to her father, the M.P.

1859 . . .

My dear Mr. Fox,

Our Times of to-day—well of yesterday—well, to-morrow it will be of some day in dream-land, for I am past power of counting—

Our Times of to-day has taken away my breath—Who —What, Where, Wherefore, Why—oh! do be a woman, and give me all possible details—Never mind the House of Commons: it can keep—but my, our, curiosity CAN'T.

Oh! please telegraph back anything about him— how long known what is he—what has *he (I live in Manchester city sacred to Mammon,) when did she* first *see him—Where are they going to live—Whole love story, &c., &c., &c.*

Write for 26 hours consecutively, and you can't write enough.

WELL TO BE SURE
I THINK I AM
VERY
GLAD.

Yours most truly,
E. C. GASKELL

42, Plymouth Grove,
Manchester
March 10th.

The relations with Dickens were not always too smooth. To tell the truth Mrs. Gaskell wished to get free of *Household Words* and the Dickens control. This extract from another pen shows how he regarded the matter. It is a dangerous matter for one writer to alter the work of another.

*   *   *   *   *

You have guessed right! The best of it was that she (Mrs. Gaskell) wrote to Wills, saying she must particularly stipulate not to have her proofs touched, " even by Mr. Dickens." That immortal creature had gone over the proofs (North and South) with great pains—had of course taken out the stiflings—hard plungings, lungeings, and other convulsions—and had also taken out her weakenings and damagings of her own effects. " Very well," said the gifted Man, " she shall have her own way. But after it's published show her this proof, and ask her to consider whether her story would have been the better or the worse for it."

Mrs. Gaskell carried on a long correspondence with Charles Eliot Norton, of Harvard, and his wife. The Nortons became great friends in Rome where they met continually. Mr. Norton later visited Mrs. Gaskell in Manchester. She writes of their little daughter's birth. " If I had been in time I should like her to have been called after me and, though Elizabeth is not the prettiest of names, yet it has very pretty abreviations and pet names." The next child was named after Mrs. Gaskell.

Mr. Norton in his letters expresses the greatest appreciation of her work and says, " I learned every day to feel towards her a deeper affection and respect. She is like the best things in her books. . . . I have known few men who seem to me to have such lovable qualities."*

> *Monday, June 10th, 1881.*
> *Dining room in Plymouth Grove,*
> *breakfast things not as yet removed,*
> *your letter came at breakfast.*

My dear Mr. Norton :

Yesterday—a quiet Sunday, with somhow less of bustle about than Sunday School and Ragged School usually make, Meta and I were having a long yearning *talk about America, and our dear friends there. I am not sure that we did not shake hands upon a resolution that if we lived we* would *go over to America. I know we calculated time and expense, and knocked off Niagara, because we would rather see friends. (That is to say Meta did. I was not so clear in my own mind about going up Niagara, so I won't pretend I was). Then we talked over your politics and could not understand them ; and I half determined to do what I am doing now—take myself and Meta for average specimens of English people,—*most *kindly disposed to you, our dear cousins, hating slavery intensely, but yet thoroughly puzzled by what is now going on in America. I don't mind your thinking me dense or ignorant, and I think I can be sure you will give me a quiet* unmetaphorical *statement of what is the end proposed in this war.*

*   *   *   *   *

Every one looks and feels sad (—oh so sad) about this war ; it would do Americans good to see how warm the English heart is towards them, although we may all be blundering in our minds as to the wisdom or otherwise. No ! Mr. Field—our dear, dear Jack never writes to us,—which hurts us only we love him

* " Letters of C. E. Norton, 1913," by His Daughter, Vol. I, p. 172.

just as much as if he did. Mind, you always *tell us about them, for it is our only way of hearing till we go to the Clam-Bake on the Shore which he promised us. Mr. Wild where is he ? You owe me a* Personal *as well as a* National *letter. Put me right where I am wrong,—(You'll say I'm wrong throughout—) You would see — — — I have been called off and forget what I was going to say. Your account of your lovely Sunday does sound so peaceful and charming. What is the Golden Robin ? Oh ! don't you long to go back to Rome. Meta and I were so talking about you, and Rome and America yesterday, the Pamphilia Doria gardens especially, and about your face as we first saw it,—and this morning comes your letter. The reason why she and I were tête-à-têteing in this way was that Mr. Gaskell was gone to Liverpool to preach. Marianne was visiting our friends at Knutsford and so, as the younger ones were occupied by themselves, Meta and I talked over " old days," partly àpropos of conversations she had had with Katie Winkworth at Malvern. Katie W. has been very ill again, and as her father Mr. W. was also dangerously ill and required all his family about him, Meta offered to take Katie to Malvern and nurse her there under Dr. Gully's directions—so the two have been together there for the greater part of a month, quite alone, and when Katie was able to bear it, the two had long serious conversations about many things. The doctrine of Atonement on the one hand—old Roman days on the other. Besides which we have just been reading Elsie Venner and we were altogether* very *American yesterday : and our love and sympathies most alive for you all. We go to Silverdale in the first week of July ; I think you must address your answer there. Mrs. G., Silverdale, near Lancaster, will find us and we are so glad of letters there, for not a book is to be had but what we take with us,—and we are so eager for reading of all kinds there. Marianne (did I tell you?) won't be there; she is going South to pay a series of visits, as she is not " one of the Silverdale ones." (Meta and Julia are* the *enthusiasts for Silverdale.) We shall all meet at home about the middle or end of August ready for the British Association here at the beginning of September. Oh Mr. Norton! Meta and I do* so *wish there was time for you to write to Mr. Gaskell and ask him to America before the* 1st Sunday in July,—*but I am afraid there is not. Yesterday the congregation gave him an entire holiday for* July and August ; *and this morning one of his friends has sent him £50 and begs him " to put the sea between himself and England." Now he hates the Continent ; and has always fancied America ; and I suppose a fortnight and two or three days would be enough for the sea-voyage both ways. And the change would be so complete! I do* not *know all Henry Vaughan's poems,—I know well " They are all gone into etc." and parts of Silex Scintillans. I wish you would come over to see us again. I wish you were to be with us at Silverdale,—it would be* just *the place for charming long lounging talks.—Elliott* has been very poorly and we have had to nurse her, and now she is going to a little country inn near Bolton Abbey for a fortnight's rest before joining us at Silverdale. Hearn has been to Paris for* 10 *days as attendant to a friend of ours who wanted a maid. But I must not cross. Meta sends you her kind love.*

Your ever affectionate friend,

E. C. Gaskell.

Mr. Norton had written to J. R. Lowell suggesting

* A maid.

that Mrs. Gaskell should write for the *Atlantic Review*. He told her that she would be paid at least half as much again as she received for *Household Words*. However the conditions did not satisfy her.

Plymouth Grove,
Monday, May 10th.

My dear Mr. Norton,
Your letter, half begun on Sunday evening—April 26th, and finished the next day, has just come in. Just after our early dinner, Meta and her Papa being the first set of people to whom it was read,—Marianne reading it now, even while I answer, on the rebound (as it is always so much easier to answer—) Oh! if you were here how much we should have to say! And do you suppose we forgot the Torcello Sunday? No! not to the material fact of our hunger and cold when we came in! Our sky here was so like the sky over the Lagoons on that day, and the lovely Stars of Bethlehem, and the stones, all carved, and square cut below the water level of the Canal Banks; and the Cathedral—oh happy lovely day,—I wish you could come over again. And the Campagna " bits " in your letters always give one a sort of heimweh,—" Give our love to Mr. Field; he won't like it the less for coming through you. But don't forget it. I do love him; it is no form of words." How I wish we could see our " Romans " again, including François. Be sure you tell us about him. . . . (Oh how much I have to say! that comes in like a burden of an old song,—I feel to want to write of the old Roman days, and yet I must earn that pleasure by working through business.) First, because most disagreeable about Mr. Underwood. I want (as I know you will see my letter to him), to put you up to what made me feel it necessary to give

*up writing for the " Atlantic " for him. So I shall
just give you an extract premising that I quite understand an Editor's desire to please his readers but that
I can not (it is not will not) write at all if I ever
think of my readers and what impression I am making
on them. " If they don't like me, they must lump me "
to use a Lancashire proverb. It is from no despising
my readers. I am sure I don't do that, but if I ever
let the thought or consciousness of them come between
me and my subject I could not write at all.*

    *   *   *   *   *

*On June 17th we are all going (except Mr. Gaskell,
who will I think go a pedestrian tour with his brother)
to Silverdale (near Lancaster)—you must have heard
us speak of it—close to Lancaster Sands and Morecambe Bay, and Annie Austin comes to stay with us,—
and there we shall remain for six weeks, and all get
as strong as horses, it is to be hoped. We live in a
queer pretty crampy house, at the back of a great farm
house. Our house is built around a square court
[here follows a plan of the house]. We have all that
is shaded, the rectangular piece is two stories high, the
little bit by the lane one story, said little bit being
kitchen and servants' bed rooms ; the house is covered
with roses, and great white Virgin-sceptred lilies, and
sweetbriar bushes grow in the small flagged square
court, across which we merrily call for " hot water,"
" more potatoes," etc. in very primitive fashion to the
kitchen. It is well for our dinner when it does not
rain, otherwise what is meant to be hot, has to be
carried carefully under an umbrella, if our visitors are
very particular people. The soil about the place is all
sandy and heathery, and you know what delicate little
plants grow in it ; and hedgehogs, and glow-worms
abound. In the garden, half flower, half kitchen is an*

old square Tower, or "Peel"—a remnant of the Border towers. Think of the perils our legs of mutton undergo! First they are kept in the larder, or lower story of the Tower. Rain or fair they have to be carried to the kitchen to be cooked. Rain or fair they have to be carried hot across the court. And to begin with Silverdale is so wild a place we may be happy to get a leg of mutton at all. I have had to dine 15 people, as hungry as hounds, on shrimps and bread and butter,—and when they asked for more had to tell them there was no bread nearer than Milnthorpe 6 miles off, and they had to come down to oatcake and be thankful! Then at the very end of the garden is a high terrace at the top of the broad stone wall, looking down on the Bay with its slow moving train of crossers led over the treacherous sands by the guide, a square man sitting there on his white horse, (the better to be seen when daylight ebbs). The said guide, Carter by name, is descended lineally from he who guided Ed. 1st over on his march to Scotland, and was by him given a coat of arms, and a grant of land. On foggy nights the guide (who had let people drown before now, who could not pay him his fee, but who writes "gentleman" after his name, thanks to Ed. 1st), may be heard blowing an old ram's horn trumpet, to guide by the sound,—

But I dare say you are tired of all this,—only write to us there, for it will seem like introducing Newport and Silverdale together. We shall be there from June 17 for 6 weeks; and our address will be Lindeth Tower, Silverdale, near Lancaster.

It is a long hot walk to the post office, and it is so disappointing to find no letters there when you get there.

*   *   *   *   *

Tuesday. I am so far from strong that my only

piece of work yesterday, (writing this letter), utterly knocked me up, and I have been quite unable to sleep —whereupon, as events travel in circles, I have been thinking during the night of no end of things I want to say to you. First (uncomplimentary), I don't like American biographies. Dr. Kane's life* is unordered, —and why do you give us all those speeches and obsequy things at the end? It is very ungrateful of me to say this, for Dr. Elder sent it me. Next—who is Mr. Parton who writes biographies on your side of the water? Barnum, and Aaron Burr†—the first I literally could not read, just for the want of any moral feeling at all in it,—the last I have just read, because I wanted to get some knowledge of American Society in the last century and beginning of this,—and to know who Aaron Burr was? There is just the same or worse want of any idea of simply right or wrong,—but I don't come out clear as to what could have been Aaron B's real character—was he not always acting a part,—writing to Theodosia not as he really felt I thought, but as he wanted to persuade the world, and himself, that he did think and feel. And after all did he not (in the Mexican affair) only forestall " vous autres " by fifty years. But it is strange to see the whole world rising up against him as against Cain,— who was a far finer fellow, because he humbled himself before God, and dared to be true, and to cry aloud.— You may depend upon it Cain was human and loveable compared to Aaron Burr. I must go back to the March Atlantic (I see by the May number) for the review of this A. B.'s life. Do tell me something distinct of the man's character. Next—our Venice

---

* The Arctic explorer whose Life had just been written.

† The American statesman who fought a duel with Alexander Hamilton. He was tried for treason for endeavouring to raise a force to conquer Texas.

seeds,—do you remember giving them to us,—have been sown this spring, and are coming up famously. Our Academy Exhibition this year is minus the Pre-Raphaelites. Meta who was in London in March, saw through the favour of Mr. Ruskin, Holman Hunt's new picture of Christ disputing with the Doctors,— which is not finished, and won't be this three months. Meta did so *admire it—and him himself, and a sculptor of the name of Munro to whom Ruskin introduced her, as well. There! that's as much as I am going to write to-day.*

May 14. *Friday. This is the last day for posting a letter to America this week, so I shall send this off. Did I say I was going to London, to the Wedgwoods— because I am* not. *Meta is not strong, though in good spirits, and I don't like leaving her. Marianne is going to London to a dentist! Poor child! My kind regards to Mrs. Norton and your sisters.*

Yours ever most truly

E. C. Gaskell.

There was a curious little quarrel between Mrs. Gaskell and John Stuart Mill. The latter had been annoyed at certain sentences in a letter from Charlotte Brontë to her which was critical and which concluded after some appreciation, by saying : " In short, J. S. Mill's head is, I dare say, very good, but I feel disposed to scorn his heart." It had reference to an article by him in the *Westminster Review* on " The Emancipation of Women," and the matter was one respecting which John Stuart Mill was exceedingly sensitive. He seemed to think it had some bearing on Mrs. Taylor who became his wife in 1851.

The letter, published in the Biography, to which

S

John Stuart Mill so strongly objected is as follows.
It is dated September 20, 1851.

*Beautiful are those sentences out of James
Martineau's sermons ; some of them gems most pure
and genuine ; ideas deeply concerned, finely expressed.
I should like much to see his review of his sister's
book. Of all the articles respecting which you question
me, I have seen none, except that notable one in the
" Westminster " on " The Emancipation of Women."
But why are you and I to think (perhaps I should
rather say to* feel) *so exactly alike on some points
that there can be no discussion between us ? Your
words on this paper express my thoughts. Well argued
it is—clear, logical—but vast in the hiatus of omission ;
harsh the consequent jar on every fine chord of the soul.
What is this hiatus ? I think I know ; and knowing,
I will venture to say. I think the writer forgets there
is such a thing as self-sacrificing love and disinterested
devotion. When I first read the paper I thought it
was the work of a powerful-minded, clear-headed woman,
who had a hard, jealous heart, muscles of iron, and
nerves of bend* leather ; of a woman who longed for
power and had never felt affection. To many women
affection is sweet, and power conquered indifferent—
though we all like influence won. I believe J. S. Mill
would make a hard, dry, dismal world of it ; and yet
he speaks admirable sense through a great portion of
his article—especially when he says, that if there be
a natural unfitness in women for men's employment
there is no need to make laws on the subject ; have all
careers open ; let them try ; those who ought to succeed
will succeed, or, at least, will have a fair chance—
the incapable will fall into their right place. He like-*

* " Bend," in Yorkshire, is strong ox leather.

wise disposes of the "maternity" question very neatly. In short, J. S. Mill's head is, I dare say, very good, but I feel disposed to scorn his heart. You are right when you say that there is a large margin in human nature over which the logicians have no dominion; glad am I that it is so."

Doubtless Mrs. Gaskell ought not to have published a letter of this sort, certainly not intended for eyes other than her own and hurtful to its subjects. It is clear that she knew nothing personally of Mill or she would probably have acted differently. He had written to her very strongly about her action in regard to the matter, and this is her answer.

Sir,   *July* 14, 1859.

When you look at the signature of this letter you will probably be surprised at receiving it, as the only communication I ever received from you was couched in terms which I then thought impertinent, unjust, and inexcusable; which I now think simply unjust. For after reading the dedication of your Essay on Liberty I can understand how any word expressing a meaning only conjectured that was derogatory to your wife would wound you most deeply. And therefore I now write to express my deep regret that you received such pain through me. I still think you were unreasonable; but I like you better than if you had been reasonable under such circumstances. You used hard words towards me; I hardly expect now to be able to change your opinion of me; indeed I write now more with the intention of relieving my own mind by expressing sorrow for having given pain, than with the idea of clearing myself in your opinion. But still it would be but fair in you to listen to my view of the case. I knew nothing of the writer of the article in question:

I had not even read the article. Miss Brontë knew nothing either ; but the impression produced on her mind by it made her imagine that such must have been the disposition and character of the person who wrote it. This imagination told as much of her mind and judgment—if not more, than it could be held to reveal of the writer's. I do not express myself very clearly in this way. I will try and take an analogous case. I see a great picture—the painter of which is utterly unknown to me even by name. As well as my opinion of the picture I unconsciously form some idea of the painter. His choice and treatment of a subject is either pleasing or displeasing to me, individually ; and I try and discover why it is so, and to conjecture what qualities he must possess to have made it so. In speaking of these and of his character, as conjectured from his work, I believe that I should reveal as much of my own character as of his. It seemed to me that in publishing that part of Miss Brontë's letter which gave you such acute pain that no one would receive any impression of the writer of the article in question ; while to some a good deal might be learnt of Miss Brontë's state of mind and thought on such subjects.

But I will not trouble you further with recurring to a subject which I fear still must give you pain. I will not even give you my address for I do not want you to answer this. Only please do not go on thinking so badly of me, as you must have done before you could have written that letter.

Yours respectfully and truly,
                                        E. C. Gaskell.

One feels that a simple expression of regret would have met the case better.

Mill's letter in reply runs :

You entirely mistake the motive which actuated the letter to which you refer. It was not hurt feeling on a sensitive point, but a sense of truth and justice which I flatter myself would have been the same in any other case. Even now I should feel that I was acting contrary to her wishes and character by any partiality or unreasonable sensitiveness, much more than at a time when I could afford to regard these things with indifference.

The case being simply that in the exercise of the discretion of an editor you neglected the usual and indispensable duty which custom (founded on reason) has imposed, of omitting all that might be offensive to the feelings of individuals. Had what was said referred only to myself the publication of it would have been equally unjustifiable. Miss Brontë was entitled to express any foolish impression that might occur to her in a private letter. It is the editor who publishes what may give offence who is alone to blame.

Mrs. Gaskell was somewhat less *intrangisante* in her reply, but inclined, as always, to stick to her guns.

Sir,

You do me an injustice, I think, and I shall try once more to set myself partially right in your opinion, because I value it ; but I do not believe in any good result arising from this final attempt.

I wrote from Scotland, where I was away from books, and had no power of referring to the passage in the Life of Miss Brontë. I am now at home, and have it and your letter by me. Where I think you do me an injustice is in saying that " in publishing letters not written for publication you disregarded the obligation which custom founded on reason has imposed, of omitting what would be offensive to the feelings and perhaps injurious to the moral reputation of individuals . . . and the notion you seem to entertain that everything said or written by any one, which could possibly throw light on the character of the sayer or writer, may, justifiably be published by a biographer, is one which the world, and those who are higher and better than the world, would, I believe, perfectly unite in condemning."

I have expressed myself badly if you think that I intentionally disregarded the " obligation which custom or reason has imposed, &c."—I certainly did not think that " a foolish opinion,"—a mere conjecture, obviously formed on insufficient grounds for having any weight affixed to it by the most careless reader, could have been " offensive to the feelings, or injurious to the moral reputation." That is the point on which we differ ; not on the duty of a biographer to omit whatever can reasonably be expected to be offensive, &c. I acknowledge that duty ; and I believe that you are the only person who has made any complaint or remonstrance to me about the publication of any part of Miss Brontë's letters. I tried to be very careful and it was difficult to exactly tell where the limit (the necessity for which, let me say once again, I fully acknowledge) was to be drawn.

Now, having endeavoured to set you right as to my recognition of the duty you seem to think I ignore— (and some hasty expression in my last letter may have given rise to this misconception on your part) I will candidly say that on reading the offensive part over again, I believe that I ought to have omitted some part of what I inserted, in fulfilment of the duty which I acknowledge as much as you do. It may be that your letters, and the sense of having given pain has awakened my conscience ; it may be that in two or three years one's perception of right and wrong becomes juster and keener—but, if it were to be re-edited now, I should certainly *omit the final paragraph relating to yourself. " In short J. S. Mill's head is I dare say very good, but I feel disposed to scorn his heart."* It was, I see, *morally wrong to have published that. But I am not so sure about the rest.*

Do you understand ? I acknowledge the duty as much as you do. I have failed in this duty, as I now perceive in one *part. As to the* other *part, that is matter of opinion. I do not yet clearly see that I have failed in this duty with regard to that. I do not believe that a just and reasonable person ought to have been offended by the publication of such a mere conjecture as to possible character. As I said, I do* not *believe that this letter will alter your opinion of me, and of the transaction which has brought us thus unpleasantly into contact. But I write it for the chance.*

Yours respectfully and truly,
E. C. Gaskell.

42, Plymouth Grove,
  Manchester,
    August 11th, 1859.

CHAPTER ELEVEN

MRS. GASKELL had found periodical writing a tax. We have seen how she had been pressed to write for weekly publications and write to time, and in writing for *Household Words* and *All the Year Round* she had, as in " North and South," to adapt her stories to the necessities of the magazine as to space. It is easy to realise how detrimental this was to good work, especially with a woman who was constantly being held up by domestic crises, headaches and so on, and it seems a terrible pity that she consented to it. One can imagine her in that dining-room with the many doors having to clear away her papers for company, interview the cook and make arrangements for the welfare of her four girls. She began work early, being an indifferent sleeper, but after breakfast wrote at a corner of the dining-room table. It is a sad fact that much of her writing bears the mark of these invasions of her time and interest. She enjoyed good living of the simple kind (what she had was served with delicacy and refinement), travelling and pleasant company, and all these cost money. She was a good linguist, and had a scheme in her mind for escaping from the rigours of a northern climate—a scheme that she did not venture to broach to a husband whose whole life and interest was in his city or his work—work which nothing would induce him to desert.

Then there came on February 14th, 1864, a

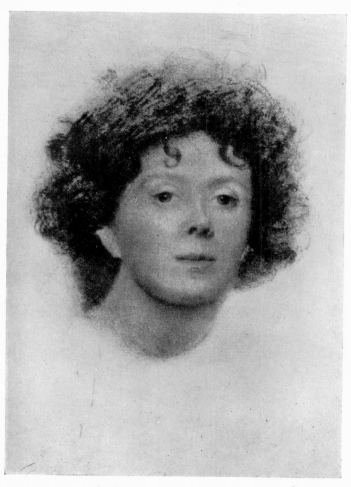

MADAME MOHL
From a pastel drawing by herself

Valentine* from Mr. Smith, the publisher. It is an amusing representation of Mrs. Gaskell as a dairy woman, while her would-be publisher is on his knees begging for his manuscript. Mr. Smith had made real friends with Mrs. Gaskell when she paid him a visit at Hampstead, and now he was not only publishing the *Cornhill Magazine* but offering specially high prices for articles produced in it, as compared with those in other periodicals, in order to get the best contributors. He went so far as to give George Eliot £7,000 for the serial rights of " Romola," and he offered Mrs. Gaskell what was then considered a wonderful price, £2,000, for a seven-years' copyright of her novel. This was a great bait, for on the strength of it she was able to supply the wherewithal for the plans she had in view, and also to allow the work of writing to be done quietly and without hurry. The end of it was that the Valentine bore its effect—that the domestic cow was to be handed over to the care of others (let us suppose) and that a tale could be written without the press or hurry of so many of the earlier ones. The result was the best real novel (for " Cranford " can hardly be called such) that Elizabeth Gaskell ever wrote. She began to write it in the summer of 1864 and the last instalment appeared in January, 1866. Unfortunately it was never finished, for the author died before she completed it ; however, the conclusion of the story is very clearly forecast.

Mrs. Gaskell's best work was done when she wrote of the people in a country town such as she knew so well in her early life ; the strange thing is that

* In the possession of Mrs. Lamb, daughter of Stephen Winkworth.

she was never quite as much at home in the great cities where she had spent most of her life, as she was in the little town of her childhood. Probably most writers of fiction find their early impressions the deepest.

In this new book she describes the life of just such a small country town with all its amusing grades of society—its county families (not often introduced by her), its doctors—not, indeed, its parsons—its country gentlemen, but above all just the ordinary people who live in the ordinary comfortable houses and do the ordinary things. Elizabeth Gaskell knew from the time she was Elizabeth Stevenson to a nicety the relation borne by the " county " to the " town "—she remembered the Egertons of Tatton Park, near Knutsford —and the annual garden parties given to the teachers of the school that they supported.

The story really hangs on the people belonging to the two estates so clearly defined in pre-war days. They were all friendly and kindly but " there was a difference." The chief woman's figure was dear little Molly Gibson, the doctor's daughter, whom we all love and whom we cannot help identifying with her creator. Molly, mercifully, has her faults —who has not?—but she is a human, natural English girl, such as luckily we are not for long without, even in these days of sophistication. It was hard for Molly as holding the first place with her father, to accept a stepmother of so different a nature from herself, as was the late governess in Lady Cumnor's family. Robert Gibson, the country doctor, and Molly's father, is one of the best male characters Mrs. Gaskell ever drew, even including Mr. Benson. He was the doctor *par excellence*, the friend of everyone in the family, the man who did his duty without thinking of the possibility of anything else, one who lived for his profession and never thought of getting on in a social sense, or doing anything to bring himself into notice. With all these virtues he married, as his second wife, a thoroughly worldly woman, to whom position was the breath of life and who did not mind descending to untruths to bring about her objects. This was naturally trying to Molly, his daughter. But the portrayal is sympathetic, so that we pity as much as blame her, and that is the attraction of all Mrs. Gaskell's work. She never, in her best work, at least, allowed one to dislike her unsympathetic characters—she always makes us feel that after all they were human beings made after God's image, even if they had turned away after other gods. She had that sure and delicate touch that women writers have at their best. When it was not there it was because the work was hurried and carelessly done.

This is an account of the relationship between the little town and its feudal superiors before the days of railways and reform bills.

" The little straggling town faded away into country on one side close to the entrance lodge of a great park where lived my Lord and Lady Cumnor : ' The Earl ' and ' The Countess,' as they were always called by the inhabitants. . . . They expected to be submitted to, and obeyed ; the simple worship of the townspeople was accepted by the Earl and Countess as a right, and they would have stood still in amazement, and with a horrid memory of the French *sans-culottes* who were the bugbears of their youth, had any inhabitant of Hollingsford ventured

to set his will or opinion in opposition to those of
the Earl. But, yielded all that observance, they
did a good deal for the town, and were generally
condescending, and often thoughtful and kind in
their treatment of their vassals. Lord Cumnor was
a forbearing landlord ; putting his steward a little
on one side sometimes, and taking the reins into his
own hand now and then, much to the annoyance
of the agent, who was, in fact, too rich and independent to care greatly for preserving a post where
his decisions might any day be overturned by my
Lord's taking a fancy to go ' pottering,' which,
being interpreted, meant that occasionally the Earl
asked his own questions of his own tenants, and
used his own eyes and ears in the management of
the smaller details of the property."

The Countess made up for this weakness by her
" unapproachable dignity." " Once a year she was
condescending. She and the ladies, her daughters,
had set up a school, not a school after the manner
of schools nowadays, where far better intellectual
teaching is given to the boys and girls of labourers
and workpeople than often falls to the lot of their
betters in worldly estate ; but a school of the kind
we should call ' industrial,' where girls are taught
to sew beautifully, to be capital housemaids, and
pretty fair cooks, and above all, to dress neatly in
a kind of charity uniform decreed by the ladies of
Cumnor Towers—white caps, white tippets, check
aprons, blue gowns, and ready curtsies, ' Please,
ma'ams ' being *de rigueur*."

We have the writer at her best in describing the
relations between Hyacinth Clare, who married the
doctor, and Cynthia, her daughter. Both had their
good points, as shallow, tactless, tiresome people

have. Their foibles are tolerated because they
are often ready to do kind deeds. Cynthia loved
simple Molly and was ready to help her, though
they were made of so different a clay that it was
difficult for the one to understand the other. The
contrast between the girls is drawn with great
subtlety and truth. So with the other men besides
the honourably straight Robert Gibson. There are
two young men in the story—Osborne Hamley,
who made a secret marriage and brought much
trouble on himself; and his brother, Roger Hamley,
who first loves Cynthia, a beautiful girl who had
the faults and virtues that most appeal to the other
sex, and then the more staid Molly. Both are given
real individuality and masculine character. Roger
is a scientist, and when thwarted in love he goes
on an expedition which recalls the expedition of
Charles Darwin as recorded in " The Voyage of the
Beagle." Indeed, Roger Hamley is supposed to
have been actually modelled on Darwin, and there
is some likelihood in the conjecture inasmuch as
the Darwin family were in touch with the Gaskells.
Mrs. Gaskell did not have the knowledge of the life
of young men at the University that she might
have had, supposing she had had sons of her own,
and hence the account of how the rather backward
Roger developed suddenly into " the Senior Wrangler
of the year " is rather unconvincing.

Naturally people looked for, and found, similarity
to the characters of existing persons in the book.
That was to be expected. There was not much
harm in identifying the excellent Dr. Gibson, but
there was some unhappiness in the description of
the Miss Brownings when they went to a party at
Cumnor Towers. For their supposed prototypes

did wear white satin shoes when they took their luncheon at the great house, and there was natural resentment at the account of the fact ! These things are difficult to avoid in this type of writing.

Altogether this novel, written as it is simply and without mannerisms, enhanced its author's reputation as a woman of letters. Thackeray credited her with some of the truest and best works of fiction in the English language—rather an exaggerated estimate, of course—and this is supposed to be her masterpiece. It has a good plot, well developed, and all the characters are interesting. George Sand admired it, and it is easy to see the reason. She writes of it as a " book which might be put into the hands of any innocent young girl, while it would rivet the attention of the most blasé man of the world." It is not certain that the staid Molly was autobiographical. Mrs. Gaskell had more of the sprightliness of Cynthia in her make-up. But then no one is a good judge of their own mentality, and it may be that Molly was to Elizabeth Gaskell what Maggie Tulliver was to Marian Evans. There is a certain resemblance in this novel to " Middlemarch " in that both are faithful representations of rural life as it was in the middle of last century, and also inasmuch as there is the same play of character upon character in both. Mrs. Gaskell is not as profound ; we are spared philosophical and moral reflections such as are given us by George Eliot. But if the characters are not as subtly portrayed, they are depicted with equal care and understanding and, strange to say, the book is not as sad as "Middlemarch," while its humour is as true. Mrs. Gaskell loved tragedy and violent and sudden deaths, but here we find everyone leading normal lives and dying normal deaths—there are no great tragedies or even miseries, beyond those common to us all. The human element permeates the whole and is not dragged in : there are no lessons to be taught or morals to be enforced ; yet the book stands together as a first-rate comedy with plenty of lessons if we want to learn them as we learn them in our daily course through life.

We are grateful to all writers who give us these *genre* pictures of the life of our country. We feel that it is something that can be incorporated in our history—something that will last after the so-called "facts" become dim, and this book is historical in the last degree. The writer had the gift of describing a country market town just as Trollope described a Cathedral town. Basil Champneys claims for "Wives and Daughters" that it is the best purely domestic novel in the English language. It is indeed a domestic novel ; Mrs. Gaskell has no psychological questions to puzzle us, no "problems" to discuss. Her morality is the simple morality of living the life that we should all like to live if we are decent people. Her religion is the placid religion of the day she describes ; there is no talk of the breaking through bonds of convention : that was to be the fashion in a later age. Her sense of humour recognised the absurdity of much of the social life of the time, the subservience of the lower to the upper classes; the efforts to stand well with the world ; she described it all with the hand of a master of the craft, so that we know without being told. The irony is as hidden as is the irony of Jane Austen. And hence we find her restful, and are never made to wish to controvert or question as we are in most modern novels, but accept what is given as in the course of nature. Perhaps this militates against its popularity in these days : perhaps the young require stronger fare and cannot be troubled with the old days when women knew their place and intermittently kept to it, and men were beings apart who regulated the outward course of life if not the inward. Still to those of us who do not look too far afield and who believe that there is nothing common-place even in the most ordinary and humdrum life it is refreshing to browse in the peaceful fields of English life a hundred years ago.

" Wives and Daughters " is in a way four-square—the story of two sons and two daughters. It is the story of two generations and their relations to one another. Indeed the first idea was to call it " The Two Mothers." The books of the day were beginning to criticise the relations of parents and children (a criticism destined to develop), but far more to satirise the relations of the classes—the higher to the middle, the middle to the lower. Of course, Thackeray gives us an outstanding example of this type of satire, but we have it in an even more subtle, though less outspoken form in Mrs. Gaskell's last book. The days of the unquestioned aristocrat were passing. Lady Cumnor's insolence was being recognised as insolence. Hyacinth Clare, the governess, was just " Clare," treated as a menial. Illness, when inconvenient, was " due to lack of self-control." " I never think whether a land-agent is handsome or not. They don't belong to the class of people whose appearance I notice," said Lady Cumnor. Clare's wedding must be put off till Christmas " to amuse the children," supposing the weather during the holidays was bad. But even Lord Cumnor protested against that, and the next generation, as personified in Lady Cumnor's daughter, was more considerate : the age of this type of snobbery was waning.

The book is not by any means all serious. There are many touches of fun in it—almost as many as in " Cranford." The author's pen had not lost its cunning. All who have read it remember the stories of the " amphibious " apprentices (so-called by Miss Browning) who held a half and half position in Mr. Gibson's household and who would persist in making love to Molly thus causing her father to think of a stepmother.

And then Mrs. Gibson, the " refined " second wife whose aim was to " do her duty." " I've that deep feeling about duty that I think it ought only to be talked about in Church and such sacred places as that ; not to have a common caller startling one with it." And again, when she is annoyed with her daughter, Cynthia Kirkpatrick, for being so tired after the ball she considers it the natural result of dancing with everybody who asked her. " Partners whose names are in the Red-Book would not have produced half the fatigue." She was vain, self-indulgent, and snobbish, yet at bottom a good-hearted woman. It is this careful drawing of character, the character that is like the characters we meet in the world, neither all good, nor all bad, but a satisfactory blending of both, that attracts us in Mrs. Gaskell's writings.

We all know Mrs. Gibson, just as we all know Molly the " born lady, uncommonly noble and generous in every thought " as Mrs. Ritchie calls her—the direct antithesis of her stepmother. When you read novels such as this, she says, quoting from another, " you feel yourself caught out of this abominable

T

wicked world into one in which it is possible for
people to live calm and wholesome lives."

The book was not written without difficulty. It
was worked out with care, and though long it does not
seem unduly long. It was perhaps the only book of
Mrs. Gaskell's written for the most part in peace
during visits to Pontresina and Paris. It did not
meet with immediate success, for it was the day of
popular novel writers and George Eliot, with her
problems such as never entered into Elizabeth
Gaskell's head, was all the craze. *The Times* almost
ignored it. And yet it has remained a popular novel
to this day just because of its humanity and what
the French call *justesse*. That is the quality which
in a story endures when the psychological or in-
formative novel passes away.

One regrets that the tale was never finished.
However this does not matter so much as seemed,
for the end is evident, and Mr. Frederick Greenwood has put it into words. When Mrs. Gaskell
died, Mr. George Smith, the friend and publisher
of so many novelists, appeared on horseback, so
it is said, at Mr. Greenwood's house at Hampstead, and asked his aid in regard to this book
—the same aid which he had given when " Denis
Duval " was left unfinished by Thackeray. In both
cases the work was admirably carried out.

Was Mrs. Gaskell herself tied down by the conventionalities she describes so well ? It is hardly
possible that anyone could so describe them and yet
be so. No doubt her own life was to all appearances
hemmed in on every side. In this sense she was a
caged bird who did not struggle against his bars.
It was a life apparently untouched by the modern
movements, quite unaffected by the ecclesiastical

have often heard some curious particulars about myself from what they chose to say."

In Society Mrs. Gaskell shone. Miss Flora Masson, in an article, quotes from the recollections of one who met her at an evening party with the Shaens in Bedford Row. " Mrs. Gaskell enters the room surrounded, it seemed to me, by a fair bodyguard of daughters. And I distinctly remember the manner in which Forster, who was there, came immediately towards her—the glad, interested friendliness of it ; and how he led her at once to one of those crescent shaped sofas or settees on which two people can sit almost facing one another and talk comfortably. and there they sat under the chandelier, the light of which fell on Mrs. Gaskell's soft, sumptuous draperies, and conversed together with animation."

We have seen how she cared for her home and its management. One day she writes that she has " seen no one but made four flannel petticoats, and I don't know how many pickles which are good and successful. I am sure it is my vocation to be a housekeeper ; not an economical one, but a jolly extravagant one." Whether or not she had a sense of beauty in furnishing one cannot tell. In the early days in the old home " Miss Jewsbury lay on the floor and read half through the Essays of Elia and called our drawing-room ' such an ugly room in which we should always be unhappy.' " But Miss Jewsbury might not be a good judge. The new house had Chippendale chairs we are told, and pretty things including Wedgwood vases which came through the connection with the Wedgwood family.

Hers was a busy life of the kind men know as busy : perhaps it could have been better organised as women's lives may be in the future, when casual interruptions are made to be less constant. "The years of one's life are slipping fast away and every year seems to get busier and busier." As time went on it seemed harder to keep pace with life. Mrs. Gaskell tried hard to get quiet for work ; she tells how in 1864, when she thought she had gained her point and found time for quiet thought, her eldest daughter fell ill in London and she had to rush off, arriving on Ascot day and finding everything difficult.

She realised that her children must have their lives free, and when they returned from school, endeavoured to see that "*they* did not fall into 'young lady-lives' and that *she* did not fall into the temptation of making them of use."

The friendship of the Winkworth family meant much to Elizabeth Gaskell. The sisters adored her from the early days when only they divined that she could "write books or do anything else in the world that she liked." "She was a noble-looking woman," once wrote Susanna, "with a queenly presence, and her high, broad, serene brow, and finely-cut mobile features, were lighted up by a constantly-varying play of expression as she poured forth her wonderful talk. It was like the gleaming ripple and rush of a clear deep stream in sunshine. Though one of the most brilliant persons I ever saw, she had none of the restlessness and eagerness that spoils so much of our conversation nowadays. There was no hurry or high-pressure about her, but she seemed always surrounded by an atmosphere of ease, leisure and playful geniality, that drew out the best side of everyone who was in her company. When you were with her you felt as if you had twice the life

in you that you had at ordinary times. All her
great intellectual gifts—her quick, keen observation,
her marvellous memory, her wealth of imaginative
power, her rare and acute instinct, her graceful and
racy humour,—were so warmed and brightened by
sympathy and feeling, that while actually with her,
you were less conscious of her power than of her
charms. No one ever came near her in the gift of
telling a story. In her hands the simplest incident,
—a meeting in the street, or talk with a factory-girl,
a country walk, an old family history,—became
picturesque and vivid and interesting. Her fun,
her pathos, her graphic touches, her sympathetic
insight, were inimitable."

This is the enthusiastic deliverance of an admiring
friend, but it is also the opinion of a woman of sense
and understanding. Miss Winkworth goes on to say
what one always feels with Mrs. Gaskell, that her
many-sided and occupied life gave her but little time
for her literary work which was done only when
" all possible domestic and social claims had been
satisfied. In one sense it might be a tragedy, but
then she was a woman and, woman-like, all these
things were a positive delight to her. She was
more proud of her cows and poultry, pigs and
vegetables, than of her literary triumphs."

The Winkworth family were intertwined with the
Gaskells ; the best known, Catherine of the " Lyra
Germanica "—the translator of so many of the best
hymns in our hymnal—was seventeen years her
junior ; there were three older sisters, Susanna,
Emily, and Selina, nearer her age. They had all
been brought up in the extremest form of Evangelic-
alism, but were of the Church of England. Mr.
Gaskell was kind enough to give the girls lessons in

Greek and literature and science, and it was the intimacy with the Gaskells that gave Catherine her knowledge of literature and her keen appreciation of style. She always declared that she owed all the literary power that she possessed to Mr. Gaskell.

Before becoming acquainted with the Gaskells the chief friends of the Winkworth family had been Francis Newman and some professors at the Independent College at Manchester ; through the Gaskells they came to know Mr. J. J. Taylor and Mr. Martineau and later on the various visitors who came to the Gaskells' house, such as Chevalier Bunsen. Intellectual society in Manchester was much developed, and, as has been said before, it was almost entirely outside the Church of England. " I cannot recall one distinctly intellectual person among them, either laity or clergy," writes Miss Susanna Winkworth. " Our Church friends were, many of them, excellent people, and perhaps on the average, superior to the *average* of our orthodox Dissenting friends in education and refinement ; but there was not one person of commanding intellect among them. The Unitarians in Manchester were, as a body, far and away superior to any other in intellect, culture and refinement of manners, and certainly did not come behind any other in active philanthropy and earnest efforts for the social improvement of those around them." Many of the more intelligent merchants of Manchester, like the Salis Schwabes, attended Mr. Gaskell's ministrations just because of his intelligent outlook. It was delightful for the Winkworth girls to have such friends who took them to lectures by Emerson or any other famous man who visited Manchester. They were remarkable girls, full of their studies, classical and theological, and excellent linguists. When one daughter, Emily, married William Shaen, the Shaens came into the party of friends.

Throughout her life, especially the latter part of it, Mrs. Gaskell travelled a great deal in Europe. In 1858 she and her daughter visited Germany and, later on, her friend Mme. Mohl at Paris. In 1860 she was in France again, as also two years later. It was then (1862) that she and her daughters went for a tour in Normandy and Brittany, partly with the idea of carrying on investigations as to the life of Mme. de Sévigné, and then to see the cathedral at Chartres. At Vitré they lived in an hotel once occupied by the famous Frenchwoman and they visited her château at Les Rochers. This was a pleasant little expedition before facing the Great Exhibition in London.

After that she returned to Manchester to find it in the midst of the Cotton Famine of 1862-3, which followed the Civil War in the United States of America. About ten million pounds were distributed at this time in relief, and Mrs. Gaskell took a prominent part in the work in Manchester. She worked, indeed, so hard that her health broke down and she was forced to go for a rest, which she took at Eastbourne, where she made notes for a story called " Crowley Castle."

Then in 1863 she made her way to Rome after the usual visit to Mme. Mohl. In Rome she met Landor and Swinburne, both of whom much appreciated her company and expressed their admiration of her in no measured terms. The really happy time in Rome was, however, during the visit of 1857, before she was oppressed by the criticisms on the Life of Charlotte Brontë. She wrote to William W.

Story, of whom she then saw much, that these happy days were " the tip-top part of our lives. I sometimes think I should almost rather never have been there than have the ache of yearning for the Great Witch who sits with you upon the Seven Hills."

Henry James, in his " Life of William Wetmore Story," gives a vivid account of those happy days in Rome and Paris. When Elizabeth Gaskell got free of the constraints of her Manchester life and the oppression of home duties she seemed to blossom forth like a plant suddenly taken from the shadow into a blaze of sunshine. She was like a different person. James tells of how she, " the author of ' Cranford,' ' Sylvia's Lovers,' ' Wives and Daughters ' —admirable things which time has consecrated," took up with Story in the autumn of 1856 an acquaintance already made or renewed in Paris the year before.

" I like," Mrs. Gaskell writes early in 1856, " to think of *our* Sunday breakfasts in Paris, and your Sunday bunches of violets, and the dear little girl, and the magnificent baby, and the Italian nurse, and the Etruscan bracelets, and the American fish-rissoles ; and then of Mr. Story, high and far above all, with his —— Island ghost-story and his puns. Oh, weren't we happy ! " Then she forecasts a possible visit to Rome at the end of the year with her daughters. " I hope to have finished my Life of Miss Brontë by the end of February, and then I should like to be off and away out of the reach of reviews, which, in this case, will have a double power to wound, for if they say anything disparaging of *her* I know I shall not have done her and the circumstances in which she was placed justice ; that is to say that in her case more visibly than in most, her circumstances made her faults, while her virtues were her own." In the end it was the spring of 1857 before Mrs. Gaskell finished her work and could escape from the " cold, dim, grey Manchester " to the happiness of the Via Sant' Isodoro, where were the Storys, whose guest she was. Under their wing she enjoyed a season of perfect felicity which, as James says, was " to feed all her later time with fond memories, with regrets and dreams." One thinks of the bliss of those days, which meant as much to the Storys who had the pleasure of giving happiness, as to the author of the newly published book brought with her—the book which was to prove such a thorn in the flesh later on. " I never shall be so happy again. I don't think I was ever so happy before. My eyes fill with tears when I think of these days, and it is the same with all of us." Poor caged bird free of her trammels, who read poetry into all her friendships and who looked back on those days later on when the crop of dragon's teeth had to be gathered in. " Oh, I so long for Italy and Albano," she writes afterwards, " that it makes me ill ! " Every bit of the life of the Storys, who had moved to the Palazzo Barberini, was of interest to her—their servants, their food—" Have you still little birds for dinner and the good ' dolci,' the cream of which it was necessary to be fore-warned, lest we should eat too much previously ? " And again, " I think Rome grows almost more vivid in recollection as the time recedes. Only the other night I dreamed of a breakfast—not a past breakfast, but some mysterious breakfast which neither had been, nor, alas ! would be—in the Via Sant' Isodoro dining-room, with the amber light

streaming on the gold-grey Roman roofs and the
Sabine hills on one side and the Vatican on the
other.' And then she, the born story-teller, writes
to Mrs. Story about a collection of tales promised
to her publishers but with which for the time she is
disinclined to proceed. " I could *tell* the stories
quite easily. How I should like to do it to you and
Mr. Story and Edith, sitting over a wood-fire or
knowing that the Vatican was in sight of the windows
behind ! "

But the Gaskell party had to depart and (befriended
by Hamilton Wild, " the man of many friends," as
James says, " who painted, who talked, who travelled, who in particular endeared himself " and who
helped them through difficulties regarding a visit
to Siena and such like) to plunge into England and
troubles that awaited them.

In the summer of 1864 a family party made its
way to Pontresina, where much of " Wives and
Daughters " was composed ; and in 1865 Mrs.
Gaskell went abroad twice, paying her last visits to
her friend Mme. Mohl. At this time we are told*
she made some contributions to the *Pall Mall
Gazette* in order to help Mr. Smith, who had found it
a serious financial burden. Before returning she
paid a short visit to Dieppe.

Mme. Mohl, who has been spoken of, and who
had been a friend for many years, was by birth
Mary Clarke, a lady half Scottish and half Irish,
but wholly French by adoption, " full of ésprit and
of espièglerie : well-read and artistic, yet wholly
devoid of pedantry," as says Mr. E. T. Cooke in his
Life of Florence Nightingale, for Miss Clarke had
been a warm friend of the Nightingale family and

* Mr. A. Stanton Whitfield in his Life of Mrs. Gaskell.

a constant correspondent of Florence. Other of her friends were Dean Stanley and his wife Lady Augusta. She was odd to look at, extraordinarily untidy in dress, but a remarkable woman in many ways and with an attraction of her own.

Her husband, Jules Mohl, was one of the first Orientalists in Europe, and he drew round him men like Cousin, Miguet, Guizot, Tocqueville, Barthélmy St. Hilaire, and Thiers, the latter having been one of Miss Clarke's earliest admirers. Mme. Mohl held a sort of *salon* in the rue du Bac in a house which had once been that of Mme. Récamier and was that in which Chateaubriand died. Visits to her friend in Paris had become almost annual after 1854, so far as Mrs. Gaskell was concerned, for Mme. Mohl had a wonderful power of attraction, and she found it possible to carry on her work in her house undisturbed, " standing by the fire-place and using the mantelpiece as a desk." But Paris in early spring is cold ; it was so during her last visit, and the food was not that to which she was used and perhaps the cheerful but eccentric Mme. Mohl did not understand her needs. Though her guest wrote cheerfully she was not well in health, and possibly there was a risk in living in unwonted circumstances however interesting the surroundings.

Henry James, in his life of W. W. Story, says of Madame Mohl: " The eminently social (as well as the eminently individual) figure of Mme. Mohl, with its high antiquity and its supreme oddity, looks out at me, characteristically, from one of Mrs. Gaskell's letters [to W. W. Story]. But this remarkable shade has enjoyed copiously the honours of commemoration—walks in fact with a public effect with which no light touch of private testimony can hope to compete. . . . What a fortune indeed would have assuredly awaited any chronicler able to produce her image, by the light of knowledge, quite intact and as a free gratuity to his readers ; produce it in its habit as it lived, in its tone as it talked, with its rich cluster of associations, and above all, with the mystery of the reasons of its eminence—a mystery admirable, almost august, from long duration, and enhanced by the complete absence, at any moment, of any weak attempt on the lady's part to clear it up."

Of the same lady Mrs. Story writes : " I can see her now, just arrived, her feet on the fender before the fire, her hair flying and her general untidiness so marked as to be picturesque—since she showed a supreme indifference to the details of dress. . . . Her little dinners were amusing beyond any others, thanks to the quantities of clever talk. She was always at home on Friday evenings, which were occasions we so liked that we never, when in Paris, omitted one. She knew how to manage her clever people—it was what she was most remarkable for, putting them always on their strong points and effacing herself except for appreciation."

This is a letter written from Paris by Mrs. Gaskell to Emily Shaen, describing the life with the Mohls :

Paris, 27 March, /63.
120 Rue du Bac.

I think you will like to hear how I am going on in Paris. It is a very amusing life ; and I'll try and describe a day to you. Mme. Mohl lives on the fourth and fifth stories of a great large hotel built about 150 years ago, entre cour et jardin, " cour " opening into the narrow busy rue du Bac, " jardin " has a very large (10 *acres*) *plot of ground given by Cardinal Richelieu to the Missions Etrangères—and so not built upon, but surrounded by great houses like this. It is as stiffly laid out in kitchen garden, square walks, etc., as possible ; but there are great trees in it, and altogether it is really very pretty. That's at the back of the house and some of the rooms look on to it. On the fourth story are four lowish sitting rooms and Mme. Mohl's bedroom. On the fifth slopes in the roof, kitchen, grénier, servants' bedrooms, my bedroom, work-room, etc. ; all brick floors, which is cold to the feet. My bedroom is very pretty and picturesque. I like sloping roofs and plenty of windows stuffed into their roof anyhow ; and in every corner of this room (and it's the same all over this house)* French and English books are crammed. *I have no watch, there is no clock in the house, and so I have to guess the time by the monks' singing and bells ringing (all night long but) especially in the morning. So I get up and come down into the smallest and shabbiest of the sitting-rooms, in which we live and eat all day long, and find that M. Mohl has had his breakfast of chocolate in his room (library) at ½ past 6, and Mme. Mohl hers of tea at 7, and I am late having not come down (to coffee) till a little past 8. However I take it coolly and M. and Mme. come in and talk to me ; she in dressing gown and curlpapers, very, very amusing, he very sensible and agreeable, and full of humour too. I'll give you one or two specimens of Mme. Mohl's witty expressions. Speaking of* men *cooks in great families she calls them " tom-cooks." Another day " Let me see what year it was when M. Mohl* worried the baker." " What do you mean ? " " Oh, *you know we stayed with Hilary Carter at Kensington and a baker kept the post office, and he never had any*

U

foreign stamps, and M. Mohl wanted them every day, and was always going for them, till at last the baker said, ' Sir, Sir, you will worry me to death—' " and he did die soon after (M. Mohl the most good-natured of men stands by and smiles) ! . . .

Then, after my breakfast, which lingers long because of all this talk, I get my writing " Wives and Daughters " and write, as well as I can for Mme. Mohl's talking, till " second breakfast " about 11. *Cold meat, bread, wine and water and sometimes an omelette—what we should call lunch, in fact, only it comes too soon after my breakfast, and too long before dinner for my English habits. After breakfast no* 2 *I try to write again ; and very often callers come ;* always on Wednesdays *on which day Mme. Mohl receives. I go out a walk by myself in the afternoons ; and when we dine at home it is at six sharp. No dressing required. Soup, meat, one dish of vegetables and roasted apples are what we have in general. After dinner M. and Mme. Mohl go to sleep : and I have fallen into this habit ; and at eight exactly M. Mohl wakes up and makes a cup of very weak tea for Mme. Mohl and me, nothing to eat after dinner ; not even if we have been to the play. Then Mme. Mohl rouses herself up and is very amusing and brilliant ; stops up till one, and would stop up later if encouraged by listeners. She has not been well, but for all that she has seen a good number of people since I came ; she has generally a dinner-party of* 10 *or* 12 *every Friday, when we spread out into all the rooms (and I am so glad, for continual living and eating in this room and no open windows makes it very stuffy) and " receive " in the evening.*

Guizot has dined here and Miguet and Montalembert since I came ; and many other notabilities of less fame. But everybody stays up the first half of the

*night, as I should call it. When we go out for the
evening we go to dress directly after our dinner nap and
tea; and just cross the court-yards even in snow, or step
to the Porter's Lodge opening into the Rue du Bac, and
send him for a coach. We " jigget" to some very
smart houses (for all Mme. Mohl's friends are very
smart people and live in very grand houses) curtsey
as low as we can to the Master of the house, and shake
hands with the Mistress, sit down and in general have
a great deal of very beautiful music from the masters
of the Conservatoire, quartettes and quintettes; make
a buzz of talk, look at the fine dresses, and I come
home hungry as a hawk about one a.m. I am going
out a great deal to dinner: last night I dined at a
Russian house, a real Russian dinner. First soup
made of mutton, and sour kraut; very nasty and
horrible to smell. Then balls and rissolles very good;
fish, rice, eggs and cabbage, all chopped up together,
and cased in bread. Then caviare and smoked fish
handed round with bread and butter. Then sweet-
breads done in some extraordinary fashion, then eels,
chopped up with mushrooms, lemon juice and mustard.
Then rôti of some common sort; then gelinottes or
Russian partridge, which feed on the young sprouts
of the pine trees, and taste strong of turpentine. Then
a sweet soup, ball of raisins and currants like plum-
pudding, boiled in orange-flower water. I think that
was all—it was all I took at any rate. The gentlemen
hand the ladies back to the drawing-room, just as they
have handed them in to dinner. The other night M.
Guizot and M. de Montalembert dined here; the
latter speaks English as easily as he does French;
and was very eager about the American war; abusing
the English for their conduct towards the Northerners
and professing the warmest interest in the North. We*

never see any newspaper here so we don't know what is
going on. Guizot (who is 78) looks much older since
I saw him last. Good bye my dearest Emily for I am
suddenly called off.

Your own affec. friend E. C. G.

Towards the end of her not very long life, a time
of weariness came. Over the finishing of the new
novel she felt this severely. " Oh, I am so tired of
my story (" Wives and Daughters "), I dream about
it," she writes, and yet the story shows no signs of
strain. She had undertaken a responsibility which
entailed a serious tax upon her strength. This she
describes fully in a letter to Mr. Norton in 1865 :
" And then I did a terribly grand thing and a secret
too ! Only you are in America and can't tell. I
bought a house and 4 acres of land in Hampshire—
near Alton—for Mr. Gaskell to retire to, and for a
home for my unmarried daughters. That is to say,
I had not enough money to pay the whole £2,600,
but my publisher (Smith & Elder) advanced the
£1,000 on an ' equitable mortgage.' And I hope to
pay him off by degrees. Mr. Gaskell is *not to know*
this till then unless his health breaks down before.
He *is* very well and very strong, thank God ! but
he is sixty, and has to work very hard here. His
work is increasing with his years, and his experience,
and in the winter he feels this."

She hoped to let the house for three years, i.e.
until the mortgage was paid off, as she explains,
and " when we get it *free* we plan many ways of
telling him of the pretty home awaiting him."

The plan was kind and considerate, and Mrs.
Gaskell looked forward to it gleefully, but one always
has the feeling that the two, Mr. and Mrs. Gaskell,

never quite understood one another. It is hardly probable that Mr. Gaskell, whose whole life was in his work, and to whom Manchester meant the sphere of his work, would, at the age of sixty-three, resign the occupation he loved and retire to any bower of bliss, however beautiful. He would certainly have pined and died. Mrs. Gaskell, on the other hand, loved the south country ; its soft air suited her, and the life would have given her the rest and quiet she longed for. She always wanted to get away from the smoke and turmoil and constant round of callers and domesticities that wore her down. When possible she went abroad. If that was not feasible she made for her beloved Wales, and the house with its tower at Silverdale by the sea. " I think, and it is pleasant to think, that one never is disappointed in coming back to Silverdale. The secret is I think in the expanse of view—something like what gives its charm to the Campagna—such wide plains of golden sand with purple hill shadows, or fainter, filmy cloud-shadows, and the great dome of the sky." They sat up in the tower all night when the nights were tranquil and enjoyed it all immensely.

There is something of Ruskinese in this intense feeling for sky or cloud, and Ruskin was much in touch with the little company of north country friends, Winkworths, Shaens and Gaskells. His " simplicity and nobility " were spoken of after his visit. He was really much more to Mrs. Gaskell's mind than Carlyle.

On returning to Manchester she found innumerable things to do. She tried to keep up with her social duties, to keep her notebook ready to note inspiration from which she could weave a story as was her wont, and so complete her novel. But it was all a struggle. She wrote to Mr. W. S. Williams to ask his opinion about her novel when two volumes were written : " If somebody (out of my own family) would be truly interested in my poor story it would give me just the fillip of encouragement I want." Mr. Williams had said so far not a word. She was restless and yet wanted quiet and peace such as could be got in a country home.

After leaving Manchester she went to stay at her attractive little house which was called The Lawn, at Holybourne, near Alton, in Hampshire ; she did not want permanently to occupy the house till the three years were out and Mr. Gaskell was told. She felt better after her time of feebleness and was happy. She had been at church (for her tenets did not prevent her attending the services of a body not her own), and her son-in-law and daughters were seated at tea in the drawing-room when she fell forward dead. This was on Sunday afternoon, November 12th, 1865.

Though she was only fifty-five years of age, surely this was just the kind of death Elizabeth Gaskell would have chosen. The place is lovely in the sort of scenery she cared for : the parish church which she attended the morning of her death has a picturesque lych gate, and she appreciated beautiful old buildings. It is indeed just the Helstone described in " North and South." She had no suffering. The alterations being made in house and garden were nearly complete, and all seemed to promise for happiness. Mr. Gaskell was away, preaching in his own chapel in Manchester, so that the sad news had to be taken to him by his son-in-law.

Her body was laid in Knutsford in a spot she herself had chosen within sight of the old Unitarian chapel. It was the only place where she could rightly lie, and it was amongst her people—the people she had made the friends of the English-speaking world.

There is a memorial tablet erected in her husband's chapel in Manchester, a County Council tablet on the house where she was born in London. There is a portrait by Richmond in the National Portrait Gallery and a bust in the library of the Manchester University, taken from the bust done in Edinburgh in 1832, when she was a gay and beautiful girl. In her portrait she is shown to be what we know she was, a beautiful woman. Henry Greville (no mean critic) says in his diary : " Mrs. Gaskell is remarkably pleasing, unaffected, and easy in her manners, with a melodious voice in speaking."

For those who wish to study her works and books concerning them there is a complete collection of them, once at the Moss Side Public Library, Greenheys, the spot described at the beginning of " Mary Barton," and now in the great Public Library of Manchester.

IT is now sixty-five years since the day when Mrs. Gaskell passed away in her peaceful home in Hampshire, and 120 since she was born, in no very propitious way, for six of her family predeceased her in infancy and her mother survived her but a year. And yet with all the omens against her physically she not only bore a family of six, of whom four survived her, but she was besides a most efficient housewife and mother, and in addition had a long list of novels and tales to her credit, some of which, it is safe to predict, will survive for generations to come. It was a life of which Victorian womanhood has reason to be proud : it was also one which gives cause for reflection, in respect that had circumstances been more favourable even more might have been accomplished, and some of what was accomplished might have been of better quality.

Now, of course, we cannot but compare her with contemporary and preceding novelists of her sex, for whatever the future may bring forth, the quality of the woman novelist has something quite different from that of the man. It is true that in an age of great novelists Mrs. Gaskell's excellence could not fail to be overshadowed by such men as Dickens and Thackeray, and their successors Meredith and Hardy. Her place, however, in the galaxy of talent was a different one. Of women novelists Jane Austen was, undoubtedly, a much greater writer, though one with whom, from the nature of her work, one cannot help comparing Mrs. Gaskell; but even she lacked the tender charm of the latter at her best, and her technique, if perfect, was exercised within a limited range. Miss Yonge and Mrs. Oliphant of later days have less artistic feeling, though the latter had great gifts as a writer when she took the necessary pains. / Her sense of fun and real humour was more developed than with the Brontës, though she would never have placed herself on their level as an artist. She had, indeed, what women writers more often miss than men, a true appreciation of the humorous side of life—an appreciation which is kindly, charitable and human, and such as every one can understand. / Possibly she was devoid of real wit, but that is another matter.

Elizabeth Gaskell had indeed the power of writing with what a competent critic, Louis Cazamian, calls a descriptive realism that knows how to keep supple and free, and this is because the range of her work is kept within what she herself knows to be true. " The value of her art," he says, " is enhanced by its just and finely tempered quality." / She does not soar to the heights, and probably never could have attained to them. But though she kept within the average bounds of human life, she was capable of interpreting it and showing its true pathos. / Sometimes she was no doubt carried away into a diffuse commonplace as in the end of " Ruth " and in many of her short tales. Also, as in her first novels, there is the tendency to preach which spoilt so many novels of the day. / Her preaching, however, if inartistic, was with some effect, for she wrote with real knowledge, and the didactic element passed away in time : it is absent altogether in her last novel. So it is impossible to say that Jane Welsh

Carlyle's criticism that there was an attitude of moral dullness about her was just, when we think of the best part of her work. She was apt, no doubt, to be impersonal, to fail to grapple with realities, and to be content with conventional understanding. But it is not so when she comes to write of the very poor or of the faithful, crabbed servant. She showed no dullness there—no " lady-like " refinement.

Mrs. Gaskell struck a new line in writing of the Black Country with its surroundings of dim green fringing into real country ; all this was natural to her, as were the voices, expressions and feelings of the people. With their dialect she took enormous trouble. Other writers have suffered from their lack of this intimate knowledge. Her books cannot be read without the inward assurance that they are written from life and not just from information worked up for the occasion. When she describes the rage of the crowd in " North and South " we feel quite convinced that she has seen and understands a crowd of angry men ; and when she describes fierce characters like Thornton's mother we know that she believes in them and is not consciously exaggerating ; also that the rather savage exterior is not the whole man or woman. That is to say, she is an artist, and can make us do her will. Even in the scenes of passion amongst the factory workers in " Mary Barton " we know that while describing them the author is still mistress of herself, and is not carried off her feet by her emotion. The pity is that often enough she finds it difficult to end her tales without falling into somewhat sensational tragedy or comedy as the case may be ; in her case tragedy predominates. But the tragedy, the happy ending does not come into the picture. Impressionism and Realism we talk of, but of course they cannot be divorced. The realism of our older novelists probably accounted the "facts" of existence as too important, just as the scientific men of their period counted their facts as unassailable. Both had to learn their lessons—the literary man that their romances were far away from real life as it is led by men and women in the world ; and the scientist that a new outlook would arise that would show that the "ascertained facts" were built on foundations of sand, or were only true within certain rather narrow limits.

But though the modern novel may and does have more interest for the modern reader who delights in problems of a psychological sort, even he turns back to the old devices with a sense of rest and relief. After all it is true that we must take the occurrences around us in a matter-of-fact, rather abstract way, as events in time succeeding one another in somewhat arbitrary fashion. We cannot always pause to dwell on their psychological significance, or on the spiritual and ethical phases passed through. So we thoroughly enjoy the romances of Scott and the narratives of Trollope with the comfortable assurance that there are no difficult problems to perplex us and that whatever anxieties we may pass through all will be well in the end.

Mr. Shorter notices what is very true, that in Mrs. Gaskell's writing a certain ill-natured satire which is found in most women writers of genius—in Jane Austen, in Charlotte Brontë, and very markedly in George Eliot, is absent. That indeed amongst both sexes of authors the quality of good-natured toleration, such as one finds in Goldsmith and Lamb, is a rare one. In any case, it is present in Mrs. Gaskell and that is why her writings are sometimes compared with those of Lamb.

It is, however, certain that although Mrs. Gaskell gives us in the main a sense of rest in her writings, we can see how she is being moved and driven by the new winds that are troubling the waters and threatening many things that are only so far dreaded. She is of a period of transition—transition from the story-tellers of old days to the problem writers of to-day. She is, after all, however truly a Victorian, a portent of what is to come. We cling to her because she is still simple and direct, but the life that followed was to be neither simple nor direct, and so she is read as part of history—but a very important part of it as well as a very delightful one.

THE END

1837—Sketches among the Poor (with Mr. Gaskell).

1840—Clopton House.

1847—Libbie Marsh's Three Eras.
The Sexton's Hero.

1848—Christmas Storms and Sunshine.
Mary Barton.

1849—Hand and Heart.

1850—The Heart of John Middleton.
Lizzie Leigh.
The Moorland Cottage.
The Well of Pen-Morfa.

1851—Cranford.
Disappearances.
Mr. Harrison's Confessions.

1852—Bessy's Troubles at Home.
The Old Nurse's Story.
The Shah's English Gardener.

1853—Bran.
Cumberland Sheep-Shearers.
Morton Hall.
My French Master.
Ruth.
The Scholar's Story (Poem).
The Squire's Story.
Traits and Stories of the Huguenots.

1854—Company Manners.
Modern Greek Songs.
North and South.

1855—An Accursed Race.
Half a Life-time Ago.
Hand and Heart.

1856—A Christmas Carol.
The Poor Clare.

1857—The Life of Charlotte Brontë.

1858—The Doom of the Griffiths.
The Manchester Marriage.
My Lady Ludlow.
The Sin of a Father, or Right at Last.

1859—The Ghost in the Garden Room or The Crooked Branch.
The Half-Brothers.
Lois the Witch.
Round the Sofa (including previous tales).

1860—Curious if True.

1861—The Grey Woman.

1862—Six Weeks at Heppenheim.

1863—The Cage at Cranford.
Cousin Phillis.
A Dark Night's Work.
How the First Floor went to Crowley Castle.
An Italian Institution.
Robert Gould Shaw.
Sylvia's Lovers.

1864—French Life.
Wives and Daughters.

Rome, 291 *seq.*
Roscoe, 32.
Ruskin, 83, 84, 87, 255, 265, 283, 301.

S

Sand, George, 278.
Sanders, Gerald de Witt, *Pref. Note.*
Sandlebridge, 17, 20.
Schwabe, Mrs. Salis, 71, 78, 116, 236, 290.
Scots Magazine, 15, 25.
Scott, Mr., 246.
Scott, Walter, 3, 14, 25, 309.
Senior, 49.
Sévigné, Mme. de, 174, 291.
Shaen, Annie, 120, 128.
Shaen, Margaret, *Pref. Note.*
Shaen, Mrs., v. E. Winkworth.
Sharpe's Magazine, 162.
Shaw, Mrs., 154.
Shaw, Robert G., 209.
Shepheard, Rev. H., 171, 172.
Sherlock Holmes, 194.
Shorter, Clement, *Pref. Note,* 53, 72 *n.,* 128, 189, 284, 286, 309.
Shuttleworth, Lady, 128.
Silverdale, 118, 120, 233, 259, 262 *seq.,* 301.
Smith, Adam, 118.
Smith, George, 65, 132, 133, 168, 182, 206, 273, 282, 300.
Smith, Mrs. G., 132.
Smith, Reginald, 190.
Smith, Sydney, 15.
Smollett, 1.
Southey, 4, 127.
Spectator, 63.
St. Hilaire, 295.

Stanley, Dean, 295.
Stephen, Leslie, 206.
Stephenson, George, 24.
Stevenson, John, 18.
Stevenson, William, 13 *seq.*
Story, Mrs., 294, 296.
Story, W. W., 115, 116, 170, 292, 295.
Stowe, Mrs. Beecher, 65.
Stratford-on-Avon, 21.
Swinburne, 79, 291.

T

Taylor, J. J., 290.
Taylor, Mary, 179.
Taylor, Mrs., 265.
Taylor, Sir Henry, 240.
Taylor, Tom, 236.
Tennyson, 123, 124, 211, 230, 231, 235.
Thiers, 295.
Thomson, Isabella, 13.
Thornycroft, Hamo, 25 *n.*
Times, The, 282.
Tocqueville, de, 295.
Trollope, 18, 39, 279, 309.
Turner, William, 23.

U

Unitarianism, 4, 17, 18, 77, 138.

V

Vaughan, Henry, 260.

W

Walpole, 228.
Ward, Mrs. Humphry, 109.

Watts, G. F., 235 *seq.*, 250, 283.

Wedgwoods, 17, 22, 26, 241, 265, 287.

Wesley, C., 217.

Westminster Review, 130, 266.

Whewell, 48, 103.

Whitby, 210 *seq.*

Whitfield, A. Stanton, *Pref. Note*, 70, 192.

Wild, Hamilton, 259, 294.

Williams, W. S., 46, 121, 128, 167, 179, 189, 229, 302.

Winkworth, Catherine, *Pref. Note*, 154 *seq.*, 158 *seq.*, 170, 174, 180, 184, 225, 259, 285, 289.

Winkworth, Emily (Mrs. Shaen), 70, 89, 179, 184, 251, 289 *seq.*, 296.

Winkworth, Mr., 259.

Winkworth, Susanna, 47, 180, 253, 254, 288 *seq.*

Wolstonecraft, M., 240.

Women's Medical Education, 284.

Woodsworth, Mrs., 183.

Wordsworth, 71, 131.

Wright, T., 236, 237, 238.

Y

Yonge, Miss, 305.